# JUDY

## A LEGENDARY FILM CAREER BY JOHN FRICKE

# JUDY

## A LEGENDARY FILM CAREER

BY JOHN FRICKE

RUNNING PRESS
PHILADELPHIA • LONDON

## Acknowledgments

Books comprised of so many individual elements of text and art invariably become their own community project. Therefore, gratitude must be expressed to the many extended family members who made possible this venture: Fred McFadden and Dennis Cleveland for their generosity, hospitality, and customarily selfless contributions; Ranse Ransone for the eternal scanning, photo editing, and subsidizing; Steve Sanders, Jonathan Shirshekan, Ricky Coombs, David Rambo, Scott Roberts, David Price, and Ken Young for their contributions. For additional tangibles and intangibles: Lorna Luft, Jesse and Vanessa Richards, Colin Freeman, Joseph Luft. Ned Comstock and the University of Southern California Cinematic Arts Library. The Academy of Motion Picture Arts and Sciences/The Margaret Herrick Library: The Victor Fleming Scrapbook, art on pps.102–105. Susan Lacy and the American Masters executives and staff, PBS-TV. Richard Pena and Tom Michel, rhe Film Society of Lincoln Center (NYC). Ron Simon and Barry Monush, rhe Paley Center (NYC). And Woolsey Ackerman, Russell Adams, Andreas Bauer, Nancy Barr Brandon, Willard Carroll, Frank Degregorio, William Patrick Dunne, Marcus Geisler, Sam Gratton, Tom Larro, Kim Lundgreen, Leonard Maltin, Christian Matzanke, Frank McCullough, Rick Meadows, William Mowbray, Nathan Neihardt, Ron O'Brien, Amanda Osborne, Robert Osborne, Sue Parry and family, Les Perkins, John Perri, Gwen Potter, Max O. Preeo, David Rebella and Jim Downs, Clay Schiebel, Ken Sephton, Michael Siewert, Donald F. Smith, Lorna Smith, James H. Spearo, Justin Steensma, Martha Wade Steketee, Charlotte Stevenson, Seth Stuhl, Charles W. Triplett, Jerry Waters, Tom Watson, Ben Wetchler, Reverend Raymond Wood; Barry, Marc, Marty, Gregg, and Scott; and the late Bill Chapman, Dana Dial, Al DiOrio, John Graham, Pat McMath, Hugh Martin, Jim Squires, and Betty Welch. Special acknowledgment is extended to the International Judy Garland Club (judygarlandclub.org), Gary Horrocks, Dr. Justin Sturge. The International Wizard of Oz Club (ozclub.org). Daniel Berghaus, Robin Binsk, and thejudygarlandexperience@yahoogroups.com. Steve Jarrett, the late Mark Harris, and thejudylist@googlegroups.com. JohnKelsch and the Judy Garland Birthplace and Museum (judygarlandmusem.com). And_ everythingoz@yahoogroups.com; friends_In_OZ@yahoogroups.com. At Warner Bros.: George Feltenstein, Ned Price, Ronnee Sass, Kathleen Wallis. At Stay All Night The Movie.com: Steve Lippman, Mary Wharton, George Hahn. At Running Press: Cindy De La Hoz, Susan Van Horn, Seta Zink, Craig Herman. Finally, heartfelt appreciation for their all-important and ongoing family faith to Brent Phillips, John Walther, Patty Fricke, Erin, Noel, and Haley Fricke, Michael and Linda Fricke, Dottie Fricke . . . and, as ever and always, Kellen Lindblad. Walther, Patty Fricke, Erin, Noel, and Haley Fricke, Michael and Linda Fricke, Dottie Fricke . . . and, as ever and always, Kellen Lindblad.

To Fred and Dennis—professionally, personally . . . positively!

© 2010 by John Fricke
Published by Running Press,
A Member of the Perseus Books Group

All rights reserved under the Pan-American and International Copyright Conventions
Printed in China

*This book may not be reproduced in whole or in part, in any form or by any means, electronic or mechanical, including photocopying, recording, or by any information storage and retrieval system now known or hereafter invented, without written permission from the publisher.*

Books published by Running Press are available at special discounts for bulk purchases in the United States by corporations, institutions, and other organizations. For more information, please contact the Special Markets Department at the Perseus Books Group, 2300 Chestnut Street, Suite 200, Philadelphia, PA 19103, or call (800) 810-4145, ext. 5000, or e-mail special.markets@perseusbooks.com.

ISBN 978-0-7624-3771-9
Library of Congress Control Number: 2010943211

E-book ISBN 978-0-7624-4368-0

9   8   7   6   5   4   3   2   1
Digit on the right indicates the number of this printing

Designed by Susan Van Horn
Edited by Cindy De La Hoz
Typography: Filosofia, Gotham, and Trade Gothic

Running Press Book Publishers
2300 Chestnut Street
Philadelphia, PA 19103-4371

Visit us on the web!
www.runningpress.com

# contents

▷ THE FEATURE FILMS ▷     ▷ THE FEATURE FILMS ▷     ▷ THE FEATURE FILMS ▷

JUDY A LEGENDARY FILM CAREER

JUDY A LEGENDARY FILM CAREER JUDY

# INTRODUCTION: A LOT OF SOMETHING EXTRA

*You've got "that little something extra" that Ellen Terry talked about. Ellen Terry—a great actress, long before you were born. She said that that's what star quality was: "that little something extra."* —NORMAN MAINE (JAMES MASON) TO ESTHER BLODGETT (JUDY GARLAND), *A STAR IS BORN*

Moss Hart's dialogue for that moment in *A Star is Born* (1954) both propelled the plot of the picture and fed directly into the estimations of any audience viewing the film. They—and James Mason's character—had just experienced Judy Garland's rendition of "The Man That Got Away"; surrender, as one critic later offered, could only be unconditional. And with pleasure and trepidation, the average moviegoer was then able to anticipate the success that Esther Blodgett's undeniable talent was sure to achieve for her.

Life imitates art. Across the four decades of her career, Judy Garland enjoyed astounding levels of accomplishment in every entertainment medium. Those achievements have since proved to be joyously timeless, and her legacy is constantly discovered and shared—or rediscovered, remastered, and reissued. Much of her television work (four specials, a twenty-six episode series, and a number of guest appearances) stirs rapturous response on DVD and YouTube. Her studio, "live," and radio recordings are heralded as key representations of "The Great Popular Songbook." And those who participated in the electricity of Judy in person on the stage retain memories of the most pure and potent of all exposures to her genius. It was as a movie star that she first came to international fame and where—thanks to home video and cable television—she is still most likely to be initially encountered.

There is a pyramid-like construction to any overview of Garland's film work. At its pinnacle, one finds *The Wizard of Oz*—the best-loved, best-known, and most widely seen motion picture of all time. Lined up just below *Oz* are three more classics: a family story told with song (*Meet Me in St. Louis*), an archetypal, ebullient musical comedy (*Easter Parade*), and an outstanding drama about a singer in Hollywood (*A Star is Born*). Beneath them, a firm foundation is provided by that raft of happily memorable, if slightly lesser, screen achievements (*The Harvey Girls, For Me and My Gal, In the Good Old Summertime*, and *Summer Stock*); a number of early, exhilarating costarring vehicles for Judy and Mickey Rooney (including three of the *Andy Hardy* series and four full-fledged song-and-dance shows); and the all-star extravaganzas, in which Judy's contribution is invariably one of the best components. Even the atypical, middle-period deviations from the norm (*The Clock, The Pirate*) are equally effective in their own ways, and if only one of her final four movie efforts was a commercial success, each possessed intrinsic social or artistic value. In review, there seems to be little (if anything) in the Garland filmography about which she could manifest regret, whether about her work or her participation.

When first released, all of those films (or Judy's segments in them) were at least critically endorsed; many were venerated, but much of that enthusiasm eventually came to be considered of its time. When Garland died in 1969, earlier show business history was in the process of being written off or cavalierly dismissed. (Her passing occurred less than a year prior to the infamous auction and sale of the holdings of her "home" studio, when any tangible piece of Metro-Goldwyn-Mayer was dismantled, disbursed, destroyed, or destined to serve as southern California landfill.) Two days after Judy's funeral, film critic Vincent Canby published *The New York Times*'s opinion piece about her life and work; also of its time, it was appreciative, somewhat uninformed, and needlessly psychological. Notably however, he observed, "When I looked [this week] through several comprehensive film books, I found only several references to Judy Garland, and then only in incidental connection with the films of Vincente Minnelli and Stanley Kramer. . . ." He concluded, "She did not make movies important by simply inhabiting them."

If Canby was correct about film books circa 1969, his final statement has proved to be blissfully inaccurate. No one could have known it then, of course, but revisionist recognition and the reclamation of a specific era of entertainment were only five years in the future. Though it remains true that just the four titles at the top of her aforementioned pyramid can be stringently defined as "classics," the rest of Garland's pictures have come to be regarded as noteworthy and significant, if only because Judy appeared in them. It should be added that, in her main oeuvre, she had full support from the nonpareil MGM creative troops, but it took her alchemy to coalesce and convey the much-vaunted magic of a Garland-film experience.

The change in public perception of the traditional movie musical can be credited to MGM's *That's Entertainment!* (1974). Written, produced, and directed by "son of Tin Man," Jack Haley, Jr., his compilation of vintage clips and new narration traced three decades of screen numbers as originated at Metro. The studio's film library, regarded by its contemporary owners as a collection of "old movies" with "old stars," was suddenly worth a fortune. (According to apprentice editor Michael Sheridan, *That's Entertainment!* "made forty million dollars on a $985,000 investment.") Executive editor Bud Friedgen has since elaborated on the film's focus: "We had to do Judy, Gene [Kelly], and Fred [Astaire]. They were the Golden Triangle of MGM; they deserved sequences all their own." Garland, in fact, rated two.

As a result, *That's Entertainment!* offered incontrovertible proof that Judy—in her teens and twenties—was the preeminent female performer of Hollywood's greatest studio. The general public excitedly embraced that reminder and was unwittingly primed for the next level of revelation. In 1983, historian/archivist Ron Haver presented a nearly complete restoration of *A Star is Born*, which had been manhandled in post-premiere editing by Warner Bros. thirty years before. The media and sold-out benefit audiences were swept away by a thirty-two-year-old Judy, still in inestimable command of her talent and the motion picture screen. It's somewhat poignant to note that such substantiation of her gifts was then essential, given the much-reported stresses of her final years, incessant and ongoing tabloid journalism, and the mostly disproportionate biography to which her life was subjected after she died.

Of course, those who had been fans at any point during Judy's lifetime needed no reminder of her professional standing. Nor, as it turned out, did most of those who'd worked with her. Shortly before his own premature death in 1970, Garland's lifelong musical and personal mainstay Roger Edens told an interviewer, "The discovery of Judy Garland was the biggest thing to happen to the MGM musical." He was quite literally correct, as can be seen through the simultaneous progression of her career and the studio's output. In her first three seasons at Metro, Judy's prodigious talent saw the young girl more than hold her own opposite Sophie Tucker, Fanny Brice, and Mickey Rooney. A year later, when songwriter Arthur Freed realized his ambition to become a film producer, it happened specifically in Garland's company. Freed proudly admitted, "I made my bet on Judy, [and] she helped me as much as I helped her. She makes any producer look good."

What came to be known as "The Freed Unit" initially flourished at Metro between 1940 and 1950, with Garland as its cynosure. He produced thirteen of her twenty pictures during that decade, while Edens wrote songs and arrangements and refashioned scripts on her behalf. MGM's preeminent orchestrators and conductors worked on the scores of those films, and Judy had new numbers written for her by everyone from Irving Berlin and Cole Porter to Johnny Mercer, Harry Warren, E. Y. Harburg, Burton Lane, Hugh Martin, Ralph Blane, Mack Gordon, and Saul Chaplin. She was the delight of the great Broadway/Hollywood choreographer Robert Alton; later on, his protégé Charles Walters would stage, dance with, and direct Judy both on film and on Broadway. It was at Garland's request that Gene Kelly made his film debut opposite her in *For Me and My Gal*—an auspicious launching pad for the Broadway hoofer/choreographer. Five years later, when Kelly broke his ankle, Fred Astaire came out of retirement specifically to dance with Judy in *Easter Parade*, leading to a string of further film triumphs for the veteran entertainer.

[It's historically important to note that some of the most accomplished "Freed Unit" productions—including *An American in Paris*, *Singin' in the Rain*, *The Band Wagon*, and *Gigi*—were still in the future when Judy was dismissed by MGM in 1950. But as has been theorized by film archivist/author Brent Phillips, "Much of the warmth and integrity of the Metro musical went with her. The studio still had its stylized sopranos, a spunky ingénue (Debbie Reynolds), and a new gamin (Leslie Caron). But no longer did they have an all-around musical comedy actress of range and innate musical ability. This was particularly noticeable in Freed's output in the 1950s, where dubbing the singing voice of a female star became the norm rather than the exception. He produced twelve musicals following Garland's departure. Eight of these supplied counterfeit vocals for their leading lady; two others offered no female vocalizing whatsoever. As a result, audiences no longer witnessed an authentic or complete musical performance, and in some way, they must have sensed this manufactured artificiality. The 'integrated' film musical— so brilliantly championed by Freed and brought to such heights by Garland in the 1940s—relied upon a seamless blend of story, song, and dance. Without Judy, MGM no longer had a superstar female artist under contract who could supply all three ingredients with her combination of natural ease and skill."]

While Garland was inspiring the imaginations and emotions of her coworkers, she was having the same effect on movie critics. The erudite James Agee consistently appreciated her in his mid-1940s reviews for *The Nation* and *Time*, and an anonymous British journalist in 1946 was equally sagacious: "Judy has a much wider range than is called for by her work in the ['Judge Hardy's Family'] films, but I emphasize her part in these pictures because she brings to them a very rare quality. That quality is hard to describe except in negatives, yet it is in itself anything but negative. It is not beauty, although she can appear beautiful; not wit, though she can point a line with style; nor is it acting ability, though she is obviously an actress of considerable skill. What it is can only be described as vitality, though the word hardly conveys all it should. Eagerness, drive, or gaiety would answer as well, and her acting has them all." Individual press quotes about each of Garland's films appear with their specific entries in this book; they offer ample proof that she equally impacted on the popular media of her time. These excerpts were specifically selected as a cross-section of contemporary comment and include opinions from the then-pervasive trade papers (with their intra-industry perspective), national and major metropolitan publications, the "local" press of Middle America, and several international forums.

Judy was fervently appreciated by most of her coworkers as well, and each of her motion pictures is additionally defined here by their observations. One of the most salient estimations of Garland's worth, however, came from someone with whom she never appeared. Historically, Laurette Taylor is frequently referenced by other theatricals as the most unforgettable, communicative, and gifted stage actor they ever saw. (In his outstanding documentary, *Broadway: The Golden Age* (2004), Rick McKay parades a venerable host of legends who speak to that effect, including Harold Prince, Uta Hagen, Marian Seldes, Maureen Stapleton, Ben Gazzara, Gena Rowlands, Patricia Neal, and Martin Landau.) Taylor died in 1946; she only knew Judy from Garland's first years of screen work and a handful of social encounters. When they met during Taylor's Broadway run in *The Glass Menagerie* in 1945 she told Judy quite simply, "You have the greatest talent ever wrapped up in one little package."

As noted, Judy appeared only sporadically on the big screen post-MGM. "I've done some movies," she told a 1962 concert audience and then added with a grin, "They let me back in." But it's significant that both Garland and her film themes had matured with the times. The four major pictures in which she appeared between 1954 and 1962 dealt with (however theatrically) somber issues never imagined by the Freed Unit: alcohol abuse, the Holocaust, the education of mentally challenged children, illegitimacy, and the uncompromising pressures of stardom. At random moments, Judy could, like many others, be her own worst enemy (i.e., the "By Myself" dress in *I Could Go on Singing*). She nonetheless garnered deserved consideration for these final installments in her motion picture career.

Decades after the fact, the range of Garland's motion picture work continues to command respect from her peers. Her avowed admirers extend from the new generation including Scarlett Johansson, to young veterans like Marlee Matlin, to those who survive from Judy's era. Elaine Stritch has repeatedly acknowledged, "I watch a Judy Garland movie before my opening nights. Now, a lot of people think it's rather strange that you look at 'The Trolley Song' to do Edward Albee. But what that does for me is this: it tells me not to tell a lie for the rest of the evening . . . to tell the truth when I get out there. Because to see her up there—to see her reach over to an audience with the absolute 100 percent truth—is something else. Never have I caught her in a lie. And never have I caught her 'acting.'"

Such professional reaction to Garland's efforts has now also been underscored in terms of historical perspective. She ranks high on the "best" lists—most notably at number eight in the American Film Institute tally of the Greatest Female Stars of All Time. Her films achieve additional recognition in the AFI general and genre polls, and she holds five spots in their selection of the hundred greatest songs in American cinema; "Over the Rainbow" is in first place. Thus far, four Garland movies have been selected by the Library of Congress for protection and preservation under the National Film Registry as "culturally, historically, or aesthetically significant" achievements: *The Wizard of Oz*, *Meet Me in St. Louis*, *A Star is Born*, and

*Love Finds Andy Hardy*. (At different times, under varying circumstances, Judy's own personal favorites among her screen credits were cited as *Oz*, *St. Louis*, *Star*, *Easter Parade*, *A Child is Waiting*, *The Clock*, and "any picture with Mickey Rooney!")

With these years of retrospective honors have come a multitude of written and oral appreciations. It would be impossible to tabulate all of the intelligent journalism about Judy Garland's career that has been put forth in books, essays, or on the lecture circuit in recent decades. Film historians point with amazement to the "long takes" sustained by Garland on camera, whether acting, dancing, or lip-synching singing. Furthermore, for all her tempestuous reputation, their archeological research into her career has turned up very little actual evidence of temperamental behavior, whether on-set or in a recording studio. Finally, the longevity of her fame and familiarity over that of her fellow female film musical stars is a matter of obvious record. As a result, Judy has won knowledgeable perspective and praise from (among many others) Ethan Mordden, Michael Feingold, Ron O'Brien, David Hajdu, Ken Bloom, Coyne Steven Sanders, Roy Hemming, Vito Russo, and Robert Osborne.

A multi-decade Hollywood correspondent and an active observer of and participant in the film industry, Osborne is the esteemed host of cable television's Turner Classic Movies. He has unconditionally stated, "Judy Garland was the all-around, most talented person that's ever been in films to date. And she's one of the few stars of yesteryear . . . who seems to be gaining more fans of every age bracket." After referencing her "great power and yet great vulnerability," he adds an echo to the earlier comment by Elaine Stritch: "What makes Judy timeless is the fact that every moment she has on screen is an *honest* one. She was a brilliant comedienne, an unmatched singer—she had the best singing voice of any Hollywood star—a terrific actress, [and] a surprisingly good hoofer. She could do it all."

Osborne's recognition of Garland's ongoing, cross-generational appeal is cheerful proof of the active presence she manifests for each new generation. It usually starts with Dorothy Gale, of course. Ironically, when *The Wizard of Oz* celebrated its fiftieth anniversary in 1989, many thought that public appreciation for the film had peaked. Lining the parade routes at nation-wide *Oz* festivals that year were thousands of little girls, bedecked in blue-and-white gingham, real or faux-braids, and countless variations of ruby-colored shoes. It didn't seem possible that such passion would sustain itself. But those events have since continued on an annual basis, and the little girls of today who emulate Judy Garland are, in many cases, the daughters of the Dorothys of more than twenty years ago.

There are also noteworthy reactions to Garland from the opposite sex, attesting to her non-*Oz* appeal. An Indiana family still marvels at the recent inexplicable reaction of a five-year-old boy, consumed and preoccupied with trains throughout every day. Sitting on the carpet of the TV room and fixated on his toy engine, cars, and track, the child was oblivious to the adults in the room as they watched a telecast of *That's Entertainment!* In the opening moments of the film, Cliff Edwards and then Jimmy Durante deliver "Singin' in the Rain," followed by a swift segue to Judy's rendition of that song from *Little Nellie Kelly*. At the moment she began to sing, the child's head snapped up. For the first time in months, his trains were totally ignored; everyone else in the room was instantly aware of that unusual phenomenon—and his complete captivation by the voice and presence on the video screen. When Garland disappeared (and the number was taken up by Gene Kelly, Debbie Reynolds, and Donald O'Connor), the child immediately turned to his uncle and plaintively asked, "Where did she go?" Then he quietly demanded, "Make her come back!"

In a similar recent instance, a nine-year-old boy wandered in and out of the living room where his parents and friends were watching *I Could Go on Singing*. Not unexpectedly, the adult drama held no fascination for him. He happened to reenter the room just as "Jenny Bowman" was revving up in the wings of the London Palladium, preparatory to taking the stage for her opening-night performance. The combination of Mort Lindsey's orchestration on the soundtrack and the energizing Garland on the screen caught the child's complete attention; he stood, transfixed and beaming ever brighter, throughout her building rendition of "Hello, Bluebird." As Judy belted out the final, growled word—"HELL-LOHHH!"—the dam broke. Emotionally propelled, with eyes, smile, and face alight, the boy whirled on the roomful of grownups and exclaimed, "How does she DO that?!"

This book is intended as a history behind those Garland films and all the others; as an expansion of the foregoing statements; and as a collection of photographs and reminiscences attendant to the *"lot* of something extra" that Judy selflessly poured into her celluloid career. Perhaps most of all, it comes as a heartfelt, hardbound response to those of any age who will watch a Garland movie and—in time-honored tradition—eagerly request, "Make her come back!" or joyously wonder, "How does she DO that?!"

—**JOHN FRICKE**, NEW YORK CITY, APRIL 2011

## JUDY: OUR FEATURE PRESENTATION

With typical self-deprecation, Judy Garland once declaratively joked, "I was never 'born in a trunk.' Can you imagine the shape I'd be in, if I had been born in a trunk?" But given her family's theatrical endeavors, her stage debut at thirty months, the Roger Edens/Leonard Gershe song written for her film *A Star is Born*, and the forty-five years she spent as an entertainer, Judy's "born in a trunk" association is somehow legendarily valid.

Garland's extraordinary gifts and achievements were perhaps best summarized by an adulatory Elaine Stritch, who told a 1998 Carnegie Hall audience, "Everything Judy did was so *real* that there was almost no such thing as a text in her life. It was just off the top of her head, the whole damn career!" And Garland's professional and personal evolution was virtually that natural. Her parents themselves had grown from children who performed in the family parlor—Frank Gumm in Tennessee and Ethel Milne in Michigan—to professionals, who (admittedly) never made it beyond the lowest rung of the "picture show" and small-time vaudeville circuits. They met when she played piano for his sing-alongs in a Superior, Wisconsin theater, were married in 1914, and then settled down to manage a silent movie house in Grand Rapids, Minnesota. Between 1915 and 1921, they raised two daughters and continued to perform in the area—sometimes as the more euphoniously named "Jack and Virginia Lee."

A third daughter, Frances Ethel Gumm, was born on June 10, 1922, and spent the first dozen years of her life answering to the nickname "Baby" or "Babe." After cutting her teeth on backyard entertainments with her siblings, Baby made a formal debut at her father's New Grand Theatre on December 26, 1924. The enthusiasm of the hometown audience was such that the girl refused to get off the stage, and her mother accompanied her in chorus after chorus of "Jingle Bells." Finally, her maternal grandmother strode out from the wings and carried off the tot, who lustily protested, "I wanna sing some more!" Baby began semi-regular stage appearances soon thereafter, both on her own and with her sisters. In 1926, the Gumm family entrained west for a California vacation, stopping along the way in a handful of tank towns to perform at local cinemas. The Devil's Lake, North Dakota paper for June 9 touted, "Jack and Virginia Lee and Kiddies . . . in a Group of Classical, Semi-Classical and Popular Songs. See the 3-Year-Old Wonder Lee Kiddie Dance

**OPPOSITE:** Frank Avent Gumm (1886–1935), shown here in 1926, and Ethel Marion Milne (1893–1953) at an MGM sitting in 1941. They'd wed in 1914 and had daughters Mary Jane and Dorothy Virginia in 1915 and 1917, respectively. By the time Ethel became pregnant a third time, in 1921, there were so many difficulties in the marriage that she and Frank had to be persuaded not to pursue a then-illegal and dangerous abortion.

**ABOVE:** Baby Gumm at home in Grand Rapids. More than thirty-five years later, she reflected, "I'm sure that the first three years of my life were the happiest I ever had. It's amazing to me that I do remember so much; I'm sure it's because it was the only tranquil period of my life with my family. There is complete joy in everything I can remember."

ABOVE AND LEFT: After moving to Los Angeles in late 1926, the Gumms briefly settled in this house at 3154 Glen Manor. The following spring, they relocated to Lancaster, where Frank ran the local movie theater, Ethel accompanied the silent films at the piano, and the whole family periodically entertained between features. | By the late 1920s, the girls were regularly trundled on the six-hour round trip to Los Angeles by their mother in the family car. Judy remembered, "She became conscious of our 'career.' She decided we had to be stars."

the Charleston. Hear Virginia Lee at the Piano. These People Are Just from the F. & R. Circuit on Their Way to the Coast."

By the time the Gumms returned to Minnesota, they had decided to relocate to the more entertainment-oriented and climate-friendly city of Los Angeles. The Grand Rapids *Herald-Review* of October 6, 1926, portentously announced their departure: "Mr. and Mrs. Gumm . . . have been active in the business and social life of the town and have responded willingly to the many demands made upon them for their services. Both are versatile entertainers and have taken part in a great many plays, concerts, and other home talent affairs. They have been training their children along similar lines, and the appearance of the Gumm Sisters has always been a drawing card at any entertainment." The article noted that the Gumms had not sold their house, and "their host of friends in Grand Rapids and vicinity . . . hope that someday they may decide to return." Such journalism was both heartfelt and generous if not universally endorsed. By 1926, Frank Gumm had experienced precipitous or semi-enforced leave-takings from a number of the small towns in which he'd worked, as rumors or accounts of his sexual exploits with young men had begun to circulate.

The family officially launched their new start in spring 1927 by settling in Lancaster, California. But the drama continued, good and bad, onstage and off. Over the next eight years, Frank managed the local Valley Theatre, where Ethel accompanied sporadic "live" entertainment and (until the addition of sound equipment in 1930) silent films. The three girls sang at countless local and regional events; gradually, more and more of their act fell to Baby Frances. Much of this was due to her youth, diminutive size, vocal power, and precocity, but from all reports, there also was an already-apparent, inherent charisma about her.

By December 1928, the Gumm Sisters were appearing at the Los Angeles Loew's State Theatre with other moppets from the Ethel Meglin Dance Studios. Lancaster's *Antelope Valley Ledger-Gazette* proudly reported, "Judging from the storms of applause at every performance, Frances has been one of the biggest hits on the Christmas program, and the packed houses have shown their appreciation of the exceptional voice of this tiny tot." Over the next six years, Ethel's increasing ambition on behalf of her daughters would see the girls placed in motion picture "short subjects," on local radio, in several training/performance groups for youngsters, and in scores of live theater engagements. Baby won mostly raves and all of the attention in every instance. She was one of nine juveniles supposedly (if briefly) signed by Universal in 1931 "for places in the coming production of children's pictures." That same year, her appearance in Maurice Kusell's *Stars of Tomorrow* stage revue won *Filmograph*'s commendation: "Baby Gumm's watery blue [sic] eyes should conquer the world 'or some millionaire.'"

Unfortunately, all this ran counterpoint to Frank's renewed activities with young men. If his daughters remained oblivious to the scandal, his wife did not; the couple endured repeated, vociferous arguments and separations. Marcella Bannett would wed longtime Gumm confidante Dr. Marcus Rabwin in 1934 and come to know the family well. She remembers that, "Ethel spoke openly of Frank's homosexuality but did not leave him. She sublimated herself in promoting the careers of the three little girls . . . [and] even if she was a stage mother, I knew she was trying to be as good a mother as she could." Most of Ethel's aspirations were held for Baby, and the child grew to detest the many days away from her father and childhood friends when she was dragged off to Hollywood for classes and forced into frequent auditions at her mother's behest.

The little girl's separations from Frank served only to enhance the bond that existed between them. Baby cherished him: "We were very close. I adored him, and he had a special kind of love for me. Daddy had a wonderful voice, [and] he had a funny sense of humor; he laughed all the time—good and loud, like I do. He was handsome and temperamental and fun, and he loved music and theater and everything about it. In the evening, before he went to the theater, while I sat on his lap in a little white flannelette nightgown, he used to sing 'Danny Boy' and 'Nobody Knows the Trouble I've Seen.' [Later,] all the times I had to leave him, I pretended he wasn't there; because if I'd thought about him being there, I'd have been full of longing."

There was one other new complication at this time—beyond the enforced performance trips for the Gumm Sisters and their mother's understandable (if unexplained) hostility toward Frank. According to Garland biographer Gerald Clarke, it was Ethel who now introduced her daughters to stimulant medications: "I've got to keep these girls going!'" Though amphetamines per se weren't available until the mid-1930s, there were variations of ephedrine, caffeine, and other herbals mass-marketed for weight loss and energy boosting beginning in the late 1920s. Medical researcher Jonathan Shirshekan adds, "As early as 1930, the American Medical Association registered major concern regarding dependency and the use of ephedrine which was, at the time, indicated for the treatment of asthma (along with the previously described off-label uses). It's now uncertain what Ethel could have specifically given the girls, but in retrospect, it's definite that there was no safe formulation available even then to provide her desired effects."

The concepts of medication and overwork thus became sometime-features of Judy Garland's life when she was still a preteen. But ever-greater was her capacity to delight (and to delight in) virtually any audience, anywhere. In summer 1934, Ethel took the Gumm Sisters to work in Chicago, where they were "discovered" and renamed the Garland Sisters by entertainer George Jessel. His patronage led to additional midwest bookings; Ed J. Weisfeldt was the manager of Milwaukee's Riverside Theatre and would exclaim twenty years later, "[Baby's] talent was unmistakable! She could put over a song and a smile like a million, and when she sat on the piano in the Helen Morgan manner, she scored a real hit." A critic in Kansas City defined the tiny Garland as "a young show-stopper . . . on [her] first performance [of 'Bill'] . . . and then repeated later with 'Little Man, You've Had a Busy Day.' The girl has personality (as have her sisters, not to neglect them), and the act gets long and loud applause."

The Garland Sisters returned to increasing triumph and recognition in Los Angeles in fall 1934. Over the next seven months, they played (among other venues) Grauman's Chinese, the Wilshire-Ebell, and the Paramount, where Baby continued to decimate both the general public and any partaking professional. At age twelve, she was invariably the "highlight of the show. . . . Her inimitable songs proved quite a sensation, and her evident willingness to please called for several encores" (Los Angeles *Evening Herald and Express*). As a result, the girls were auditioned by Decca Records, and auditioned and briefly signed at Universal Studios. Baby was twice summoned to Metro-Goldwyn-Mayer—first with her sisters under the auspices of test director George Sidney, producer/director Joseph Mankiewicz, and executive secretary Ida Koverman—and later on her own, sponsored by songwriter Burton Lane. Sidney photographed her screen test in a musical baseball routine. A few months later, with Lane at the piano, studio chieftain Louis B. Mayer had Baby tour the lot and sang for everyone. She created her customary sensation, but no one had any idea what to do with her; for all her talent, she was neither a titan tot like Shirley Temple nor a bosomy ingénue. Meanwhile, in spring 1935, and amidst burgeoning Lancaster rumors about his behavior,

Frank lost the lease on the Valley Theatre and was informally but directly invited to leave town. Ethel and the girls had already relocated to Silver Lake. Frank moved back in with the family and took over a cinema in nearby Lomita.

Further developments grew out of a summer booking for the girls at the Cal-Neva Lodge. Mary Jane, the oldest Gumm Sister, changed her first name to Suzanne or Susie and found a fiancé in musician Lee Kahn. Dorothy Virginia, the middle Gumm Sister, changed her first name to Jimmie and found a fiancé in actor Frankie Darro. Finally, Baby changed her first name to Judy (from a contemporary Hoagy Carmichael/Sam Lerner pop song) and found an agent in Al Rosen. In August, Susie married, and she and Jimmie retired from the family act. Rosen was thus free to peddle Judy as a single, which he began to do with a vengeance in August 1935. A month later, his efforts led to her third MGM audition, where everyone was finally in accord: even with no specific project in the offing, the girl belonged at Metro. Judy Garland started work on the Culver City lot on October 1,

With Judy as the vocal and focal point of the act, the Gumm Sisters began to gain real recognition by 1934. The "Old Mexico" at the Chicago World's Fair abruptly closed after their third week (they'd only been paid for the first), but a subsequent booking at the Oriental Theatre led to work throughout the Midwest and a formal sitting at the Bloom studios.

FROM LEFT: Duluth was the largest nearby Minnesota city to Garland's Grand Rapids birthplace. She demonstrated some retroactive local patriotism by posing with their newspaper while on the set of *Broadway Melody of 1937*. | At the MGM Studio School, December 1935. Judy had only been with Metro for two months and found more pleasure in working on vocal arrangements with Roger Edens than attending class. (She'd later joke, "The teacher, I think, was Ma Barker.") From left: actor hopefuls Robert McClung, Judy, June Wilkins, Mickey Rooney, Garett Joplin, and instructor Mary MacDonald.

1935, at $100 per week. Her seven-year contract included salary raises whenever the studio exercised one of its options—the first after six months, the remainder on an annual basis. If she wasn't dropped from the MGM roster along the way, she would be making $1,000 per week by late 1941.

Metro's first move was to introduce her to a national radio audience. On October 26, Judy sang on NBC's *Shell Chateau Hour*, and her appearance was remembered thirty-five years later by Miles Kreuger, president of the Institute of the American Musical: "Her performance of 'Broadway Rhythm' on that broadcast literally defies belief; for her poised assurance, effortless vocal control, sense of dramatic dynamics, pathos, and skill at syncopation were as fully developed as they would ever become. At the age of thirteen, she was a consummate performer." Garland returned to *Shell Chateau* three weeks later and recalled that second show for more personal reasons: "I did a show with [Wallace Beery] the night before my father died. Before we went on, the doctor telephoned that dad would be listening. I guess I knew he was going to die, because he'd been too sick to have a radio. I sang my heart out for him. By morning, he was gone."

Frank Gumm's frailties had played havoc with his family's stability. But his death (from a virulent meningitis) effectively eliminated the emotional center of Baby Gumm's life, and the loss of him weakened any minimal grasp she might have had of the reasons for her parents' problems. Decades later, she would ask journalist Vernon Scott, "Did you ever hear anything about my father being homosexual? I only heard it once, from my mother, and then I think she said it to sort of alibi her relationship with Will Gilmore." Ethel had long since begun an extra-marital affair with Gilmore, a Lancaster neighbor whose wife had been crippled by a stroke, and who—for reasons unknown—delighted in tormenting Baby Gumm. The Ethel/Will involvement was a poorly kept secret, even while Frank Gumm was alive; then, four years to the day after his death, Ethel married the widowed Gilmore, which only fed Judy's resentment of both the man and her mother.

Saving grace came with work. In addition to attending school on the MGM lot, Garland began daily coaching with Roger Edens. The Texas-born Edens had studied locally and in Paris before winding up as a Broadway musician, notably providing accompaniment and then vocal arrangements for Ethel Merman. He'd come to Metro not long before Judy and championed her from the onset. In addition to their ultimately three-decade professional association, Edens filled a personal gap for Judy; a few years later, the teen acknowledged, "I know no one could really take my father's place, but Roger comes nearest."

It was Edens' outstanding capacity to create special material—melodies and lyrics—that quickly defined Judy's public persona. By decade's end, he had worked with her on songs for commercial recordings, seven feature films, and more than seventy-five radio shows. One of his numbers proved to be her first signature tune and first record hit for Decca, "Dear Mr. Gable." (In all, Garland recorded twenty-one singles for the label between June 1936 and October 1939, with "Over the Rainbow" her first "charting" disc. Two earlier audition records for Decca had been rejected by the label, and only the first of these—pre-MGM, from March 1935—is now known to survive. If Judy's "On the Good Ship Lollipop" and "The Object of My Affection" now seem intentionally coy and affected, she sings them solidly and effortlessly. Meanwhile, her "Dinah" is astoundingly precocious and mature; as is "Bill," an audio souvenir of the song that had become her vaude-ville mainstay. First heard publicly in 2010, the tracks were celebrated by Will Friedwald, who appreciatively offered in *The Wall Street Journal* that Judy was "even at age twelve, already larger than life." Roger Edens and MGM would refine the Garland sound, approach, and ability—and present it to the world—but her God-given talent obviously predated their involvement.)

To further boost Judy's visibility, Edens also accompanied her on sixteen weeks of personal appearance tours for the studio in 1938 and 1939. She sang four shows a day, from Loew's State on Broadway to Miami, Chicago, and points in between. In every instance, Garland received what one wag later noted was "the same review she got for her whole career": "[Judy's] just about the grandest bundle of personality ever presented . . . the audience doesn't want her to leave the stage. [They're] blistering their hands at her grand singing . . . [in] a great big voice that does justice to hot-cha melodies or ballads" (Pittsburgh *Press*, March 26, 1938).

By the end of the decade, Judy had risen to full-fledged star status on the MGM roster. But the earlier specters of overwork and medication were frequent partners in her ascent. No one seemed to comprehend the fact that the genuine vulnerability and sensitivity that made Garland's multi-talents so exceptional also left her ill-equipped to withstand the relentless career flogging dictated by her abilities. Given a determined campaign to reduce the girl's naturally plump, four-foot eleven-inch frame to a camera-thin ninety-five pounds, the studio began to supply her with Benzedrine as a weight suppressant. Its enervating effects were then counteracted with barbiturates.

In the early 1970s, Judy's sister Jimmie would protest, "[Our] mother didn't think it was bad. If she had, she wouldn't have let Judy take it." This statement was perhaps as much an attempt to neutralize the notorious stage-mother image that Ethel had earned as it was an honest recollection. However, it's true that there was little initial knowledge about the addictive or nerve-destroying qualities of such easily obtainable "miracle" prescription drugs; or that increased dosages would be required as a user developed a physical tolerance to them; or that the young Judy was being detrimentally hastened without let-up from film to broadcast to recording studio to personal appearance. In a statement that was part-hindsight and part unwittingly self-damning, an anonymous MGM executive admitted in 1960, "I see now that we exploited Judy in many ways. We treated her like a property instead of a kid. [But] at the time, we thought we were doing her a favor. She had come up from nothing—nothing at all. We set her up for a lifetime of money and success. If the rest of us expected to ride along with her, that was only natural."

Yet through it all and across countless performances to come, Judy conveyed an almost limitless joy to any audience, onscreen and off. Such natural ebullience often extended to all of those in her personal orbit as well. Mrs. Ira Gershwin once reflected, "Wherever Judy went, there was laughter." Marcella Rabwin could later look back at Garland's increasingly troubled times and assert, "She wasn't born for tragedy. Her laughing face as a child could brighten up the whole neighborhood. Her sense of humor made her a favorite companion. She was the life of every party." With a gift for succinct summation, Garland's daughter, Lorna Luft would retrospectively offer, "Yes, tragic things happened to my mother. But *she* was not a tragedy."

As the new decade began, Garland and her mother had much to make them happy. They reveled in a spacious Bel Air home. Judy's new (and Louis B. Mayer-approved) agents negotiated for her a better contract and salary increase, befitting an Oscar honoree and top ten box-office name. Her onscreen magic in *The Wizard of Oz* and *Babes in Arms* had lifted MGM songwriter Arthur Freed to the status of "producer"—a title he would enjoy through two decades-plus of superlative motion

picture entertainment. Roger Edens was his right hand, the power behind the Freed throne, and for ten years, Garland was their principal muse. Astoundingly, she starred or guest-starred in twenty feature films between 1940 and 1950. In that same period, she also made more than a hundred broadcasts, plus nearly three dozen gratis appearances on behalf of World War II Armed Forces Radio. (Virtually all of the programs involved special songs, sketches, and material that had to be rehearsed apart from Judy's film work.) Between 1940 and 1947, Judy also cut forty-two Decca sides and three separate "movie cast albums"—*Girl Crazy*, *Meet Me in St. Louis*, and *The Harvey Girls*.

**CLOCKWISE FROM TOP LFET**: Jackie Cooper was Judy's first Hollywood "beau." Here he beams as she signs an autograph at the premiere of MGM's *Captains Courageous* (March 23, 1937). | June 26, 1940: Just eighteen and determined to enjoy some "real girl" experiences, Judy attended the graduation ceremony at University High School, accompanied by her mom. | Making a personal-and-autograph-signing appearance at the 1941 Chinese Moon Festival with fellow MGM star Robert Young.

Judy Garland was one of the very first movie stars to entertain the troops during World War II. In January 1942, just weeks after the attack on Pearl Harbor, she and husband David Rose interrupted their already-deferred honeymoon to tour army camps from Michigan to Texas; the stint was interrupted only by Garland's hospitalization with strep throat. (Rose can be seen at right at the piano for Judy's rehearsal with the band at their first stop, Fort Custer, Michigan. For the performance, she shed her coat and acquired an alternately rapt or vociferous audience of military men, along with a few of their family members and associates.) Later in the year, she led the "Judy Garland Community Sing" on the steps of the Los Angeles Victory House in Pershing Square, attracting twenty-five thousand citizens who joined her in patriotic numbers from the concurrent *For Me and My Gal*.

Finally, Judy did another army camp tour on her own in summer 1943 and then joined an all-star cast for the Hollywood Bond Cavalcade/Third War Loan. The latter trek encompassed sixteen cities and sold over a billion dollars in bonds. In each locale, the stars did a daily motorcade parade, random afternoon appearances, and then an evening stage show in the largest possible venue. The cast included Lucille Ball, James Cagney, Dick Powell, Betty Hutton, Kathryn Grayson, Paul Henreid, Greer Garson, Harpo Marx, Jose Iturbi, Kay Kyser and His Orchestra, and (shown at right as they entrained from city to city) Judy, Mickey Rooney, and Fred Astaire.

Concurrent with her prodigious film activity, Garland's private life evolved from that of a girl to that of a young woman. But given her inherent emotionality and the conflated reality/fantasy of the Hollywood star existence, her transition was commensurately more painful. Judy's teen crushes and publicity dates in the late 1930s had included Jackie Cooper, Billy Halop, Freddie Bartholomew, Robert Stack, and Mickey Rooney. As the decade turned, her gravitation toward father figures—or, at best, facsimiles thereof—led to fascination and obsession with Oscar Levant, Johnny Mercer, and particularly Artie Shaw. Garland was psychologically devastated when Shaw rejected her to marry fellow MGM star Lana Turner on their first date. (Turner was forever the physical standard of beauty to which Judy compared herself—or to which she felt she was compared by the studio.) Meanwhile, men and boys managed to walk away from Judy unscathed, except for songwriter Mercer. It's recently been asserted that many of his most declarative love lyrics were inspired by several seasons of torching for Garland: "That Old Black Magic," "This Time, the Dream's On Me," "One For My Baby," and "I Remember You" among them. But Mercer was already married, and Judy—on the rebound from Shaw—was seriously dating composer David Rose.

In an attempt to establish her independence from both mother and Metro at age nineteen, she married Rose on July 28, 1941. Rose did excellent orchestral arranging and conducting on Judy's behalf and accompanied her on her first tour of military camps in 1942. But, in the words of Garland scenarist Fred Finklehoffe, the musician proved to be "cold and undemonstrative. . . . He would not respond to her love in quite the way she offered it . . . young, romantic, eager." Whatever her

Judy at home with her first husband, composer/conductor David Rose, circa late 1941. He was a dozen years her senior and a fine musical adjunct to her radio and recording work. But their romantic match was a fleeting thing, and Rose was incapable of withstanding the power plays perpetrated by MGM and Judy's mother when those forces decided that she should abort their child.

husband's reticence, Judy eventually found herself pregnant. Rose offered no support when Ethel Gumm (with the full force of MGM behind her) took Judy to have the pregnancy terminated. This effectively ended their union, and they were divorced in 1944.

Through it all, Judy was expected to work, work, work, and she suffered her first nervous breakdown in early 1943. (There would be similar illnesses in 1947, 1948, 1949, and 1950.) Around the same time, she sought solace in passionate affairs with two married men, enduring a second abortion during a relationship with actor Tyrone Power, and then ever-after referencing Joseph Mankiewicz as the major love of her life. If bad luck seemed to infuse her personal life, there were countless happy milestones in any professional endeavor. Her films were box-office champions. Her first formal concert drew the largest audience in the twenty-six year history of the original Robin Hood Dell in Philadelphia. On a smaller scale, Garland enjoyed the same rapturous reception when performing "live" at army camps, service hospitals, and on an all-star bond tour.

In late 1943, she began to work full-time with director Vincente Minnelli. He had been peripherally involved in several of her film musicals in the preceding three years, but *Meet Me in St. Louis* was their first real project together. Off-camera, they slowly began an affair that culminated in a June 15, 1945 wedding. Garland saw the association as a fresh beginning. She vowed to rid herself of medication,

which was a gesture Minnelli welcomed. What was less auspicious—for him and for Metro—was her plan to divest herself of a long-term studio association after her MGM pact expired in 1947. In healthy determination to avoid any more overwork, Judy hoped to freelance, do one film a year, and perhaps tackle a stage musical and/or radio series. When her intentions were made public, corporate chaos reigned at Loew's, Inc., Metro's parent company: Garland was immeasurably valuable as the studio's star among stars. They quickly worked to romance her into a new five-year deal, raising her salary to the basic industry maximum: $5,619.23 per week, with an annual forty-week guarantee. Encouraged by Minnelli, she signed the contract, which went into effect when she returned to work after a maternity leave. Daughter Liza May was born on March 12, 1946.

Within months, Garland regretted the new pact with MGM. All the pressure she'd sought to circumvent was back. Her health was compromised by the birth of Liza, the earlier years of emotional defenselessness and physical addiction, and the growing realization that her marriage and husband were ineffectual. (Minnelli himself would come to concur with the last estimation.) Gentle, protective, solicitous, and professionally gifted, the director was perhaps too much the quintessential father figure of Judy's adulthood. Garland blamed herself as well, given a regrettable ability to unrealistically ascribe to the men in her life whatever characteristics she most desired of them. During her courtship with Minnelli, she had ignored indications and counsel that the man was bisexual. Metro dancing star Ann Miller put a more knowing—if cavalier—spin on the director's effeminacy by exclaiming in 1996, "Vincente Minnelli! You had to close the window, or he'd fly right out!" Judy's suicidal reaction when later discovering him in a compromising situation with a male employee is somber history.

FROM LEFT: First Class Seaman Guy Madison escorts Judy to the Carthay Circle premiere of *Since You Went Away* (August 1944). Madison launched his acting career with a brief bit in the film and was later best known as TV's "Wild Bill Hickock." | Already a mutual-admiration society: Nearly a decade prior to *A Star is Born*, Judy bonds with director George Cukor at the 1944 party hosted by Elsa Maxwell to celebrate the liberation of Paris during World War II. | Howard Dietz plays host to Judy and Hedy Lamarr at a 1945 MGM party held for the staff of *Modern Screen* magazine. Broadway lyricist Dietz was also Metro's director of public relations.

FROM LEFT: Judy spent her twenty-third birthday posing for new portraits at MGM and was given a surprise party by the publicity staff and members of the various studio crews. She had just completed *The Harvey Girls*; fiancé Vincente Minnelli was wrapping up *Yolanda and the Thief*. | Born on March 12, 1946, Liza drew her first name from a popular song by George and Ira Gershwin and Gus Kahn. Over the years, Judy celebrated her daughter by performing that number on radio, stage, and television.

Whatever the specifics, the Garland/Minnelli relationship became increasingly complex, and there were separations and reconciliations through the end of the decade. Judy resumed lengthy sessions in psychiatry, sometimes working with her doctors and at other times bolting from what seemed a futile process. Mayer had put a halt to such visits for her earlier in the decade, a decision he now regretted. She was in and out of sanitariums, treated for exhaustion and medication withdrawal, and had to be replaced in three films. After a much-publicized dismissal from *Annie Get Your Gun*, Judy was advised to recuperate at the Mayer-recommended Peter Bent Brigham Hospital in Boston. Broke, she turned to Loew's, Inc. for an advance to pay for the trip and treatment. When they refused ("We are not running a charity organization"), Mayer ashamedly offered her a personal loan. Ultimately, Loew's opted to provide her the necessary funds but extracted reimbursement when she once again began working. Meanwhile, even while on suspension, Judy made arrangements for her mother to receive the weekly stipend she'd drawn out of Garland's salary ever since the girl had started at MGM. Unfortunately, the two were now estranged over Judy's fears that Ethel had begun to subject baby Liza to a series of familiar stage-mother patterns.

Once again (typically) the six Garland feature films and thirty radio broadcasts that accompanied these four years of personal upheaval were expressions of jubilance, excitement, and happy song, dance, and laughter. When able to work, she remained the studio's greatest asset. But after another suspension over the film *Royal Wedding*, and an internationally headlined suicide attempt, Judy was finally released from her MGM contract in September 1950. There was a mix of frustration, compassion, and emotionless cold in their gesture, but it all came under the advisement of Dr. Marcus Rabwin, who told Mayer, "This girl is going to die if she doesn't get away from here."

Judy's own feelings were similarly jumbled. Sixteen years of security were over. At age twenty-eight, she was overweight, financially insolvent, and—in the dramatized press of the day—written off as unemployable. What she came quite quickly to discover, however, is that she remained "box office," and increasingly so. Reflecting on the evolution of her own career, fellow MGM star Rosalind Russell later wrote, "It's a funny thing about audience acceptance. If you don't have it, there isn't much you can do about it. If you do have it, it can nourish you. I remember talking to Judy when she was playing the Palace. 'Well,' I said, 'You're knocking them out of your seats; isn't it great?' 'Yes,' she said. 'And I've found out one thing. I've found out I have an audience, and no one can take that away from me.' It was true. Even though she'd been dropped from films, she had an audience until the day she died."

In 1950, the Palace and any Garland return-to-films were all in the unforeseeable future; but there were other, instant helping hands. In Judy's own words, "Bing asked me to be on his radio show. You can't see a fat person on the radio. He knew I couldn't find work, but he treated me like a star. What a wonderful man." (Crosby's response: "We've got a spot for Judy every week, if she can put up with us.") Between October 1950 and March 1951, Garland appeared on eight Crosby programs. There were other radio appearances as well, rumors of recordings, and discussions about Broadway work with no less than Richard Rodgers and Oscar Hammerstein II. But the most logical route to travel for "Baby-Gumm-grown" led Judy Garland back to the vaudeville stage and to a nineteen-year career in "live" entertainment. Her ultimate impact in this field of endeavor was subsequently recapped in one sentence by an entertainment historian: "If it can be measured by the pitch of excitement in the auditorium, Garland was the greatest artist of the [twentieth] century." Repeatedly across those years, she received what countless theater managers and booking agents described as "the greatest ovation I've ever seen or heard."

Some percentage of that audience exhilaration may have been motivated by nostalgia or empathy. But it's safe to say that their basic reaction was compelled by a distillation of Garland's overwhelming gifts. The professional critics would exult over the fact that "What she does is always real singing, and often singing of a high caliber"—so much so that "She could sing in front of Mt. Rushmore, and you wouldn't even notice the heads." One journalist was pleased to note, "She moves with grace and elegance," while others felt wonder and glee at discovering and disclosing "her secret: at heart, Judy's a little clown" and "an untiring worker—a youthful personification of ageless show business."

The omnipresent charisma and Garland's somehow ever-growing capacity to entertain were apparent as well: "There is something that comes through that makes people enthusiastic—a type of radiance; people streamed down the aisles to applaud as near to the star as possible." Other reporters went for poetry-in-prose: "Hers was a triumph of the art that conceals art," "Her magnetism is easily capable of lifting several tons of scrap iron," "She is a universal treasure" and, finally, "She could have walked on water." The quotes are drawn from world-wide press and span the years 1951–1969; they cover Judy's first adult stage appearances to her last. There were difficult nights along the way, of course. She suffered occasions of overmedication, exhaustion, or illness, resulting in canceled, aborted, or disastrous concerts. But during those nineteen years, Garland completed—in pretty much unprecedented triumph—something over 93 percent of her scheduled bookings: 1,100 "live" shows.

These were launched in 1951 by her courageous decision to start her return at the top, if out of the country. London's premiere variety house had been clamoring for Judy for several seasons; MGM, naturally, wouldn't let her consider the idea of such an absence or interlude. As a free agent now, Garland was available to open a month's worth of shows at the Palladium on April 9, 1951: fifty-six thirty-five minute performances in all. Her success led to six weeks of equally victorious touring in England, Ireland, and Scotland, as she proclaimed: "Now I know I can do it; I'm going to pick up where I left off. I am going to sing my heart out." She would additionally exult, "The wonderful warmth of all those people gave me a whole new grip on life"—so much so that, on her return to the United States, she gambled further by planning to bring a similar vaudeville bill to Broadway.

The legendary Palace Theatre was originally the hallowed showplace of live entertainment, but in the face of radio, film, and (eventually) television competition, it had become a threadbare movie house. With an act written by Roger Edens and staged by Chuck Walters, Judy reopened a refurbished Palace on October 16, 1951, and sang her way into theatrical history. The scheduled four-week engagement—which cynical showmen and columnists declared in advance would never sell—had to be extended to nineteen weeks. Overnight, scalpers were peddling tickets at four and five times their face value; Garland ultimately won a special Tony Award and took the production to Los Angeles and San Francisco. A subsequent coast-to-coast tour was scrapped when she became pregnant.

OPPOSITE, COUNTER CLOCKWISE FROM TOP LEFT: Born November 21, 1952, the alliteratively named Lorna Luft is here barely a month old and already gives as good as she gets. | "Happiness is a thing called Joe"—Joseph Wiley Luft arrived on March 29, 1955, and served as the finest possible gift for a mother who would lose the Best Actress Oscar a few hours later. | November 27, 1957: Judy, Lorna, and Joe return to the United States on board the Queen Mary after Garland triumphs at the Dominion Theatre and Palladium "Royal Variety Show" in London. | Considering a permanent move to London in autumn 1960, Judy and Sid Luft leased Carol Reed's house and brought Liza, Lorna, and Joe abroad to test the experience with them.

On June 8, 1952, she married manager Sid Luft, who'd been escorting her for the preceding twenty months and whose emotional support was credited for her comeback. (The preceding September, with the Palace opening at hand, Judy had been forced to undergo a third abortion. A marriage to Luft at that time was inconceivable, as Garland's divorce from Minnelli had not been finalized.) Daughter Lorna Luft was born on November 21, 1952; by then, preproduction work on Judy's return to films had already begun, despite an emotional setback when her long-estranged mother died on January 5, 1953. *A Star is Born* would be the only motion picture in which Garland appeared in the 1950s, but it was and remains one of the most challenging and best fulfilled popular showcases afforded any actor.

FROM LEFT: "Dorothy" greets "The Scarecrow" (Ray Bolger) at a Los Angeles Masquers dinner for Arthur Freed in 1954. | Director and costars congratulate Judy on the set of *Judgment at Nuremberg*, March 1961. From left: producer/director Stanley Kramer, Burt Lancaster, Spencer Tracy, Richard Widmark, and Maximilian Schell. | Jane Fonda, Roddy McDowall, and Judy at Robert Goulet's Cocoanut Grove opening, 1963.

Joseph Wiley Luft, Judy's third child, was born on March 29, 1955. She spent most of the rest of the decade in work. There were annual theatrical tours, each with a different revue program or format, and all of which broke records or set some new level of industry excellence. In 1956, Garland became the highest-paid performer in Las Vegas history and then returned to the Palace for seventeen weeks. There were successes in London in 1957, at the Cocoanut Grove in 1958, and in a 1959 tour of opera houses, including the Metropolitan in New York. Judy "live" was, in effect, Judy in her natural habitat. She drew cross-generational fans (one wag later described Garland audiences as ranging in age "from fetal to fatal") and inspired the kind of standing, shouting ovations that were customary for opera divas but totally unheard of as a response to popular entertainers.

For her 1950s shows, Garland mixed the standard songs expected by her audiences with new material, often drawn from her latest recordings. After the early Decca successes, Judy had appeared on a series of well-received MGM soundtrack albums, signed a mysteriously unfulfilled 1951 contract with RCA Victor, and cut four singles and the *Star* soundtrack for release by Columbia. Her classiest and most timeless discs were made during a profitable and mostly exceptional decade on the Capitol Records label, beginning with the 1955 "greatest hits" assemblage aptly titled *Miss Show Business*. Subsequent "concept" albums included *Judy* (a 1956 collection of standards new to Garland), *Alone* (a torchy, mostly tender 1957 ballad compilation), *Judy in Love* (a 1958 mélange of happier romantic classics), and *The Letter* (an original 1959 "musical" written for records). Less propitiously, Capitol also taped Garland live on her closing night at the Grove, but after fourteen concerts in less than two weeks, her vocal weariness was reflected in the resultant album.

Television had clamored for Judy from the time she departed Metro, and all-time record fees were offered for everything from a guest appearance on *The Arthur Murray Party* to a TV adaptation of *The Heiress*, starring Garland and James Mason. Under Luft's aegis, she finally launched a video career with her own specials in 1955 and 1956, but the strain of "live" television led her to over-medicate, impacting her voice and nerves. Critical reaction to both shows was mixed, but public response to Judy and the overwhelming ratings success of the programs swiftly led her into a long-term deal with CBS. The pact was dissolved in 1957 when the network failed to live up to its contractual obligations for a third special, and Garland summarily refused to perform. Subsequently, an at-home visit with the Lufts on *Person to Person* was canceled, and attempts to reconcile Judy and the network went unfulfilled until 1961, despite proposals for TV versions of an expanded "Born in a Trunk" or a video version of *The Letter*, opposite Mickey Rooney.

By then, even greater problems had grown from Judy's ever-more-compromised physical and mental health. "I played some very big dates in 1958 and 1959," she would later reflect. "[But] I staggered along in a nightmare, knowing something was vitally wrong—but what? I was a virtual automaton, with no memory." Despite dieting attempts, Garland had bloated to 180 pounds; near-death in November 1959, she was clapped into a New York hospital. History is divided as to whether she was afflicted with hepatitis or cirrhosis. (It's worth noting that, defying years of press conjecture and outright accusation, Judy's autopsy a decade later showed no trace of either alcoholism or cirrhosis.) Whatever the diagnosis, her liver was more than four times its normal size, inflamed by two decades of pills and tonics and crippled by years of personal and financial pressure and overwork.

Though she and Luft genuinely cared for each other, his business acumen was seemingly nonexistent. Well-known as a gambler and clotheshorse, he'd left an endless trail of unpaid bills, despite Judy's top salaries in every medium. He was also known for scooping money out of the till at the theaters in which he'd booked his wife, thus eliminating any payment for them at the conclusion of an engagement. Luft frequently self-referenced himself—and was thought of—as Garland's savior during the 1950s. What has seldom been put into perspective is the theory that she would have required much less saving if he hadn't so mismanaged her funds and energies. During Judy's near-fatal illness, he worked out one of the deals for which he prided himself: a contract for her autobiography with publisher Bennett Cerf. The advance money was intended to tide over the family while Garland recuperated; Luft purportedly lost the entire sum at the track on the day it was paid over.

Meanwhile, across seven weeks of hospitalization, twenty quarts of fluid were slowly drained from Judy's body. She slowly, almost unexpectedly, recovered and, at age thirty-seven, was told she could never work again. Garland's reaction was perhaps the first sign of healing: "You want to know something funny? I just didn't care. All I cared about was that my children needed me. The children have always been terribly close to me. No matter how ill I've been, I've always been able to make sense with them. Perhaps because they're my security—not only because of the love they give me, but because of the love I find I can give them, that I want to give them. But the pressure was off. I just thought: no more pills, ever. I'm free. I'll find a way to be happy."

Early 1960 brought six months of recuperation, interrupted only by some low-key recording work for Columbia Pictures' *Pepe* and a new Capitol album, *That's Entertainment*. On holiday in London in August, Garland did additional recording and then showed real proof of her new-found health by presenting her first one-woman concert. It was the onset of a fresh performance format: the programs ultimately read "Act One: Judy/Act Two: More Judy," as she offered upwards of thirty songs in each show. She toured abroad for the last four months of the year and somehow, miraculously, created even greater excitement than at any past career point. ("The miracle," explained Roger Edens at the time, "is that she enjoys singing again, as she did when she was a child.")

In December, Sid sold her career over to Freddie Fields and David Begelman, who were then launching a new management agency. The motivated duo leapt on the resurgent Garland; in the first two years of their association, Judy did more than eighty live performances, and from the Hollywood Bowl to the Newport Jazz Festival, she broke attendance and box-office records everywhere. The highlight of the tour—and one of a dozen or so Mount Everest-like peaks in the overall Garland career—came on April 23, 1961, when she played New York's Carnegie Hall. Later heralded as "the greatest night in show business history," the concert was recorded live, and Capitol's *Judy at Carnegie Hall* became the fastest-selling two-disc set in history. On the charts for ninety-seven weeks—thirteen at number one—it garnered five Grammy Awards, including Album of the Year and Best Female Vocal Performance. (Over the last five decades, it has been released on vinyl, then tape, and then compact disc and has never been out of print.)

During the same forty-eight months, Fields and Begelman booked Garland to complete four feature films. She also recorded another album and two singles for Capitol. She starred in the highest-rated TV special in CBS history, committed to another special, and (with all three major networks in the bidding) signed contracts for her own weekly series. *The Judy Garland Show*, set to premiere in the 1963–1964 season, was later defined by head of CBS Programming Michael Dann as the biggest talent deal in the history of the medium: "Twenty-four million dollars over four years—the most money ever paid for a single variety star." In December 1959, Garland had been a thirty-seven year old invalid. In December 1962, she was forty,

and the biggest, hottest, and most revered name in the industry. Judy was overjoyed at the upswing and grateful to both Begelman and Fields. Fields—sage but self-congratulatory—would state, "If there's one thing we've done, it's been to make Judy's career a business. You wouldn't run Macy's with lackeys or relatives."

Garland to some extent endorsed the frenzied schedule as a means of clearing her debts and establishing funds and a home for her children. But she was also charmed into the overwork by the ambitious and already-married Begelman, who both romanced her to ill effect and, in the later words of columnist Liz Smith, "systematically robbed [her] blind." He and Fields built their careers and their Creative Management Associates on Judy's comeback, willfully heedless of the detrimental effects such a grind would have on her health. By the time her TV series went into preproduction in spring 1963, they were booking their clients on the show (both in front of and behind the cameras), and extracting commissions for one and all. If they were greedily aware of such monetary benefits, their lack of experience in the early days of CMA also worked against Judy.

At New York's Kennedy Airport, Judy, Liza, and Mark Herron await the arrival of Lorna and Joe Luft, December 29, 1964. The two youngsters, pawns in the divorce case between Judy and Sid Luft, had been hidden away by their father in defiance of a court order that he send them east to their mother for Christmas.

Mike Dann later stated, "In television, we all know that where a show is scheduled is more important than even the content of the show. And Begelman didn't ask about what time period she would be put in." Slotted against NBC's top-rated *Bonanza*, Garland's series was instantly in jeopardy; her chances were further diminished by an interfering network. Dann summarized her predicament: "Here's a woman who has spent her whole lifetime developing a style. And imagine the president of the network [James Aubrey], with no record in the variety area at all, telling her, 'You've got to change.' She was the victim of bad advice as to the structures of her show; she had to reduce herself to the forms we were suggesting. The failure of the show was [caused by] the absolute difficulties we presented to her." Though venerated by many critics and "viewers who seek showmanship and sophistication," *The Judy Garland Show* was canceled after twenty-six episodes.

Back on the road, and long since back on medication to meet the demands of her career, Judy spent the last five years of her life on a dizzying and devastating roller coaster. There were nearly two hundred additional concerts—some embarrassing, but most triumphant, despite the drying effect that prescription drugs could have on her vocal chords. Garland had been placed on Ritalin as a "mood elevator" after her 1959 illness. Unfortunately, it was just as likely to incite addiction as any of the stimulants she'd been prescribed in the past.

Between 1964 and 1969, she made nearly two dozen TV guest appearances, but these also vacillated wildly in quality, and the viewing audience was more and more confronted by a Judy whose excesses were publicly unexplained and inexplicable. The confusion was compounded when difficulties in her personal life continued to hit the press with wearying frequency. There were apparent suicide attempts; a dozen hospitalizations; a custody battle with (and divorce from) Luft; and marriages to two younger and bisexual men: actor Mark Herron, on November 14, 1965, and musician/entrepreneur Mickey Deans, on March 15, 1969. Garland was continually dunned for the back taxes Luft had never paid on her late 1950s earnings—a sum that ran to nearly $400,000. Fields and Begelman ended their association with her in 1966, and almost immediately, Judy futilely joined Sid in an embezzlement lawsuit against them.

Ironically, once again entrusting Luft was her only recourse, and he would be responsible for booking Garland's final United States concerts in 1967 and 1968. (These included a happy, record-breaking return to the Palace and an amazing outdoor stand on the Boston Common that drew 108,000 people.) Judy had agreed to undertake such a workload when assured by Luft and those in charge that it would solve her financial problems. But by 1968, she was even more in debt; understandably, the monetary machinations of Luft and some of his cohorts finally disillusioned her, and she refused to accept further bookings from them. In turn, Luft impounded

After playing to her largest single live audience—108,000 people on the Boston Common—Judy and Joe enjoyed the attractions at Paragon Park on Nantasket Beach, September 1967.

her orchestrations, taking the stand that if Judy wouldn't work for him, she couldn't work for anyone else. This left Garland pretty much adrift; with her permission and regret, Luft took Lorna and Joe to live with him in California.

Desperate for funds, Judy briefly returned to the Fields and Begelman camp, dropping her portion of the lawsuit against them to obtain a comparatively small check for accumulated royalties that they'd been holding. In December 1968, with fiancé Deans in tow, she sought refuge in England. Her final appearances that winter—in London, Sweden, and Denmark—ranged in quality from excellent to fair, but most of them left audiences enraptured and on their feet, thrilled with her still-potent artistry. She did, however, suffer one night of indignity at London's Talk of the Town, when she arrived late, and a handful of irate, rowdy patrons tossed garbage on the nightclub stage. As with a delayed arrival for a Melbourne concert five years earlier, Garland took the stage thinking that management had made her requested apology in advance, explaining the genuine illness that had delayed her. In both cases, no such announcement had been made.

Those who befriended Judy across those final years were always quick to note that she rose to the occasion as often and as best she could. Unfortunately, much of the beneficial medical intelligence since devised wasn't even imagined in the 1950s and '60s. There were no comprehensive facilities or comprehending authorities to aid in substance abuse issues—or to relieve the apparent bi-polar extremes Garland sometimes exhibited. Regardless, in her efforts to withdraw from prescription drugs, Judy semi-regularly entered such treatment centers as existed in the 1960s. Up through her last major attempt, just eleven months before her death, she once again diligently worked to avoid self-medication; witnesses remember her resultant renewed mental and physical health and voice. But as in the past, there was no ongoing, adequate support or foundation on which she could continue to rebuild herself or her life. She invariably crumbled or angrily lashed out—escaping to hide again in medication—when confronted by her lack of funds; "her" massive debt incurred by those with whom she entrusted her business affairs; her physical frailty and emotional confusion; her separation from (and inability to support) her two teenage children; the distancing manifested by her eldest daughter; the loss of her home; and a multitude of past guilts.

As one of countless international headlines expressed it, Judy Garland died of "the pills she needed to live" in her London cottage on June 22, 1969. CBS newsman Mike Wallace later astutely defined that accidental overdose of Seconal as "one sleeping pill too many for a body that had become too frail, too vulnerable." (According to the pathologist who conducted her autopsy, Garland was then delicate to the point of malnutrition, which as much as anything else contributed to her passing.) Her subsequent wake in New York City drew 22,000

Judy reflectively waits for the onset of an interview during a Chicago press conference, September 13, 1967. She, Lorna, and Joe played for the next three evenings at the Civic Opera House; closing night saw Garland deliver eighteen songs, four encores, and a two-hour-plus performance that remains legendary in the history of that venue.

mourners of all ages, and—as a sometimes surprised media observed—they'd gathered not out of pity but to quietly honor someone who was genuinely loved. James Mason followed their lead at Judy's funeral on June 27 and pointedly eulogized his *A Star is Born* costar as "the most sympathetic, the funniest, the sharpest, and the most stimulating woman I ever knew. I traveled in her orbit only for a while, but it was an exciting while during which it seemed that the joys in her life outbalanced the miseries."

As one looks back over the forty-seven year arc of Judy Garland's life, it's important to acknowledge that the joys did, indeed, outbalance the miseries. Such perception is perhaps most true to Judy herself; as late as January 1969, it was the stance she took when healthily reviewing her successes and failures. The latter were definitely in the minority in terms of overall career achievement, and it's safe to say that Garland would base any appraisal of her personal happiness on the love she shared with her children. Individually and collectively, Liza, Lorna, and Joe have always championed their mother's memory, as have virtually all who observed her with them. In 1998, Marcella Rabwin wrote, "Judy deeply loved her children; they had so much fun together. Her children may have suffered from certain physical and emotional deprivations, but they will tell you, in spite of everything, they had a wonderful life with 'Mama' because of her humor and warmth. When Judy was 'ill,' the children would look after her and wait until she could be their mother again. That took a lot of character from youngsters. They watched from the sidelines as Judy's money, her earning power, her talent were all exploited and consumed; but through all these travails, they adored her and knew her as a good-hearted and loving mother."

In illness—or confusion or anger—Judy Garland could at times create genuine havoc for those who traveled in her orbit. There were nocturnal phone calls, sudden bursts of temper, suicide attempts; her behavior could be irrational or even monstrous. But to her credit, the vast majority of those with whom she worked or was associated have gone on to reference their alliance as an incomparable lifetime highlight. Thousands of personal reminiscences in books, documentaries, oral histories, and the press echo the 1994 declaration of one of Garland's colleagues, who pronounced, "No one was more talented. No one ever spread more joy. And no one was better loved." Finally, such affection as expressed by her children and coworkers must be augmented by the loving reaction Garland has now inspired in film, music, theater, and television devotees across more than seventy-five years. In his 1970 memorial address for Judy, the Reverend Peter Delaney classified her adherents as "the millions . . . throughout the world who will not and *cannot* forget Judy Garland"—a tally that has done nothing but increase in succeeding decades.

Waiting to say goodbye, June 26, 1969: The quadruple-stacked lines extended west from 81st Street and Madison Avenue to Fifth Avenue, north to 82nd Street, and around that corner. Twenty-two thousand quiet and ofttimes tearful mourners stood in line for up to four hours, simply to—as the press noted— pay their respects and express their thanks to someone they loved.

Given the theme of this book, perhaps a film critic and a film character should have the final words. Garland's last motion picture was *I Could Go on Singing* (1963), and in his London *Daily Express* critique, Leonard Mosley pondered, "Her voice is the same—yet different, somehow. Different and better. She still sings with her whole heart. It just seems somehow as if the heart were bigger." In turn, Mosley's assessment can be clarified by no less an expert than the Wizard of Oz himself, who once offered: "Remember . . . a heart is not judged by how much you love—but by how much you are loved by others."

Between February 1937 and June 1940, Judy appeared as a regular on three different radio series: the *Jack Oakie College*, MGM's *Good News...*, and *The Pepsodent Show Starring Bob Hope*. Audiences thrilled to the manner in which the teen put across Roger Edens' vocal arrangements of her movie songs, standards, and special material. Here, in 1937, she banters with *Oakie* announcer Bill Goodwin, who'd also appear with her and Hope during the 1939–40 season.

Across a score of broadcasts, Judy appeared as Bob Hope's resident girl singer and comic equal. The actor later wrote, "She was the sweetest, most unspoiled little girl who ever topped me in a comedy sketch. Judy was supposed to have a crush on me, and I was always nervous about being so much older than she was. I asked her once, 'Do your young friends think I'm in the groove?' And her diplomatic answer was, 'Well, they think you've got one foot in it.'"

For *Mail Call* #38, recorded on May 19, 1943, Garland was scripted to "act" with Jack Benny.

June 3, 1944: The AFRS *Command Performance* #122—Judy with Frank Sinatra and Bing Crosby. The latter would exalt, "Judy is one of the greatest talents, male or female, in Hollywood. She laughs infectiously. She's the perfect illustration of the 100 percent professional. You can't help being drawn by her magnetism. And it rubs off on you, too. Nobody can be professionally indifferent when [she's] part of the act."

From left: Adolphe Menjou, Ronald Colman, James Cagney, Judy, and Mickey Rooney at the all-star *Bundles for Britain* benefit program, January 1, 1941.

Groucho Marx did sketch comedy with Judy on *Mail Call* #19, recorded January 9, 1943, as one of the Armed Forces Radio programs, specifically produced for servicemen and women around the world.

An all-star gal chorale joins forces for a *Command Performance* Christmas Show prerecording in October 1944. From left: Dorothy Lamour, Ginny Simms, Dinah Shore, Judy, Virginia O'Brien, and Frances Langford.

"I could listen to her all night" was Al Jolson's atypical praise for another performer when he listened to Judy. She sang and traded banter with him on *The Kraft Music Hall*, September 30, 1948.

Rehearsing with John Scott Trotter for three programs with Bing Crosby in May and June 1952. Recollecting some two dozen broadcasts with Judy, Crosby proclaimed, "The weeks we did on radio were the best I ever had."

Garland's TV performance debut came at the behest of Henry Ford himself, who requested that she launch his company's monthly series of color programming. Broadway's David Wayne served as master of ceremonies for the September 24, 1955 premiere of *Ford Star Jubilee*; it won the largest audience for a television "special" to that date.

Seen here in rehearsal, photographer/visual consultant Richard Avedon and dancer/choreographer Peter Gennaro contributed to Judy's second CBS show, a half-hour concert sponsored by General Electric. It was a different era: the April 8, 1956, "live" telecast was precluded from some later filmed syndication when bluenoses criticized Garland's costumes for showing too much leg.

Judy capped her greatest comeback with *The Judy Garland Show* (February 25, 1962). The Norman Jewison production was reviewed by the Los Angeles *Times* as "absolutely inspired. . . . A magnificent job . . . capturing that errant [Garland] spirit." The high-priced, high caliber guest talent—Dean Martin and Frank Sinatra—faded into comparative obscurity, and the night and audience belonged to Judy.

Cigarette in hand, Garland rehearses for the program finale. Jewison later defined Judy as the preeminent talent of his directorial experience: "No one [else] comes close to her. She was open, curious, earthy, and very funny."

# THE JUDY GARLAND SHOW

**OPPOSITE:** At her first TV series taping, Judy debuted a memorable new Mort Lindsey orchestration of "When the Sun Comes Out" and concluded with a subtle nose-thumbing at MGM by singing "Too Late Now" from *Royal Wedding* and "Ol' Man River" from *Show Boat*—two of the films from which the studio had dropped her in 1950. **RIGHT FROM TOP:** "I can't do the first show with anyone but Mickey," trumpeted Judy. "He's my partner!" Rooney concluded the taping by offering, "Judy's the love of my life. My wife knows this...my wives know this!" | Seventeen-year-old Liza Minnelli had just enjoyed an off-Broadway success in a revival of *Best Foot Forward* when her mother invited her to share an episode of the series. | Regular Jerry Van Dyke (left) was colossally ill-served by the material provided for him by the Garland show writers and left after ten programs. Judy's old vaudeville compatriot Donald O'Connor guested on the debut telecast (September 29, 1963); it drew qualified reviews, but most echoed the New York *Herald Tribune* estimation: "Sparkling . . . magnetic . . . irresistible. Miss Garland worked a wizard's spell." **ABOVE:** Across the twenty-six episodes, Judy enjoyed memorable duets with Lena Horne, Tony Bennett, Peggy Lee, Vic Damone, Jack Jones, Steve Lawrence, Diahann Carroll, Mel Torme, Martha Raye, Steve Allen, Chita Rivera, Jane Powell, June Allyson, Ray Bolger, and Dick Shawn. Here, she and Bobby Darin trade banter prior to a medley of traveling songs.

TOP SPREAD FROM LEFT: "This was the most enjoyable night I've ever had," opined Jack Paar when Judy appeared as special guest on his weekly program (December 7, 1962). At her host's behest, Garland delivered uproarious anecdotes about her vaudeville, movie, and concert careers; unlike most movie stars, Judy proved to be even more entertaining as herself than when playing a scripted role. | Her March 19, 1963 CBS special found Judy in a solo revival of "Get Happy"; this go-round, there were no complaints about her legs. Larry Gelbart contributed excellent sketch comedy for Garland and guest Phil Silvers; here she plays a hopeless Broadway hopeful whose preparations for a singing audition push an impatient producer to snap, "No arrangements! Just do the song!" | Judy made her final United States TV appearances as guest and guest-hostess during two episodes of The Merv Griffin Show. Griffin welcomed her to the first, and Garland then took over the show for one night during his vacation. She interviewed everyone from Van Johnson to Moms Mabley and Rex Reed, finally duetting a charming "If You Were the Only Girl in the World" with program announcer, Arthur Treacher.

BOTTOM SPREAD FROM LEFT: Rehearsing with host Perry Como and costar Bill Cosby for The Kraft Music Hall (telecast February 28, 1966). Como's conductor Nick Perito later raved about the opportunity to pair him with Garland: "How great it was to accompany these two fabulous singers, who were relaxed and giving perfect interpretations of the lyrics they were singing. [And] no matter whether Judy was singing or acting, she represented the truth." | Garland guested for two consecutive weeks on the short-lived Sammy Davis, Jr. Show (March 18 and 25, 1966). On the second program, as "a couple of song and dance men" they performed a mélange of nearly twenty vaudeville classics. (A lifelong friend, Davis had a photo of young "Baby Gumm" on his nightstand throughout his long final illness in 1990.) | During the 1965–66 TV season, Judy worked twice as hostess of the popular Hollywood Palace. She opened the second appearance (telecast May 7) with "What the World Needs Now," in which an anonymous vocal arranger took a light, totally atypical Garland song and built it through several key changes into a rousing, go-for-broke showpiece.

# concerts

**THURSDAY, JULY 1**
Robin Hood Dell Orchestra
**ANDRE KOSTELANETZ,** Conductor
**JUDY GARLAND,** Soloist

A. *Berlioz* ................ Excerpts from "Damnation of Faust"
     a. Minuet of the Will-o'-the-Wisps
     b. Waltz—Danse of the Sylphes
     c. Rakoczy March

B. *Strauss* ........................................ Emperor Waltz

C. *Miss Garland*
   Group I
     1. *George Gershwin* ............ Four Love Songs
       a. "Someone to Watch Over Me"
       b. "Do Do Do"
       c. "Embraceable You"
       d. "The Man I Love"
     2. *George Gershwin* ........ "Strike Up the Band"

**INTERMISSION**

D. *Gershwin-Bennett* ............ Porgy and Bess Fantasy

E. *Miss Garland*
   Group II
     1. Medley of Judy Garland Songs
       a. "You Made Me Love You"
       b. "Our Love Affair"
       c. "Nobody's Baby"
       d. "For Me and My Gal"
       e. "Over the Rainbow"
     2. "The Joint Is Really Jumping Down at Carnegie Hall"

The STEINWAY is the Official Piano of Robin Hood Dell Concerts, Incorporated
Sound Re-enforcement by ALGENE SOUND AND RADIO COMPANY

**CLOCKWISE FROM TOP LEFT:** Judy's very first concert, in Philadelphia in 1943, attracted thirty thousand customers, who overflowed a sixty-five hundred seat amphitheater and its surrounding terrain. Crowds of them rushed the stage to be close to her at the show's conclusion. | Enthused journalist Jim Burton on Garland's 1951 Palace performance: "She is the one artist of our era who has achieved the stature of the beloved stars of the past generations. She makes [audiences] stand up and cheer at an age when most of the others were just getting started." | Judy worked briefly with The Wiere Brothers as the surprise finish to one of their routines during her 1955 "Seven City Tour." The revue garnered headlines that noted "Judy Rocks 'Em Again," "Garland's New Show Called Triumph at Opening," and "Judy Garland rises to thrilling heights."

**FROM LEFT:** Judy returned to the Palace in September 1956, winning front-page reviews in the New York dailies. By popular demand, her month-long engagement was ultimately extended to seventeen weeks. No longer two-a-day, Judy played the standard Broadway schedule of eight weekly performances. Management noted, "We could have sold out Madison Square Garden if we had it." | Between 1955 and 1959, Garland toured with five different "live" shows, incorporating new songs from her Capitol albums, new dance routines by Robert Alton, Chuck Walters, or Richard Barstow, and new vocal arrangements by Roger Edens. She tallied nearly five hundred performances across those five seasons, appearing everywhere from the Minnesota Centennial to the Royal Variety Show in London.

**TOP SPREAD, FROM LEFT:** At the Sahara Hotel, 1962. Judy made history in many ways during her nine Las Vegas engagements. In 1956, she became the highest paid performer ever to work the desert. On at least two occasions, the other major nighteries shut down for Garland's opening night so that their entertainers could attend her show. Later, she was the first to be given a one (rather than two or three) performance-per-evening booking—and then the first to sell out a series of concerts at 2:30 am. | Seriously ill and bloated in May 1959, Garland nonetheless was the first popular vocalist to appear at the famed Metropolitan Opera House. She carried a supporting cast of comic Alan King, soft-shoe vaudevillian John Bubbles, a singing-and-dancing chorus of thirty, conductor Gordon Jenkins, and fifty musicians. But as *The New York Times* noted, "The show, of course, is Miss Garland." And the *World-Telegram and Sun* offered a humorous aside: "The audience began crying 'more' as soon as she had completed her first number."

**BOTTOM SPREAD, FROM LEFT:** Judy and Liza in rehearsal, November 1964. Their two mother-daughter concerts at the London Palladium were sold out before they could be advertised. Unfortunately, none of the badly edited or assembled vinyl, cassette, compact disc, or home video releases of the show convey the excitement and joy of the occasion | Once more on the comeback trail, Judy returned to the stage for the first time in nearly a year in June 1967. *Billboard* reviewed her Westbury (New York) Music Fair opening: "Wherever Judy Garland performs, she transforms the stage into a land of make believe. Her presence, even before she delivers one note, sweeps the audience into near-hysteria." | Judy was a Las Vegas mainstay from 1956 through 1967, and veteran columnist Ralph Pearl never failed to exult over her shows. Among his comments: "[She] gave the single and greatest performance I've ever seen in all the years here. I keep remembering her tremendous recital that made the spine tingle and the heart all but stop. Her plaintive, sobbing, tonsil-torching reached everyone within the sound of her voice."

# THE ROAD TO OZ

1936–1939

J udy Garland's contract with Metro-Goldwyn-Mayer studios went into effect on October 1, 1935, and her feature film career was launched ten months later, when MGM loaned her to Twentieth Century Fox for *Pigskin Parade* (1936). But this was not Judy's first experience in motion pictures. Between 1929 and 1935, she had appeared with her two siblings in five short subjects. The Garland Sisters were also cast in a 1934 two-reeler that never went into production and signed for (and then dropped from) a major feature film in early 1935.

MGM was delighted to have Judy under contract: "We have just signed a Baby Nora Bayes," exhorted their publicity machine, linking the girl with one of the most famous singing vaudevillians of an earlier generation. But despite that initial excitement, Metro let Judy sit idle for most of the next seven months. At the time, George Sidney was overseeing screen tests for the studio. Later a respected feature film director, he was one of many who authoritatively recalled that MGM "just didn't know what to do with a thirteen-year-old girl who sang like a thirty-year-old woman." Nevertheless, Garland was immediately discussed for roles in two Metro features, as well as a loan-out to Hal Roach for a mini-musical. None of those projects came to fruition for her, but—in spring and summer 1936—Metro finally built two brief films around Judy and fellow teen singer Deanna Durbin: a short exhibitor's reel and the "tabloid musical," *Every Sunday*. [See "Selected Short Subjects" (page 116) and "The Rumor Mill" (page

208) for specific details of all the early and potential Garland pictures.]

It was after viewing the exhibitor's reel that the hierarchy took more decisive action. Apparently feeling that the Culver City lot wasn't big enough for two young female vocalists, Louis B. Mayer sent down word: "Get rid of the fat girl." This supposedly referenced Judy, but it was Durbin's option that MGM neglected to pick up. Just prior to his death in 2002, Sidney for the first time pinned responsibility for the gaffe on casting director Billy Grady: "He made the mistake. . . . he got rid of the pretty girl—and we got stuck with the ugly girl." Perhaps Grady's "mistake" was intentional—or at least based on personal omniscience. In his 1972 autobiography, he rhapsodized, "A star to my mind must be all-embracing in the arts. Their talents must be such that they are unforgettable; they must inspire. The greatest woman star I have ever seen, past or present, is Judy Garland. She excels in everything she attempts. And I mean excels."

Judy may have remained at MGM, but they still weren't ready to cast her in a feature. This began to create serious frustration; she despised the inactivity and asked to be released from her contract. Meanwhile, thanks to vaudeville, benefit appearances, and studio parties, Garland was an admired quantity in the film community. Mayer was under fire from both her champions at MGM and even some of the trade press for Judy's professional dormancy. In 1970, preeminent musical film and theater authority Miles Kreuger shed light on the situation: "The truth is that she was a personal favorite of Louis B. Mayer; and, as Judy informed this writer the year before her death, the staff producers were afraid that if her first appearance in one of their pictures failed, their heads would roll. For this extraordinary reason, Judy was loaned-out to Twentieth Century Fox."

Even though Fox had specifically requested her, Judy's role in *Pigskin Parade* was, understandably, only a supporting one, though she managed

to shine in it. Meanwhile, within days of the lapse of her own Metro option, Deanna had been signed by Universal and enjoyed instant national acclaim in her first vehicle, *Three Smart Girls*. Judy was initially distraught, sobbing to Mayer's executive assistant Ida Koverman, "I've been in show business ten years, and Deanna's starred in a picture, and I'm nothing!" Soon thereafter, however, Garland was quick to publicly credit Durbin's success for

paving the way for teens in the movies: "Before Deanna, fourteen-year-old girls didn't have a chance at all. You might have thought, the way [producers] acted, there were no such things."

In 1965, with nearly three decades of additional hindsight, Judy added, "Deanna and I were at an awful age where no one existed. You either had to be seven years old or twenty. There was

no teenage—nothing. So we just hung around and went to school—and didn't know what we were there for. Finally, [MGM] fired Deanna, and they were going to fire me, too. But Universal picked up her contract and . . . made a star of her." With typical humor, she concluded, "And MGM got so mad at Universal, they just said, 'Well, *we've* got a girl that age, too!' And that's the only reason I really got a job—because Deanna Durbin was a big star!"

In truth, Metro had substantial corporate faith and pride in Judy, and in the glow of her *Pigskin Parade* success, it was announced in late 1936 that she would appear in *Broadway Melody of 1937*. While the film was in preproduction, George Sidney acknowledged, "The overall feeling about Judy at MGM was that [the public would think] it was a lie: how could that big voice come out of that little girl? So MGM sent her over to . . . radio [where] she could sing her head off, and the audience never saw her." It was the studio's rationalization that such appearances would give the public an opportunity to acclimate themselves to both Garland's mature sound and juvenile persona.

Thanks to her undeniable talent, their theory worked. By February 1937, Judy had been offered a regular slot on the weekly [Jack] *Oakie's College* program for the remainder of the season. She was soon at work on *Broadway Melody* as well—into which was interpolated a showcase sequence

specifically crafted for her. Earlier that year, Roger Edens had prepared a special material routine which Judy was to sing as a tongue-in-cheek paean of affection to orchestra leader Ben Bernie on his radio program; it was built around the 1913 standard "You Made Me Love You." Then Edens had to hastily rewrite the number when Ida Koverman managed to slot Judy as the in-house entertainment at a birthday tribute to MGM's biggest star, Clark Gable. Gable had just been in the headlines as the defendant in a trumped-up paternity case; the mother of his supposed child had been writing extortion-style letters to the actor, each with the salutation, "Dear Mr. Gable" (which only heightened the comedy of Edens' lyric). Judy delivered the song to him at a studio party on the set of *Parnell*. "I was frightened to death, and my knees were shaking, but somehow I managed to sing. Then we were introduced. I thought I'd faint, but I saw there were tears in his eyes. So then I felt better!" Gable embraced her, "Thanks, honey; that was a real thrill," and then he turned to proclaim to the assembled stars, executives, and crew, "Someday, this little girl will be a great actress!"

By late summer, the "Gable" song and Judy's signal success in *Broadway Melody* had won her both a Decca Records contract and her second radio series. Throughout the 1937–1938 season, she was heard regularly on

MGM's weekly program, *Good News of 1938*. She was also working simultaneously that autumn on two secondary film features, in roles crafted specifically for her. (As with later properties, some of these pictures had been in the works on her behalf for a year or more, and Garland's rising stardom meant that they now could be put into production.) *Thoroughbreds Don't Cry* cast her with Mickey Rooney, but even before it could be completed, Judy was also working in *Everybody Sing*. Such back-to-back or overlapping schedules soon would prove to be detrimental to her health, but this was not yet a consideration on the part of MGM.

Over the summer of 1938, she reteamed with Mickey in *Love Finds Andy Hardy*; Metro had decided to build the picture around a role for her rather than write the already-established Freddie Bartholomew into the script. Judy rallied to complete the film on schedule, despite an auto accident that landed her in the hospital with a punctured lung, sprained back, and three broken ribs. Then, without a break, she went into *Listen, Darling*—again, long in the works as a Garland vehicle, costarring with Bartholomew himself.

But *Listen, Darling* was basically a B-picture stopgap when preproduction on *The Wizard of Oz* extended itself from January into early autumn 1938. Although tests were launched in July, principal photography didn't begin until October and then ran into March

1939. It took at least five directors, three choreographers (plus two assistants), and fourteen writers to bring in the picture. Written for Judy, the role of Dorothy Gale was both taxing and exacting. The girl from Kansas figured in almost every scene of the film and was only off-screen for such fleeting moments as the bicycle rides of Miss Gulch; the approach of the tornado to the farm; random cutaway shots of the Wicked Witch in her tower; and the sequence depicting Dorothy's friends en route to rescue her from captivity. Both in 1939 and ever after, her *Oz* coworkers acknowledged Judy's power and achievement. "Tin Man" Jack Haley recalled her "rare, remarkable" talent and summarized Garland as "the dearest soul. [*Oz*] would have suffered without her. You believed that she *really* wanted to get back to Kansas. She carried the picture with her sincerity."

*Oz* took its toll, however. Even in those more guarded days of studio-controlled publicity, reports of Garland's exhaustion filtered out to the press. But instead of giving her a vacation MGM booked her for a five-week vaudeville tour as soon as the picture was finished. Then, within hours of her return, she began rehearsal for *Babes in Arms*, another full-scale musical and her first real role opposite Mickey Rooney. The film wrapped production at the end of July. On August 6, the two teens were sent east to play three weeks of vaudeville

dates (four weeks for Judy), including a history-making, record-breaking engagement at the Capitol Theatre on Broadway. Between showings of *Oz* in its New York debut, Judy and Mickey did five thirty-minute performances per day—seven on weekends.

In just three years—from late summer 1936 to late summer 1939—Judy Garland had (with rapidly increasing success) appeared in eight feature films. The financial triumph of the last two would lead her to a place in the Top Ten Box Office stars for the year; the only other female on the list was Bette Davis. Additionally, Garland's most prominent film songs to date—"Dear Mr. Gable" and "Over the Rainbow"— had become substantial record successes, and the latter was both the top-selling hit tune of 1939 and the Academy Award-winning Best Film Song of the year. At the premiere of *Babes in Arms* in October 1939, Judy achieved another measure of stardom when she was invited to place her hand and footprints in cement in the forecourt of Grauman's Chinese Theatre. Concurrently, she again became a radio regular, this time as Bob Hope's girl singer and comic foil on *The Pepsodent Show* for the 1939–1940 season. Finally, at the onset of 1940, Judy received a special Oscar as the outstanding screen juvenile of the preceding year.

She was seventeen years old.

# Pigskin Parade

TWENTIETH CENTURY FOX

**CAST:**

Stuart Erwin ................................. *Amos Dodd*

Patsy Kelly ............................. *Bessie Winters*

Jack Haley ................................. *Slug Winters*

The Yacht Club Boys ..................... *themselves*

Johnny Downs ............................. *Chip Carson*

Betty Grable ............................. *Laura Watson*

Arline Judge ................................. *Sally Saxon*

Dixie Dunbar ............................. *Ginger Jones*

Judy Garland ................................. *Sairy Dodd*

Anthony [Tony] Martin .............. *Tommy Barker*

**CREDITS:**

**Darryl F. Zanuck** *(executive producer)*; **Bogart Rogers** *(associate producer)*; **David Butler** *(director)*; **Harry Tugend, Jack Yellen, and William Conselman** *(screenplay)*, **from story by Arthur Sheekman, Nat Perrin, and Mark Kelly; Arthur Miller** *(Photography)*; **Lew Pollack, Sidney D. Mitchell, and the Yacht Club Boys** *(music and lyrics)*; **David Buttolph** *(musical director)*; **Gwen Wakeling** *(costumes)*; **Irene Morra** *(editor)*

**JUDY'S NUMBERS:**

*"The Balboa," "The Texas Tornado," "It's Love I'm After," "The Texas Tornado" finale reprise. Deleted, possibly never filmed: "Hold That Bulldog"*

**RELEASE DATE:** October 23, 1936
**RUN TIME:** 95 minutes

## SYNOPSIS

By mistake, Yale University invites small-time Texas State University (instead of the University of Texas) to compete in their Armistice Day football game. The TSU student body rallies around its new coach, Slug Winters, counting on his expertise to whip their team into shape for such a challenge. When Bessie Winters accidentally incapacitates the star player, she finds his replacement in Amos Dodd, a hillbilly harvesting melons in a road-side field and hurling them to his kid sister, Sairy (JG). Amos is persuaded to enroll at the college under an assumed name to circumvent eligibility requirements. Against all odds—and with the help of every possible musical comedy manipulation (including Sairy's inspirationally powerful vocals)—TSU triumphs over Yale in New Haven.

## NOTES

*Pigskin Parade* was an amalgam of diverse film genres, blending comedy, songs, the "sports" movie, and the "college" movie to amazingly good entertainment effect in its day. In the United Kingdom, where football was a comparatively unknown quantity, the film was released as *Harmony Parade*. Buddy Ebsen, an early contender for the role of Amos Dodd, lost the part to Stuart Erwin, who also won an Academy Award nomination for his performance as Best Supporting Actor.

Twentieth Century Fox vice president Darryl F. Zanuck was very much a hands-on contributor to the studio's creative corps. Many subplots for *Pigskin Parade* were considered in his preproduction conferences and most of them subsequently dropped in development; but a month prior to the onset of principal photography, the decision was made to add Amos's singing sister to the cast. Specifically created for Judy Garland, this girl was originally named "Judy" and her singular character trait was frustration: "Why won't somebody listen to me sing?" The edgy quality was scripted to the extent that the character at one point threatened to pull her brother from the TSU team unless she was permitted to perform on the train platform as the football players departed for Yale. Fearing "Judy Dodd" would be horrible, student Chip Carson planned to have the school band drown her out. Final rewrites simplified and softened these situations, and the renamed Sairy Dodd most endearingly pled for—and got—her chance to sing.

When *Pigskin Parade* was released, the public and press recognition accorded Judy provided the final impetus for MGM to cast her in a film on her home lot, *Broadway Melody of 1938*.

**TOP AND ABOVE:** In a publicity pose for the picture, Judy wears her costume from "The Balboa" production sequence (pictured above).

FROM LEFT: Costars Tony Martin and Jack Haley flank Judy and *Pigskin* songwriter Sidney D. Mitchell. | Amos auditions: Jack Haley, Patsy Kelly, Stuart Erwin, Judy, Johnny Downs, and Betty Grable OPPOSITE, FROM TOP: Judy, Tony Martin, Dixie Dunbar, and the Yacht Club Boys at the Yale game | Confident of Judy's performing power, Fox staged the grand finale with the "unknown" Garland as its focal point.

## REVIEWS

"Although this is a football picture, its whole purpose is to burlesque film pigskin epics, which it does in an engaging manner with songs, dances, and gags galore."

—*CHRISTIAN SCIENCE MONITOR*

"With plenty of gags, with Patsy Kelly hurling wisecracks at Jack Haley, with Judy Garland's songs, and Dixie Dunbar's dancing, the film gets along very nicely, indeed."

—NEW YORK *SUN*

"JG, for my money, was the hit of [the film], although Stuart Erwin shouldn't be forgotten. . . . Garland, although only fourteen, makes most crooning ladies of more years seem like beginners."

—*SCREEN LIFE IN HOLLYWOOD*

## What They Said

*"The first time I ever saw her, she was prancing around a football field, and I wasn't sure whether she was a drum majorette or the left guard. My brother, Bogart Rogers, was making this football picture called* Pigskin Parade *for Twentieth Century Fox, and he was shooting on the gridiron at Hollywood High School. . . . Soon I saw the little girl waving a baton. As far as I could see, she was perfectly square. Then I heard her singing a fight-on song in a voice that literally sent shivers up and down my spine. But I said to myself, all college songs do that to me. Just the same, I went and asked my brother, Bo, who she was. He said, 'Oh, some kid that's been around here singing at Elks Clubs' smokers and chamber of commerce banquets. She's only about twelve or fourteen, or some such,* he said, *and she's got a voice all right, poor kid, if she was only a little more attractive."*

—HOLLYWOOD JOURNALIST
ADELA ROGERS ST. JOHNS

*"I went to the preview with my mother. I was fourteen. I thought I would look as beautiful as Garbo or Crawford, that makeup and photography would automatically make me glamorous. (They hadn't let me see the rushes, which was too bad, because if I'd seen them, I could have improved myself.) When I saw myself on the screen, it was the most awful moment of my life. My freckles stood out. I was fat! And my acting was terrible. I was loud—like I was singing to the third gallery at the Orpheum! I burst into tears. 'Mommie,' I said, 'let's leave.' I was ready to go back to vaudeville. 'You shouldn't expect a miracle,' my mother comforted me. 'Be patient. Wait, and some day, you'll look beautiful on the screen.' Well, I'm still waiting!"*

—JUDY GARLAND (1943)

# Broadway Melody of 1938

METRO-GOLDWYN-MAYER

## CAST:

Robert Taylor.............................Steve Raleigh

Eleanor Powell ................................ Sally Lee

George Murphy .........................Sonny Ledford

Binnie Barnes......................Caroline Whipple

Buddy Ebsen ................................. Peter Trot

Sophie Tucker ............................Alice Clayton

Judy Garland ............................ Betty Clayton

Charles Igor Gorin.................Nicki Papaloopas

Raymond Walburn................. Herman Whipple

Robert Benchley .....................................Duffy

## CREDITS:

Jack Cummings (producer); Roy Del Ruth (director); Jack McGowan (screenplay); Jack McGowan and Sid Silvers (original story); William Daniels (photography); Nacio Herb Brown and Arthur Freed (music and lyrics); Georgie Stoll (musical director); Roger Edens (musical arrangements); Leo Arnaud and Murray Cutter (orchestrations); Dave Gould (dance director); Cedric Gibbons (art director), Joseph Wright and Edwin B. Willis (associates); Adrian (gowns); Blanche Sewell (editor)

## JUDY'S NUMBERS:

"Yours and Mine" (underscoring a portion of the opening credits), "Everybody Sing," "Dear Mr. Gable: You Made Me Love You," "Your Broadway and My Broadway" (dance with Buddy Ebsen). Deleted: "Yours and Mine," "Your Broadway and My Broadway"

**RELEASE DATE:** August 20, 1937

**RUN TIME:** 111 minutes

## SYNOPSIS

Sally Lee is an extraordinary tap dancer, but her main interest is Stargazer, a champion horse she raised on the family farm. She loses and then regains the animal at auction, aided and abetted by Broadway producer Steve Raleigh and hoofers Sonny Ledford and Peter Trot. Even though Sally's an unknown, Steve has slated her to star in his new show, a plan that arouses the ire of Caroline Whipple, the manipulative wife of Raleigh's financial backer, Herman Whipple. Caroline fancies both Steve and Stargazer.

Meanwhile, Sally finds a Manhattan haven in Alice Clayton's theatrical boarding house. A former vaudeville star, Clayton is now grooming her teenage daughter, Betty (JG), for a stage career. At the last minute, the Whipples withdraw their support from the Raleigh musical, and it's up to Stargazer to ace a race and score the prize money to fund the show. The horse comes in a winner, largely in response to the operatic singing voice of Nicki Papaloopas over the track public address system. In the end, Nicki, Sally, Sonny, Peter, and both Claytons enjoy a smash Broadway opening.

**OPPOSITE:** Selections from a suite of photos in which MGM promoted "the most accomplished songstress in pictures . . . being groomed for stardom by her studio."

## NOTES

When Judy's supporting role was incorporated into this film it was titled *Broadway Melody of 1937*. The film took so long in planning and preproduction that, by the time it was ready to be released, the referenced year had to be changed to 1938. Her part encompassed only a few brief scenes, but she was assigned three major songs as well.

Judy's excitement about the film was rapidly equaled—if not eclipsed—by the success she was having with the specialty number, "Dear Mr. Gable: You Made Me Love You." Written for her to perform at Clark Gable's birthday party in February 1937, the routine was given a rousing reception and thereafter slotted Garland for appearances on radio, at a Hollywood benefit, an intra-corporate dinner, and for a national convention of film exhibitors. In every instance, the impact of her rendition and the material was uproarious, and the song was quickly shoehorned into an already jam-packed *Broadway Melody of 1938*.

Due to last-minute rewrites, the Garland rendition (with a children's choir) of "Yours and Mine" was cut from the final edit of the picture. A more regrettable loss came with the deletion of the three-and-a-half minute Judy-and-chorus arrangement of "Your Broadway and My Broadway." It opened the mammoth finale of the film and was purportedly trimmed because of time constraints. Listening today to Judy's prerecording (the film footage itself is not known to exist), it seems possible there may have been additional reasons for the number's elimination. It's difficult to imagine how the rest of the cast, regardless of their star power, could have followed her.

Garland came seventh in the picture's credits, but after early reviews repeatedly heralded her, MGM hastily prepared additional ad copy that positioned Judy just after the top-billed Robert Taylor and Eleanor Powell. She was touted as "the greatest little hot singer since the first talkie!" Concurrently, the "Gable" song gave her not only an immediate new level of public awareness but it also led to a successful single record and a contract with Decca Records.

*Broadway Melody of 1938* was well received, even abroad. More than 65,000 customers flocked to see it during its two-week premiere launch at the Empire, MGM's flagship theater in London.

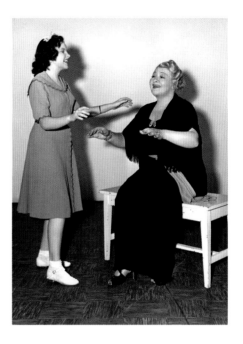

OPPOSITE FROM TOP: Judy's revival of "You Made Me Love You" provided her first signature song. | Performing a bravura "Your Broadway and My Broadway," deleted from the release print ABOVE RIGHT: Sophie Tucker bequeathed her own sobriquet to Judy: "She'll be America's next 'Red Hot Mama'!"

## REVIEWS

"The current flood of immature vocalists has brought to the screen no more startling phenomenon than Judy Garland of Metro-Goldwyn-Mayer, whose soprano [sic] apostrophe to the photograph of a certain screen actor . . . was probably the greatest tour de force of recent screen history . . . Naturally, we conceived from this artistic triumph an extravagant admiration for Miss Garland."

—NEW YORK *TIMES*

"JG puts over a number brilliantly."

—LONDON *SUNDAY EXPRESS*

"Watch JG, whose 'Please, Mr. Gable' [sic] tickled audiences all over the country. The kid has a noncancellable reservation on the Stardom Express."

—*SONG HITS*

## What They Said

ABOVE: The long and the short of it: Garland and Ebsen in rehearsal and on camera for the finale.

*"Judy must go to school on the MGM lot at least two hours a day, she must have two hours a day recreation (one of those is usually her lunch hour), and that leaves only four hours for work of the eight hours prescribed by California law for movie children. Those school sessions are something, too. Before she had finished her lunch the other day, they came for her for her French lesson . . . and while a chorus of one hundred men and women were rehearsing a song, accompanied by a record of Judy singing the same song, just outside her dressing-room door; while Sophie [Tucker] was rehearsing the scene she was later to make with Judy; and while the prop men, electricians, and technicians of one sort or another were getting the stage ready for the next scene, Judy, with her French teacher (a Spanish woman who speaks both French and English with a decided Spanish accent) hovering over her shoulder, constructed sentences in French, conjugated French verbs and what not, tapping her pencil in time to the music of her record, and glancing every few seconds into her dressing-table mirror to see that nothing had gone wrong with her makeup."*

—JOURNALIST MEL WASHBURN, VISITING THE SET

"One day, Arthur Freed came into the rehearsal hall and said, 'Meet your new dancing partner!' And there was this gangly [fourteen] year old, Judy Garland. She was very friendly, very easy to get along with, and very talented. She was a sensation in Broadway Melody; that established her as someone who was to be reckoned with. And I taught her the little shim-sham-shimmy number which we did together in the finale."

—BUDDY EBSEN

"The picture wasn't good, and I was only fair. It was okay for Eleanor Powell and Robert Taylor. For them, it was just another picture. Judy Garland was the only one in the whole cast in whom I saw great possibilities. I said so to L. B. [Mayer] and to everyone on the lot: 'Judy, if carefully handled and groomed, will be the big MGM star in a few years.' My predictions were right!"

—SOPHIE TUCKER (1945)

"Do you know what Miss Tucker did? She gave up her lunch hour every day to coach me. She taught me every trick she had learned from her years as a stage star. If I do put a song over, it's because of Sophie Tucker. The only thing I didn't like about me in Broadway Melody was the first line I had to speak: 'Aw, the Claytons are a bunch of hams!' It was so precocious. I hate anything precocious; I'm not precocious at all. I think like a grown up, and I like to be with older people and talk to older people, but I am not a grown up, and I don't want to be. So I didn't like the first line, but after that, it was all right. And I think the song about Clark Gable (which I meant!) sort of evened things up."

—JUDY GARLAND

BELOW, COUNTERCLOCKWISE FROM TOP LEFT: Robert Wildhack, Robert Taylor, Judy, Sophie Tucker, and Eleanor Powell in a deleted scene | Rehearsing "Everybody Sing": Jesse Delos Jewkes, Judy, Sophie Tucker, and Barnett Parker | The film's fade out: Charles Igor Gorin, Sophie Tucker, George Murphy, Eleanor Powell, Robert Taylor, Judy, and Buddy Ebsen

# Thoroughbreds Don't Cry

METRO-GOLDWYN-MAYER

## CAST:

Judy Garland ............................. *Cricket West*

Mickey Rooney ..................... *Timmie Donovan*

Sophie Tucker ........................... *Mother Ralph*

C. Aubrey Smith ................. *Sir Peter Calverton*

Ronald Sinclair ........................ *Roger Calverton*

Forrester Harvey ................................. *Wilkins*

Charles D. Brown .................. *"Click" Donovan*

Frankie Darro ............................. *"Dink" Reid*

Henry Kolker ........................... *"Doc" Godfrey*

Helen Troy ............................................ *Hilda*

## CREDITS:

**Harry Rapf** (producer); **Alfred E. Green** (director); **Lawrence Hazard** (screenplay); **Eleanore Griffin** and **J. Walter Ruben** (original story); **Leonard Smith** (photography); **Nacio Herb Brown** and **Arthur Freed** (music and lyrics); **Dr. William Axt** (musical director); **Cedric Gibbons** (art director), **Stan Rogers** and **Edwin B. Willis** (associates); **Dolly Tree** (wardrobe); **Elmo Vernon** (editor)

## JUDY'S NUMBER:

*"Got a Pair of New Shoes" (solo during opening; finale reprise). Deleted: "Sun Showers"*

**RELEASE DATE: December 3, 1937**

**RUN TIME: 80 minutes**

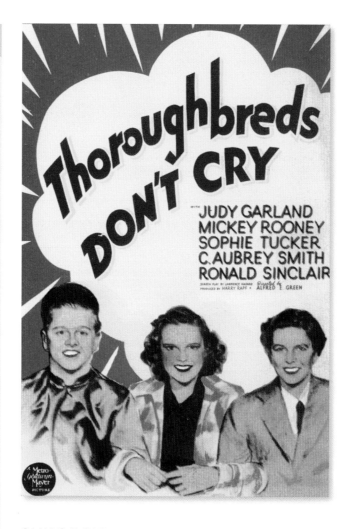

## SYNOPSIS

Sir Peter Calverton and his grandson, Roger, travel from Great Britain to America, hoping to rebuild the family fortune via their superlative racehorse, the Pookah. To implement their plan, Roger enlists the aid of expert jockey Timmie Donovan, whose ego is (barely) kept in check by Cricket West (JG), the live-in niece of boarding-house owner Mother Ralph.

When he hears of the Pookah's probable success, Timmie's estranged father, "Click" Donovan, feigns illness and convinces his son to throw the race so that the man can bet on a long-shot horse and use his track winnings for an iron lung. The shock of the Pookah's loss kills Sir Peter, sending Timmie into disgrace.

When he discovers his father's ruse, Timmie hopes to redeem himself by riding the horse in a more important race on Roger's behalf. But at the last minute, Timmie is ruled off the turf when his father's corrupt cohorts inform the track judges of the boy's earlier malfeasance. With Cricket's encouragement, Roger himself then rides the Pookah—to victory.

## NOTES

*Thoroughbreds Don't Cry* was the first of ten pictures that featured both Judy and Mickey Rooney, although this was the only time she was billed ahead of him in the credits. New Zealand teen Ronald Sinclair was listed third. After additional film roles in his youth, Sinclair slipped behind the cameras as an adult and enjoyed a successful decades-long career as an editor. Nearly thirty years later, Garland jokingly recounted the film's back story, explaining Sinclair's instantaneous rise to prominence: "They had arranged for [*Thoroughbreds*] to be made with the leading child star at the time, who was Freddie Bartholomew. But Freddie's voice was changing! So they got a new boy, Ronald Sinclair—and just put him into this starring role. And it was kind of a rough go on him, I guess; they ground him into little bits of cement or something [afterwards, as] no one has heard of him since—not even as a person!"

Although structured as a "dramedy," *Thoroughbreds* found script space for two Garland songs, both of them rejects from the Arthur Freed–Nacio Herb Brown score for *Broadway Melody of 1938*. The first, "Got a Pair of New Shoes," was prerecorded in a lengthy vocal arrangement and then considerably tightened for the scene in which it was used. The second, "Sun Showers," was completely eliminated from the release print, although Judy's soundtrack survives.

*Thoroughbreds* didn't pretend to be anything but a combination "B" picture and showcase for its worthy child stars. The film also boasted the old-pro contributions of C. Aubrey Smith, Forrester Harvey, and Sophie Tucker though. As a result, it topped double bills across the country. Another cast member was teenage Frankie Darro, who had appeared on the same vaudeville bill with the Garland Sisters in 1934 and was briefly engaged to Judy's sister, Jimmie.

Publicity sitting: Ronald Sinclair, Mickey Rooney, and Judy

## REVIEWS

"An appealing picture, especially for children. Miss Garland does several imitations nicely. Mickey Rooney gives a really fine performance."

—NEW YORK *HERALD TRIBUNE*

"Brilliant little JG again proves her right to the title of child actress. She's a fine, natural actress."

—CHICAGO *TRIBUNE*

" . . . a good hokey yarn about kids and horse racing. JG and Sophie Tucker help things along, and it's all done so sincerely that the big race at the end . . . becomes quite as thrilling as it's supposed to be."

—CONTEMPORARY NEWSPAPER REVIEW

Advertiser's Announcement  Page 2—KINEMATOGRAPH WEEKLY  December 9, 1937

# ANOTHER WINNER!

"From the stables of M-G-M comes 'Thoroughbreds Don't Cry,' an entry at the Box-Office Track which, judging by pre-view audience reaction, is due for a galloping finish at the head of its class."

Vance King in Motion Picture Herald

## "THOROUGHBREDS DON'T CRY"

with its thoroughbred cast

**JUDY GARLAND
MICKEY ROONEY
SOPHIE TUCKER
C. AUBREY SMITH**

and the new British Child Star Sensation

**RONALD SINCLAIR**

*Trade Show :* **TONIGHT** ADELPHI THEATRE **8.45**

TOP: British trade paper ad **ABOVE FROM LEFT:** Judy and Ronald Sinclair, just prior to the deleted "Sun Showers" | Judy "acts" for Sinclair during their first on-screen encounter. | Sinclair meets Judy and "aunt" Sophie Tucker.

## What They Said

*"There was a moment I thought my career had taken an upswing. I was assigned to a role in* Thoroughbreds, *and Mickey was in the picture, too. But, unfortunately, we only had two [real] scenes together, and no chance to become acquainted under business conditions. Yet the film did some good, for the studio then had a part written in for me in the next Andy Hardy picture."*

—JUDY GARLAND

*"Something that I love to do is talk about a woman that I've always adored. I never tire of it, and we'll always talk about Judy. I can give lectures on what kind of human being she was—and the talent she was."*

—MICKEY ROONEY (1994)

**TOP:** "Got a Pair of New Shoes" finale: Ronald Sinclair, "The Pookah," Judy, and Mickey Rooney **ABOVE:** Mickey's seventeenth birthday on-set, with Judy and Frankie Darro

# Everybody Sing

METRO-GOLDWYN-MAYER

## CAST:

Allan Jones .................................. Ricky Saboni

Judy Garland .............................. Judy Bellaire

Fanny Brice.............................. Olga Chekaloff

Reginald Owen ......................... Hillary Bellaire

Billie Burke.............................. Diana Bellaire

Reginald Gardiner....................... Jerrold Hope

Lynne Carver ............................ Sylvia Bellaire

Helen Troy ......................... Hillary's Secretary

Monty Woolley .......................... John Fleming

Adia Kuznetzoff ..................................... Boris

## CREDITS:

**Harry Rapf** (producer); **Edwin L. Marin** (director); **Florence Ryerson and Edgar Allan Woolf** (screenplay and original story); **James Gruen** (additional dialogue); **Joseph Ruttenberg** (photography); **Bronislau Kaper, Walter Jurmann, and Gus Kahn,** (music and lyric); **Bert Kalmar and Harry Ruby** (music and lyric to "Snooks"); **Dr. William Axt** (musical director); **Roger Edens** (music and vocal arrangements); **George Bassman** (orchestrations); **Dave Gould and Seymour Felix** (dance directors); **Cedric Gibbons** (art director), **Henry McAfee and Edwin B. Willis** (associates); **Dolly Tree** (costumes); **William S. Gray** (editor)

## JUDY'S NUMBERS:

"Swing, Mr. Mendelssohn," "Melody Farm" Bus Sequence ("Melody Farm" reprise, based on "Quartet" from Rigoletto), "Swing Low, Sweet Chariot," "Snooks, (Why? Because!)" "Ever Since the World Began"/"Shall I Sing a Melody?," "Melody Farm" (finale reprise)

**RELEASE DATE: February 4, 1938**

**RUN TIME: 91 minutes**

## SYNOPSIS:

The Bellaire household is in chaos. Actress/mother Diana is dizzily preoccupied with her stage stardom and new leading man, Jerrold Hope. Playwright/father Hillary is going broke in his temperamental efforts to complete and produce Diana's next play. Daughter Sylvia is in love with Ricky Saboni, the family cook who sings in a café to supplement his income. Younger daughter Judy (JG) has been expelled from school for singing swing music instead of the classics. And housemaid Olga Chekaloff is on call for all of them, yet eternally reminiscing about her own early dramatic career in Russia.

In the midst of everything, indefatigable Judy takes it upon herself to solve the family's problems. Without her parents' knowledge, she joins forces with Ricky and Olga in a Broadway revue. Her own career is launched and the Bellaires are happily, hammily reunited on opening night.

**ABOVE:** In a promotional lobby card, Judy exhorts her school choir to "Swing, Mr. Mendelssohn." **OPPOSITE, CLOCKWISE FROM LEFT:** Fanny Brice, Allan Jones, and Judy in promotional art | Judy as one of the "Russian Dolly Sisters," a comedy finale concept dropped before prerecording and filming. | The deleted, first version of "Melody Farm," later refilmed with Judy in overalls

## NOTES

First developed in late summer 1936 as a generically described "Judy Garland story," *Everybody Sing* was known by at least two additional titles (*The Ugly Duckling* and *Swing Fever*) before its release, nearly eighteen months later. It's the most obvious star vehicle of all the pre-*Wizard of Oz* Garland films, although she, Allan Jones, and Fanny Brice alternated first, second, and third billing in press ads and on theater marquees.

Early drafts of the story featured and then dropped roles for Mickey Rooney, Freddie Bartholomew, and "Spanky" McFarland (of the *Our Gang* series); the plot withstood similar permutations. Indeed, after two months of rehearsal, prerecording, and filming (some of it concurrent with production of *Thoroughbreds Don't Cry*), *Everybody Sing* was nearly finished, but the storyline remained unresolved, and no one seemed able to ascertain the best way to present the show-within-a-show finale. Per a studio memo of Monday, November 15, 1937, "The company is now at a standstill until a decision is made"; the communiqué then blithely and blindly concluded, "We are preparing to record and shoot this Friday and Saturday." Meanwhile, a performance troupe called the Apple Dancers had been imported from New York and were on a weekly salary of $3,000, but no one knew how to best use them once they'd arrived. Ultimately, they never appeared in the finished film.

A series of publicity photos of Garland in pseudo-Russian garb was posed and disseminated, although the number she and Brice were to share in such costumes never went beyond the rehearsal stage. It was replaced by the Fanny/Judy routine in which the former brought her prized radio characterization of "Baby Snooks" to the screen for the first time. That duet and the two individual finale numbers for Jones and Garland weren't even prerecorded until the second and third weeks of December. At the last minute, it was also decided to retake Judy's bravura solo, "Melody Farm," with the girl garbed in overalls (she had worn a simple dress in the original footage).

By January 1938 the production had extended into a fifth month, which was highly unusual for a routine Metro musical. Despite delays and waffling, however, the final cost of the picture was less than $600,000, and MGM heavily promoted the film on Judy's behalf. She was alternately acclaimed as "the nation's new singing star" and "the acting, singing sensation of the New Year." It was no coincidence that the title finally decided upon for the movie was that of one of her hit songs from *Broadway Melody of 1938*.

OPPOSITE: "Sweet or Swing?" is the question: Judy in her finale, "Shall I Sing a Melody?"

CLOCKWISE FROM TOP LEFT: Little Lord Fauntleroy (Judy) meets Baby Snooks (Fanny Brice) in "Why? Because!" | Fanny Brice alerts Judy to backstage trouble on opening night. | Off-camera clowning: director Edwin Marin sings, and Judy and Lynne Carver disrespectfully react. LEFT: Judy, Allan Jones, and Fanny Brice in a promotional caricature from Sydney, Australia OPPOSITE: Judy and her songwriters: Bronislaw Kaper, Walter Jurmann, and Gus Kahn

## REVIEWS

"Very gay, very amusing, very tuneful. . . . I recommend [it] to everybody. Little Miss Garland, completely sure of herself at all times . . . has a number of arresting scenes. One you'll find a hard time forgetting is that where [Allan] Jones tells her *must* go back to her parents. I cried a bit right there. Judy and Fanny [Brice] tell you some interesting things to music in great style."

—CHICAGO *TRIBUNE*

"JG sings swing songs with the air of a veteran. There is no doubt that this young lady will go far."

—*PICTUREGOER*

"Good fun. JG is now unquestionably the screen's No. 2 juvenile singing-actress (she hasn't had her chance to compete wholly with Deanna Durbin), and she comes through swinging it with song and comedy."

—CLEVELAND *PLAIN DEALER*

## What They Said

"*Everybody Sing was a light, sophisticated musical comedy—and Judy was a delightful child. I fell in love with her, and I taught her all the dirty tricks a leading man could do, so that she'd be prepared. Because I knew this girl was going to have a great career. And she never forgot it. Whenever we went to a party, and she was there or came in, she'd run over and throw her arms around me and kiss me and thank me. This went on for years!*"

—ALLAN JONES

# Love Finds Andy Hardy

METRO-GOLDWYN-MAYER

## CAST:

Lewis Stone ................. Judge James K. Hardy

Mickey Rooney ......................... Andrew Hardy

Cecilia Parker ........................... Marian Hardy

Fay Holden .......................... Mrs. Emily Hardy

Judy Garland ............................. Betsy Booth

Lana Turner ........................... Cynthia Potter

Ann Rutherford ........................ Polly Benedict

Mary Howard ........................... Mrs. Tompkins

Gene Reynolds .................... Jimmy MacMahon

George Breakston ............................ "Beezy"

## CREDITS:

**Carey Wilson** (producer); **George B. Seitz** (director); **William Ludwig** (screenplay); **Vivian R. Bretherton** (original stories); **Aurania Rouverol** (characters); **Lester White** (photography); **Harry Revel and Mack Gordon** (music and lyric); **Roger Edens** (music and lyric to "In-Between"); **David Snell** (musical score); **Roger Edens** (vocal arrangements); **Cedric Gibbons** (art director), **Stan Rogers and Edwin B. Willis** (associates); **Jeanne** (wardrobe); **Ben Lewis** (editor)

## JUDY'S NUMBERS:

"In-Between," "It Never Rains, But What it Pours," "Meet the Beat of My Heart."
Deleted; possibly never filmed:
"Bei Mir Bist Du Schoen"

**RELEASE DATE:** July 22, 1938
**RUN TIME:** 92 minutes

## SYNOPSIS

As usual, Andy Hardy's life is fraught with teen angst: girlfriend Polly Benedict is going to be out of town on the night of the Christmas Eve dance. Then, in Polly's absence, Andy makes a deal to "date up" beauteous Cynthia Potter and keep her safe for her own absentee boyfriend, Beezy Anderson. Beezy is willing to pay Andy $12 for the assignment, money Andy needs to complete his surreptitious purchase of a second-hand car.

When the deal with Beezy falls through—and Polly unexpectedly returns—Andy is suddenly confronted with debt, his father's displeasure about the car, and dates with both Polly and Cynthia for the party. Compounding matters, his grandmother suffers a stroke, and Mrs. Hardy rushes to her side in Canada, leaving the family bereft and heartsick at holiday time. But Andy's problems are smoothly solved by little Betsy Booth (JG), the visiting girl next door. He considers her a mere child, yet she manages to grow up for Christmas Eve, supplant Andy's dates for the night, sing her way to a sensation at the dance, and finally effect the inevitable Andy-Polly reconciliation. Just in time for Christmas, Mrs. Hardy returns with the good news that Grandmother Forrest is well on the mend.

**OPPOSITE AND LEFT:** "Andy" and his women! Mickey Rooney with Judy, Ann Rutherford, and Lana Turner **BOTTOM RIGHT:** "Sister Marian" (Cecilia Parker) joins Andy and harem.

## NOTES

*Love Finds Andy Hardy* was the fourth in a series of sixteen movies, unwittingly and unceremoniously launched by *A Family Affair* (1937) and concluded with something of a cinematic postscript in *Andy Hardy Comes Home* (1958). At its peak, however, between 1938 and 1946, the saga of "Judge Hardy's Family" came to represent tens of millions of dollars in profit for MGM; provided the foundation for Mickey Rooney's superstar status in the late 1930s and early 1940s; and launched (or much enhanced) the careers of several young actresses (Judy, Kathryn Grayson, Esther Williams, and Donna Reed among them). The series even won a special Academy Award in 1941 for "its achievement in representing the American way of life."

By the time *Love Finds Andy Hardy* was in preparation, Metro had come to realize that it was Rooney's characterization of Andy, a titan of teenage troubles, that made the films especially palatable to contemporary, cross-generational audiences. Thus "Oh, What a Tangled Web" (a *Cosmopolitan* short story of a couple seasons earlier) was adapted to suit him and the citizens of small-town Carvel in *Love Finds Andy Hardy*. The magazine's hero, "Beezy Eaton," became Andy, and "Bets," the little girl next door who solved his problems and got taken to a dance, was cast with Judy. In order to showcase a number of Garland vocals, her character was further defined as the stage-inclined daughter of an established musical comedy star.

*Love Finds Andy Hardy* has been long regarded as the quintessential entry in the series. Appropriately, it was selected in 2000 by the United States National Film Preservation Board for preservation in the Library of Congress as a "culturally, historically, or aesthetically significant" motion picture in the National Film Registry.

## REVIEWS

"You won't want to miss this *Hardy* family picture. Judy Garland almost steals the honors from Mickey with her excellent characterization."
—*MODERN SCREEN*

"JG is a wow as Betsy. . . . She sings, too—and HOW!" —CHICAGO *TRIBUNE*

"The Hardy Family presents its most amusing and entertaining picture, a story so genuine, so natural that one feels the Hardys must be next-door neighbors. . . . JG is a decided asset in any picture in which she appears, and her work with the Hardy crew is commendable." —TACOMA *TIMES*

"JG gives the best performance of her short but busy career. Judy hasn't a big part, but she plays it in a big way. And really scores while she's doing it. Outstanding in the whole film are the songs sung in the Garland way. Best of these is 'In-Between.'"
—SANDUSKY *STAR-JOURNAL*

**ABOVE:** Beloved veteran comedian Leo Carrillo embraces the younger generation on the *Andy Hardy* set. **OPPOSITE:** Judy prepares to sing at the country club dance with "Dennis Hunt's Harmonists"; Don Castle at right

LEFT: Judy plays Cinderella and savior to Mickey, just in time for Christmas. RIGHT: Betsy" and "Andy" arrive at the Christmas Eve country club dance.

## What They Said

"Love Finds Andy Hardy—fourth and most popular of the 'Judge Hardy's Family' series—cost MGM $162,000 and is tabbed for a gross of $1,300,000, making it the smartest movie investment of the year. Proving again that down-to-earth drama about everyday people and everyday events will outsell a French revolution or a Roman chariot race, which may cost ten times as much as a 'Hardy.'"

—AUGUST 1938 WIRE SERVICE REPORT

"The thing to remember is that he wants the jalopy more than he wants the girl."

—LOUIS B. MAYER TO *LOVE FINDS ANDY HARDY* SCENARIST WILLIAM LUDWIG

"When Andy Hardy was in his infancy, 'Jootes' was there. She was a newcomer to Hollywood, jittery and frightened. But somehow she was a veteran. I think it was because she was my kind of person that I felt that way. Both of us were born into vaudeville. A career in show business was all either of us dreamed about. Even though she was new to pictures, Jootes had been trouping for years. She knew the same people I knew. She talked about the same things. She had the same hopes and was climbing the same rocky road."

—MICKEY ROONEY

"At that time, I was hopelessly discouraged with my screen work. Mickey's talent was overpowering. [I felt] I had not improved one iota. The first morning on the Hardy set, I sneaked into my dressing room to read over the lines. I didn't want to see or talk to anyone. Suddenly, there was a violent knock on the door. Mickey burst in and said, 'Jootes, I think this is going to be it. I think this picture is going to be swell. But, look—let's have a sort of pact with each other. Let's never try to steal a scene. Let's work with each other, not at each other. That's the way to make a good picture.' This philosophy put me completely at ease, and after Mickey left, I thought, 'Good heavens, Judy, you've been trying too hard. Relax. Don't throw all of your energy into every scene. Take it easy and see what happens.' Well, something did happen. . . . Watching the rushes, I saw that my scenes were more sincere and believable. I've kept that thought in mind ever since. But not until I played in that picture did I commence to enjoy myself and feel that I was beginning to find myself. . . . I learned from Mickey Rooney to be natural, to be myself before the camera."

—JUDY GARLAND

Candid capers between the first teen team of movie superstars

# Listen, Darling

METRO-GOLDWYN-MAYER

## CAST:

Judy Garland ....................... "Pinkie" Wingate

Freddie Bartholomew ............. "Buzz" Mitchell

Mary Astor .............................. Dottie Wingate

Walter Pidgeon...................... Richard Thurlow

Alan Hale................................... J. J. Slattery

Scotty Beckett........................... Billie Wingate

Barnett Parker............................ Abercrombie

Gene Lockhart .............................. Mr. Drubbs

Charley Grapewin............................ Uncle Joe

## CREDITS:

**Jack Cummings** (producer); **Edwin L. Marin** (director); **Elaine Ryan** and **Anne Morrison Chapin** (screenplay); **Katherine Brush** (story); **Charles Lawton, Jr.** (photography); **Al Hoffman, Al Lewis,** and **Murray Mencher** (music and lyric to "On the Bumpy Road to Love"); **Joseph McCarthy** and **Milton Ager** (music and lyric to "Ten Pins in the Sky"); **James F. Hanley** (music and lyric to "Zing! Went the Strings of My Heart"); **Georgie Stoll** (musical director); **Dr. William Axt** (musical score); **Roger Edens** (musical arrangements); **Cedric Gibbons** (art director), **Harry McAfee** and **Edwin B. Willis** (associates); **Dolly Tree** (wardrobe); **Blanche Sewell** (editor)

## JUDY'S NUMBERS:

"Zing! Went the Strings of My Heart,"

"On the Bumpy Road to Love,"

"Ten Pins in the Sky," "On the Bumpy Road to Love" finale reprise

**RELEASE DATE:** October 21, 1938

**RUN TIME:** 75 minutes

## SYNOPSIS

Dottie Wingate, a widow with two children, is contemplating remarriage to a man she doesn't love in order to ensure security for her family. Daughter Pinkie (JG) and her buddy Buzz Mitchell decide it's up to them to save Dottie from such a fate, and they kidnap her and son Billy in a small house trailer.

When Dottie realizes what the teens are trying to accomplish on her behalf, she agrees to a brief road trip with them. Along the way, the Wingate party encounters an admirable prospective husband in business tycoon, J. J. Slattery. Dottie, however, is more attracted to attorney Richard Thurlow, whose trailer is conveniently parked adjacent to theirs. Unfortunately, his conversation only emphasizes the carefree aspects of his approach to life; her goal, after all, is stability for herself and the children.

At Dottie's somber directive, the Wingates pack up and head home. A quick talk with Slattery convinces Thurlow of the error of his ways, and he chases down the highway until he catches the Wingate trailer and claims Dottie.

**ABOVE:** The principal cast "meets cute": Walter Pidgeon, Scotty Beckett, Mary Astor, Freddie Bartholomew, and Judy **OPPOSITE:** Judy sings "Ten Pins in the Sky" to Scotty Beckett.

## REVIEWS

"A lightweight offering that will sneak through on the lower sections of double bills. [It] has little to offer aside from three good song numbers handled capably by Miss Garland . . . she presents [them] in fine style."

—*VARIETY*

"Mildly amusing and sometimes exceptionally tuneful."

—CONTEMPORARY BUFFALO, NY NEWSPAPER

"So full of human stuff and brightness that it's a tonic for that tired feeling."

—CONTEMPORARY NIAGARA FALLS, NY NEWSPAPER

"A feeble fable." —*STAGE*

**OPPOSITE:** A *Listen, Darling* costume test **LEFT:** Deleted scenes featuring Judy with Freddie Bartholomew, Gene Lockhart, and Mary Astor

## NOTES

In the works for at least a year, *Listen, Darling* finally teamed Judy with Freddie Bartholomew. It was far from a major motion picture but it served its purpose as both suitable for "double bill" booking in thousands of 1938 movie theaters, and as a means of keeping MGM's talent well in view of audiences of the day. The film was and remains interesting for its three Garland songs and its rather cavalier use of so many superlative actors. In seventy-five minutes, in addition to Judy and Freddie, *Listen, Darling* managed to include everyone from Mary Astor, Walter Pidgeon,

and Scotty Beckett (in major roles) to Alan Hale, Gene Lockhart, and Charley Grapewin (in support).

Vocally, Judy was able to commit to film a subdued, lyrical treatment of the song she'd sung at her Metro audition three years earlier, "Zing! Went the Strings of My Heart." Interestingly, the song was also prerecorded with a remarkably hot second chorus, but that version was shelved in favor of a gentler approach. The ensemble rendition of "On the Bumpy Road to Love" typifies the catchy Depression-era tunes that were both instantly hummable and quickly forgotten.

Her third song, "Ten Pins in the Sky," had a melody by Milton Ager. He and his wife were early Garland champions, having heard her at a Cocoanut Grove function in her pre-stardom days. Ager's daughter, later the celebrated journalist Shana Alexander, never forgot her parents returning home that evening in unsuppressed rapture about Judy. Mrs. [Cecilia] Ager was an entertainment journalist and well-versed in "the show business." She compared Garland's effect as a singer to that achieved by George Gershwin, playing his own music at piano: ". . . They oxygenated a room!"

## What They Said

*"The story was light, and it was played lightly. I was Judy's mother (the first of a long career of 'Mothers for Metro') . . . and working with her was sheer joy. She was warm and affectionate and exuberant . . . and, even then, belted out her songs with more emotional quality than any fourteen-year-old [sic] should have. She was [also] young and vital and got the giggles regularly. You just couldn't get annoyed, because she couldn't help it—it was no act. Something would strike her funny, and her face would get red, and 'There goes Judy!' would be the cry. And we just had to wait until she got over it. She was a kid, a real kid. . . . During the picture, I went riding one Sunday and took a bad fall from my horse and was laid up in the hospital for a couple of weeks. When I returned, I had a gimpy walk; I did scenes where I didn't have to walk. But the gimpy walk was all Judy needed: 'I'm sorry, mom, but you just look so funny!' And there would go Judy!"*

—MARY ASTOR (1971)

*"We spent almost every Sunday afternoon at L. B. Mayer's beach house. It was sort of a command performance. I think people wanted to go, but those who didn't want to felt they pretty damn well better, anyway! But I used to love it there because he would run movies—he'd always run movies in the afternoon in the living room—and there I would sit and hold hands with Judy Garland . . . because Judy and I were very much in love. I may be phrasing that in the wrong way. I certainly was in love with Judy."*

—FREDDIE BARTHOLOMEW (1991)

**SPREAD SEQUENCE FROM LEFT:** Between-scenes conference with director Edwin L. Marin, Judy, and Freddie Bartholomew | Freddie Bartholomew, Scotty Beckett, Mary Astor, and Judy "on the bumpy road to love" | Judy and Beckett clown for publicity purposes. | Publicity photo of the principal cast: Astor and Walter Pidgeon at top, Judy and Bartholomew below

# The Wizard of Oz

METRO-GOLDWYN-MAYER

## CAST:

Judy Garland ...................................... Dorothy

Frank Morgan ....................... Professor Marvel, Emerald City Guardian of the Gate, Cabbie, Soldier, Great Head, the Wizard of Oz

Ray Bolger ....................... Hunk/the Scarecrow

Bert Lahr.................... Zeke/the Cowardly Lion

Jack Haley ....................... Hickory/the Tin Man

Billie Burke ......................................... Glinda

Margaret Hamilton ....................... Miss Gulch, the Wicked Witch of the East, the Wicked Witch of the West

Charley Grapewin........................Uncle Henry

Pat Walshe ... Nikko, Principal Winged Monkey

Clara Blandick.............................. Auntie Em

## CREDITS:

Mervyn LeRoy (producer); Victor Fleming (director); Noel Langley, Florence Ryerson, and Edgar Allan Woolf (screenplay); Noel Langley (adaptation); L. Frank Baum (original author); Harold Rosson (photography), Allen Davey (associate); Harold Arlen and E. Y. Harburg (music and lyrics); George Bassman, Murray Cutter, Paul Marquardt, and Ken Darby (orchestrations); Herbert Stothart (musical adaptation); Bobby Connolly (dance director); Cedric Gibbons (art director), William A. Horning (associate); Edwin B. Willis (set decorations); Adrian (costumes); Arnold Gillespie (special effects); Blanche Sewell (editor)

## JUDY'S NUMBERS:

"Over the Rainbow," "Munchkinland," "If I Only Had a Brain," "If I Only Had the Nerve," "We're Off to See the Wizard" (with Ray Bolger; with Bolger and Buddy Ebsen; with Bolger, Ebsen, and Burt Lahr—though dropped from the Tin Man role due to illness, Ebsen's voice remained on the soundtrack for this song), "The Merry Old Land of Oz." Deleted: "Over the Rainbow" reprise; "The Jitterbug," "Ding-Dong! The Witch is Dead" reprise (incorporating "We're Off to See the Wizard" and "The Merry Old Land of Oz")

**RELEASE DATE: August 17, 1939**
(Capitol Theatre, New York; Grauman's Chinese Theatre, Los Angeles, August 15)

**RUN TIME: 100 minutes**

## SYNOPSIS

Twelve-year-old orphan Dorothy Gale (JG) lives on a Kansas farm with her aunt and uncle. They and their farmhands—Hunk, Hickory, and Zeke—are too preoccupied with work to pay attention to the girl's great worry: her dog, Toto, has been threatened with destruction by sour neighbor Almira Gulch. To save Toto, Dorothy runs away, until carnival fakir Professor Marvel convinces her to return home. Unfortunately, the girl arrives back at the farmhouse just as a tornado barrels across the prairie.

Struck by an imploding window, Dorothy dreams herself "over the rainbow" to the Land of Oz, where she is welcomed by the Munchkins and Good Witch Glinda. All are in high spirits because the Gale home, dropped from the sky by the twister, has killed the Wicked Witch of the East. When Glinda gives the woman's ruby slippers to Dorothy, the girl becomes the sworn enemy of the Wicked Witch of the West, who craves the powers of her late sister's magic shoes. To get safely back to Kansas, Dorothy is directed by Glinda to seek help from the Wizard of Oz in the Emerald City. She is eventually joined on her journey by the Scarecrow, Tin Man, and Cowardly Lion, who plan to ask the Wizard, respectively, for a brain, a heart, and courage.

Along the way, the Wicked Witch bedevils them with poisonous poppies, sky-written threats, and winged monkeys. She finally captures them and sets fire to the Scarecrow, but Dorothy saves him with a bucket of water; in the process, the Witch is doused as well and melts away. When the Wizard proves to be a humbug, Dorothy returns home by the magic of the ruby slippers and the self-realization that her heart's desire is the company of those she loves. She awakens from her dream, surrounded by family and friends (in some of whom she recognizes their Oz-ian counterparts).

Billie Burke conducts the Munchkinland celebration upon "Dorothy's" arrival, December 1938.

TOP: Ray Bolger, Judy, and one of the less welcoming citizens of Oz, November 1938 LOWER LEFT AND RIGHT: Director Richard Thorpe's two weeks of *Oz* footage was junked when he was replaced. His "Dorothy" was a blonde, in different hairstyle, costume, and slippers; his Wicked Witch (Margaret Hamilton) wore her hair down and sported different makeup as well. Also seen: Pat Walshe as winged monkey "Nikko"

When aluminum makeup poisoning sent "Tin Man" Buddy Ebsen to the hospital, his footage was scrapped, and he was replaced by Jack Haley. The latter filmed for three days in Ebsen's shiny costume before anyone realized the character was supposed to be rusted and tarnished for this sequence. The new footage was junked as well, and filming began again. These stills show the "before and after" approach to the scene. (The oil can changed, too!)

## REVIEWS

"The combination of . . . Haley, Lahr, and Bolger . . . with Miss Garland is peculiarly fortunate, for it is the collusion of talents, highlighted by the peculiar tricks of each, which makes their efforts constantly delightful, individually and collectively. Miss Garland's singing of 'Over the Rainbow' is one of the delights of the production."

—*HOLLYWOOD REPORTER*

"Remarkable technical effects and beautiful photography create an air of sheer magic throughout the picture. The entertainment value is due not only to clever handling of the fantasy but also to the heart-warming aspects of the story. JG makes a thoroughly believable and lovable Dorothy."

—*PHOTOPLAY*

"Visually a cinematic masterpiece. . . . a piece of screen entertainment which can be shown every year from now on. To me, the outstanding feature of the production is the astonishingly clever performance of JG. All through the picture moves the little Judy, holding it together, being always its motivating feature."

—*HOLLYWOOD SPECTATOR*

"This individual, dazzling picture makes enchanting entertainment. There has been nothing like it on the screen before. JG is engaging, confident, and tuneful."

—*AUSTRALIAN WOMEN'S WEEKLY*

## NOTES

More than a score of books, documentaries, and home video and compact disc releases now trace the history of MGM's *The Wizard of Oz*, along with details of the greater *Oz* legend: the "official" series of forty books; the epochal 1902 stage musical; the filmed attempts to tell Frank Baum's stories, from 1908 to the present; the merchandising of the situations and characters; the iconic reverberations. Major points to note:

The *Oz* property was purchased by MGM specifically as a showcase for Judy Garland. The legend that Shirley Temple was nearly cast (or preferred) as Dorothy Gale is a much-exaggerated elaboration of what was at most an unofficial and brief, intra-trade discussion. The many script variations and, most importantly, the *Oz* songs, were written with Judy in mind.

Though the film broke attendance records everywhere, it lost money on its original release; children comprised perhaps two-thirds of its audience, and they paid considerably less at the box office than did adults. Additionally, much of the expected foreign market for the picture was cut off by the European onset of World War II in September 1939.

*Oz* went over budget by 65 percent; final cost for production, prints, and advertising hit approximately $3,700,000. However, its initial gross of $3,017,000 was enough to place it at number seven in 1939's top ten box office hits, and *Oz* received five Academy Award nominations, including Best Picture. It was also nominated for Best Special Effects and Best Art Direction. It won two of those Oscars, for Best Original Score and Best Song, "Over the Rainbow."

Dismissed by overanxious Metro executives, "Rainbow" was briefly dropped from the film at its second test screening in Pomona, CA, but uncredited associate producer Arthur Freed argued the song back into the picture. For all the past and present indignation and disbelief at such a situation, it's seldom been acknowledged that, without "Rainbow," *Oz* would have become a "Garland musical" without a Garland song. "The Jitterbug," her upbeat solo production number, had already hit the cutting room floor. The most successful contemporary recording of "Rainbow" was made by the Glenn Miller Orchestra. Their disc had a seven-week chart run as the number one hit in the country. Two other orchestras charted with the tune—Larry Clinton at number ten and Bob Crosby at number two. Judy's single topped out at number five during its twelve weeks on the charts.

In 1989, *Oz* was one of the first twenty five movies selected by the United States National Film Preservation Board for Library of Congress preservation in the National Film Registry as a "culturally, historically, or aesthetically significant" motion picture.

**ABOVE:** Judy frolics with Carl Spitz's female Cairn terrier, Terry, for publicity purposes. Garland, the dog, and the Munchkins received the lowest weekly salaries paid to members of *The Wizard of Oz* principal cast. **OPPOSITE:** "Dorothy" gets retouched on the Tin Woodman cottage set, November 1938.

## What They Said

*"I am grateful to pictures, but I prefer the stage. Of course, if I could have a director like George Cukor, it might be different. I learned more in the two days he was on Oz than I learned at any one time before. It isn't that the other directors aren't wonderful, but they don't know how to handle people of my age. It takes a very special kind of understanding to cope with in-betweeners. . . . And if you really want to know a wonderful man, you should meet Victor Fleming. He directed Oz— and he's perfectly marvelous. He has the nicest low voice, and the kindest eyes. Besides, he realizes that a girl who is sixteen is practically grown up. He shows me all the courtesies he would to Hedy Lamarr. That's very important to me. He notices my clothes and the way I do my hair and remarks about them."*

—JUDY GARLAND (1939)

*"Lunch was the only opportunity we had to be with each other. When I worked on the set [as her stand-in], Judy was busy with her school work. The law stated that, as a minor, you had to spend a certain amount of time on your studies. I was glad to have already graduated from Hollywood High and had all that behind me. Judy amazed me how she could do math, history, geography, and other studies; then, at a moment's notice—when she heard, 'Ready on the set, Judy'—she could suddenly turn into Dorothy Gale of Kansas."*

—STAND-IN CAREN MARSH-DOLL

*"All the little people thought very highly of Judy because they knew she had been in the theater and had already worked for so many years as a singer. She treated all the little people as troupers and, shall we say, in the same category as herself. There was never any feeling of being above or below; we were all part of the game. And whenever there was a break in the action, she would chat with us very amiably. My most treasured possession is a personally autographed picture, on which she wrote, 'To Meinhardt: a perfect coroner and person, too. Love from Judy.'"*

—"MUNCHKIN CORONER" MEINHARDT RAABE (1993)

*"I love to watch Oz. I watch it every Christmas with my children. I think it's a beautiful picture . . . and it was beautifully done. I just wish I had a 'piece' of it— just a small percentage! Or even a 16mm print; Metro won't sell me one. But now I can view it dispassionately; when I was making the picture, and when I saw it for the first time, I didn't have any objectivity about it. But after I saw it so many times, I appreciated the Munchkins—and I really wasn't afraid of the Witch. We were good friends, as a matter of fact!"*

—JUDY GARLAND (1967)

Judy later defined director Victor Fleming as "a darling man"; her teen adoration is clearly visible. Also paying attention: Ray Bolger.

# AN OZ MINI-SCRAPBOOK:

Presented here are rare, behind-the-scenes shots, scalloped by the secretary of Victor Fleming for the director's own scrapbook back in 1939.

Haley, Garland, and Bolger jokingly threaten each other with ax, acetylene torch, and watering can.

Movie-making at MGM, November 1938. Choreographer Bobby Connolly and Victor Fleming at bottom left.

Hands-on Fleming indicates Poppy Field direction for Bolger, Haley, Judy, and Bert Lahr; an assistant holds onto Terry.

"Little people" Jannette Fern (left), Jerry Maren (center), and Olga Nardone (right) join Judy and three of the performing children who "filled in" during the Munchkinland sequence: Raynelle Lasky, Priscilla Montgomery, and Betty Ann Cain.

Judy's hair is tended during a lighthearted moment in the Haunted Forest. Haley, Lahr, Bolger look on while Fleming points out the approach angle of the Winged Monkeys.

Fleming and Judy watch as a Metro technician prepares a special effect fireburst.

*Oz* filming coincided with Christmas 1938.

Judy wears comfortable slippers as she, Pat Walshe, Fleming, and Margaret Hamilton rehearse in the Witch's Tower Room.

**ABOVE:** MGM circulated many color images to promote *Oz*. Most of the transparencies have long since disappeared, but the rotogravure images remain. Here joining the rest of the cast, Frank Morgan can be seen as both "The Wizard" and "The Guardian of the Gate."

Dorothy wipes the Cowardly Lion's tears away!

**COUNTERCLOCKWISE FROM TOP:** Whether just before or after World War II—pending location—*Oz* was happily received abroad. This Mexico lobby card dates from the 1940s. | *Oz* was a box-office triumph when first reissued in 1949—despite the hand-colored lobby cards that depicted Dorothy as "the lady in red."

# Babes in Arms

METRO-GOLDWYN-MAYER

## CAST:

Mickey Rooney ......................... *Mickey Moran*

Judy Garland ............................. *Patsy Barton*

Charles Winninger ........................... *Joe Moran*

Guy Kibbee ................................... *Judge Black*

June Preisser ................ *"Baby" Rosalie Essex*

Grace Hayes ............................. *Florrie Moran*

Betty Jaynes ................................. *Molly Moran*

Douglas McPhail ............................ *Don Brice*

Margaret Hamilton .................... *Martha Steele*

Henry Hull ............................................. *Madox*

## CREDITS:

**Arthur Freed** *(producer);* **Busby Berkeley** *(director);* **Jack McGowan and Kay Van Riper** *(screenplay);* **Richard Rodgers and Lorenz Hart** *(original playwrights);* **Ray June** *(photography);* **Richard Rodgers and Lorenz Hart** *(music and lyric to "Babes in Arms," "Where or When")* **Nacio Herb Brown and Arthur Freed** *(music and lyric to "Good Morning");* **Harold Arlen and E. Y. Harburg** *(music and lyric to "God's Country");* **George Stoll** *(musical director);* **Roger Edens** *(musical adaptation);* **Leo Arnaud and George Bassman** *(orchestrations);* **Cedric Gibbons** *(art director),* **Merrill Pye** *(associate);* **Edwin B. Willis** *(set decorations);* **Dolly Tree** *(wardrobe);* **Frank Sullivan** *(editor)*

## JUDY'S NUMBERS:

*"Good Morning," "Opera vs. Jazz" [incorporating "Figaro," "Bob White (Whatcha Gonna Swing Tonight?)", "Broadway Rhythm"], "Babes in Arms," "Where or When," "I Cried for You," Minstrel Show (incorporating "Minstrel Show," "My Daddy Was a Minstrel Man," "Oh, Suzannah," and "I'm Just Wild about Harry"), "God's Country" (incorporating "The Yankee Doodle Boy," "My Day," and "Good Morning" reprise)*

**RELEASE DATE:** October 13, 1939

**RUN TIME:** 96 minutes

## SYNOPSIS

Mickey Moran, his sister Molly, Patsy Barton (JG), and Don Brice are all second or third generation entertainers, the offspring of vaudeville stars of decades past. But movies and radio have supplanted live entertainment across America, and the old-timers are unemployable. Mickey's dad, Joe Moran, decides to produce a touring comeback show for the veterans. Their children are incensed at being left out and—with Mickey's writing, directing, and composing talents as a foundation—prepare a local show of their own.

The kids are helped in their plans by sympathetic Judge Black and hindered by town busybody Martha Steele. To raise funds, Mickey is forced to re-cast Patsy's leading role with former child star Baby Rosalie. When Baby's father pulls her out of the production on opening night, Patsy and Mickey go on together as planned, only to have their outdoor theater swamped mid-performance by a hurricane. Defeated, the old-timers have returned as well, and Joe plans to sign his children into the state work school. The kids are saved by Harry Madox, a mainstream theatrical producer who attended their show and liked what he saw. He puts the babes, triumphantly, on Broadway.

OPPOSITE: In a promotional pose, Mickey Rooney gets the cold shoulder from Judy and dancer/acrobat June Preisser. ABOVE FROM LEFT: Judy and the "vaudevets"—principal among them Charles Winninger, Ann Shoemaker, and Grace Hayes | The plot thickens: Mickey and Judy meet "Baby Rosalie." Rand Brooks is her disapproving escort. | "Where or When" was originally a duet intended for Betty Jaynes and Douglas McPhail. Judy only got to sing eight bars, but it's possible a couple of different stagings were attempted for even that brief bit of song; the approach pictured here with Mickey on the violin was never seen in the finished picture.

BELOW: Up the ladder to success: Jaynes, Garland, Rooney, and McPhail polish off the film's title song. (In the actual film, Judy's role is played at this moment by a stand-in.)

The cast celebrates "God's Country" for a grand finale, briefly featuring Rooney and Garland as President Franklin Delano Roosevelt and First Lady Eleanor.

## REVIEWS

"Nothing short of sensational. It has everything that makes for enjoyment [for] classmates, young/old, rural/urban, and all in-between divisions of filmgoers. Rooney does his best job to date, and Miss Garland is an able partner."

—*MOTION PICTURE DAILY*

"It's one of the snappiest and most exhilarating films I can remember. Just what the doctor ordered for these dark days." —LONDON *DAILY MIRROR*

"Splendid. A musical that would be hard to top . . . It has swell comedy, fine tunes, good dancing, and a superb cast headed by MR and JG."

—*SILVER SCREEN*

"One of the most enjoyable pictures the movies have given us in any season. JG sings better than ever and shares in the acting and dancing honors in a big way. [She and Mickey] come just as near being 'sensational' as any star the press agent has used that word to exploit."

—SEATTLE *TIMES*

" . . . a pug-nose little Irishman, name of Mickey Rooney, [steps] right out and establishes himself as the greatest all-around performer the cinema has ever trained its cameras on. . . . JG, every day becoming less the chubby child and more the streamlined young lady, treads closely on the Rooney's heels. Giving her most versatile performance to date, Judy again demonstrates her power for poignancy in both speaking and singing roles, and shows an unexpected flair for comedy . . . *Babes in Arms* has everything. It's the sort of film you'll want to see twice—the second time because you were sorry to see it end the first time."

—CHICAGO *HERALD AMERICAN*

**ABOVE AND OPPOSITE:** Judy tests hairstyles and wardrobe for *Babes in Arms*. Oftentimes, such tests simply proved that a particular look or costume wasn't best suited to a performer, and the ensemble and hairdo in question was abandoned.

## NOTES

In 1938, Arthur Freed was one of MGM's preeminent lyricists. He'd been turning out hit songs for the studio's films for nearly a decade when he instigated negotiations for the purchase of *The Wizard of Oz* as a showcase for Judy. He then served as that picture's uncredited associate producer (to Mervyn LeRoy) while simultaneously planning his own first production, a vehicle to reunite Judy and Mickey Rooney. *Babes in Arms* was very loosely adapted from a 1937 Richard Rodgers–Lorenz Hart Broadway musical. Its success as a film, along with that of *Oz*, launched Freed's twenty-year supremacy as Hollywood's leading movie musical producer.

It took just over three months, from the end of April to the first week of August 1939, for *Babes* to flow from tests and rehearsals to prerecordings, principal photography, retakes, and looping. The picture marked Busby Berkeley's first full directorial job at MGM, following more than a decade of assignments as choreographer and/or director for Samuel Goldwyn and Warner Bros. films.

Ultimately, *Babes* boasted too many creative highlights to tabulate. Paramount among them on the film's initial release was the brief Rooney/Garland imitation of the radio demeanor and vocal inflection of President Franklin Delano Roosevelt and his First Lady, Eleanor. Metro got specific permission from the White House for the mimicry. The Roosevelts' oldest son, James, went public in his approval and deemed the sequence "hilarious."

Although Rooney's flashy role, performance, and hold on the public won him the most attention (and even an Academy Award nomination as Best Actor), *Babes* and Judy achieved their own raves. Sneak preview audiences submitted comment cards that asked for "more such pictures" and "more Judy Garland and Mickey Rooney." They cheered, "Brava, Judy," "Judy is enchanting," while at the same time wondering, "Why didn't Judy sing 'Johnny One Note'? [from the stage show]; it would have made a terrific hit." There was even concern expressed on her behalf: "there is terror in her eyes." This is perhaps one of the first manifestations of the exceptional personal bond Judy was developing with those who enjoyed her.

A final addition to the film was borne from these test showings. Audiences had seemed initially unimpressed by the principal performances in a minstrel show mélange, and the ever-savvy Roger Edens realized it was because they weren't sure which of the "babes" they were viewing. A hastily filmed insert showed Judy and Mickey applying their blackface makeup, after which the number (if of its day) played beautifully.

At a final cost of $745,000, *Babes in Arms* grossed more than $3,324,000, placing it among the top ten releases of 1939. It even bested such celebrated Metro product as *The Women*, *Boys Town*—and *The Wizard of Oz*.

## What They Said

*"My father was a great admirer of Judy's, from the time she first came on the lot. And until she died, he always thought that she was the greatest talent in Hollywood—and I think he was probably right. And I think even if it was subconsciously, he was always looking for things for her to do. The first movies he ever made [as a producer] were with Judy; he did* Babes in Arms *with her and Mickey, and* Strike Up the Band, *and* Babes on Broadway. *He did a movie with her and George Murphy,* Little Nellie Kelly. *She was the person he wanted to work with."*

—BARBARA SALTZMAN,
DAUGHTER OF ARTHUR FREED

*"It was Arthur Freed who insisted on having Judy costarred. But Judy agreed with the studio; she didn't think she deserved it. After all, Mickey was Number One at the box office. She hadn't done enough to be costarred with him. But Arthur put his foot down. Said she deserved it, if only*
*for working so hard. Said he wouldn't release the picture unless she was costarred. Fought until he got her name [beside Mickey's]."*

—CONTEMPORARY FAN MAGAZINE

*"What is the particular appeal of Mickey and Judy? Hollywood is full of young hopefuls who can sing and dance—some even better than those two kids. What have Judy and Mickey got that these rafts of others lack? 'Vitality and sincerity and experience,' Arthur Freed replied, 'and that is the proper sequence of these qualities' importance. There are hundreds of pretty and cute youngsters in Hollywood, and many of them are talented. But, to begin with, they haven't got stamina; they can't stand the grind of rehearsals and retakes. They're more interested in dates than in concentrating on their jobs. They want to be 'in the movies' for the glamour, the thrill; not 'of the movies' for the satisfaction of really contributing*
*to the business. And many of them are smarties, objecting to correction and advice. Give me kids from show business every time! Judy and Mickey have been working hard to amuse the public since they were tiny tots. Both came up the hard way of vaudeville. They're troupers. They have tremendous energy. And along with their zeal, they are sincere in everything they do—and eager to learn.'"*

—JOURNALIST MYRTLE GEBHART IN AN
INTERVIEW WITH ARTHUR FREED

**ABOVE FROM LEFT:** Garland and Rooney with classical vocalists Douglas McPhail and Betty Jaynes. The latter duo were gifted singers, but their operatic style was out of place in the (mostly) swing-happy films of the 1940s. | Generational vaudeville: Garland and Rooney with veteran greats Grace Hayes and Charles Winninger

**OPPOSITE TOP:** Though she is willing to understudy "Baby Rosalie," Judy rebels and walks out after Mickey kisses the blonde. **OPPOSITE BOTTOM FROM LEFT:** Roger Edens holds Judy's parasol, while director Busby Berkeley informally reads her palm; she's in costume for "I'm Just Wild About Harry." | The teens welcome Her Royal Highness, Crown Princess Martha of Norway to their soundstage.

**RIGHT:** *The Big Revue:* Frances, Jimmie, and Susie in the Gumm Sisters' motion picture debut. Baby punctuated their lyrical declamations with impassioned rhythmic bleats of "Yes, sir!"

## "THE BIG REVUE"

A MAYFAIR PICTURES CORPORATION RELEASE

**Two-reel short subject, 18 minutes**

**RELEASE: August 14, 1929**

Featuring "Ethel Meglin's Wonder Kiddies." Filmed in black and white, June 11–13, 1929 at Tec Art Studios, Hollywood, California. Premiere showing at the Fox Belmont Theatre, Hollywood. (Per some surviving prints, the film was later re-edited and re-circulated as the one-reel *Starlet Revue.*)

**JUDY'S NUMBER:** "That's the Good Old Sunny South" (sung by the Gumm Sisters)

**NOTES:** In company with approximately 140 other pupils from the Ethel Meglin Dance School for child talent, Judy Garland made her motion picture debut in this short, appearing in a brief song-and-dance specialty with her two older sisters. (They were introduced by another moppet performer who blithely chirped, "Now you will see a dancing and singing number by the Gumm Sisters—not the Wrigley Sisters!")

Baby Gumm had celebrated her seventh birthday only hours prior to the filming, and she is by far the most at ease of the Gumms in their routine. Her performance is notable for its focus, her second-nature command of melody, lyric, and choreography, and for the seeming effortlessness of her communication, as if singing and dancing were the natural extension of her persona. (In her eagerness to perform, Baby makes an early entrance on one vocal phrase, catches herself, and trades a conspiratorial glance with Jimmie.)

When released, *The Big Revue* as a whole was alternately tolerated or condemned and perhaps best summarized by an anonymous critic who opined, "It's an all-talking, singing, toddling juvenile extravaganza, and ought—somewhere—to please someone."

# The Vitaphone Kiddies Shorts

As evidenced by *The Big Revue*, the onset of "talkies" led several Hollywood studios to produce brief musical short subjects. Director Roy Mack built a series of two-strip Technicolor entertainments around a mélange of juvenile performers, billed collectively as "The Vitaphone Kiddies." The Gumm Sisters were seen in three of Mack's shorts, filmed between November 1929 and January 1930, at First National Studios in Burbank, California. Although the soundtracks survive for all three, actual footage thus far has only surfaced for *Bubbles*.

## "A HOLIDAY IN STORYLAND"

"VITAPHONE VARIETIES," PRESENTED BY VITAPHONE

**One-reel short subject, 9 minutes**

**Filmed in two-strip Technicolor, November 1929. Directed by Roy Mack.**

**VITAPHONE RELEASE NO. 3824:** April 2, 1930. Classification: Technicolor Flash.

**EXCERPTS FROM CONTEMPORARY PROMOTIONAL STATEMENTS:** "An enchanting fantasy of childhood dreams, pictured in the glowing hues of the rainbow," [*A Holiday in Storyland* is] "notable . . . for its color and cute antics of some of the children."

**JUDY'S NUMBERS:** "Storyland Holiday" (the Gumm Sisters and chorus), "Where the Butterflies Kiss the Buttercups Goodnight" (the Gumm Sisters), "Blue Butterfly" (Baby Gumm)

**NOTES:** The Gumm Sisters took new billing for *A Holiday in Storyland* as the Three Kute Kiddies, and plot sequences for the picture were drawn in part from two childhood classics, *The Old Lady in the Shoe* and *Cinderella*. As a result, early Garland filmographies often inaccurately referenced either of those titles as the names of early Frances Gumm screen shorts.

## "THE WEDDING OF JACK AND JILL"

"VITAPHONE VARIETIES," PRESENTED BY VITAPHONE

**One-reel short subject, 10 minutes**

**Filmed in two-strip Technicolor, circa December 1929. Directed by Roy Mack.**

**VITAPHONE RELEASE NO. 3826:** June 1930. Four Scenes/Classification: Technicolor Flash.

**A CONTEMPORARY PROMOTIONAL RELEASE:** "The gorgeous wedding of Jack and Jill, the tumbling pair of nursery rhyme fame! Beautiful rag dolls from every land are on hand for the ceremony. The talented Vitaphone Kiddies provide royal entertainment for the wedded pair. 'Dressed to kill,' they sing and dance with professional artistry. The use of Technicolor enhances the beautiful scenes of children's dreams! It will please both children and adults. Music and lyrics by M. K. Jerome and Harold Berg."

**JUDY'S NUMBERS:** "The Wedding of Jack and Jill" (the Gumm Sisters and chorus), "Hang On to a Rainbow" (Baby Gumm)

**NOTES:** The roles of Jack and Jill were played by John Pirrone (later John Perri) and Peggy Ryan (later the frequent teen screen partner of Donald O'Connor). Surviving critical comment for the short includes: "Novel in idea and treatment, weak on entertainment value" (*Variety*, May 7, 1930); "will make a big hit with kids and appeal to adults at the same time" (*Motion Picture News*, June 7, 1930); and "swell kiddie number" (*Film Daily*, June 8, 1930).

Baby Gumm and John Pirrone in a snapshot taken on the First National lot during filming of *The Wedding of Jack and Jill*.

## "BUBBLES"

"VITAPHONE VARIETIES," PRESENTED BY VITAPHONE

**One-reel short subject, 9 minutes**

**Filmed in two-strip Technicolor, January 1930. Directed by Roy Mack.**

**VITAPHONE RELEASE NO. 3898: late 1930. Two Scenes/Classification: Technicolor Flash.**

**A CONTEMPORARY PROMOTIONAL RELEASE:** "A delightful trip through a child's paradise—the magic land of dreams! A group of unusually talented children—the Vitaphone Kiddies—ranging from five to fifteen years, frolic and dance in this intriguing atmosphere of the supernatural. Beautiful scenes are made fantastically realistic through the medium of Technicolor. Both grownups and children will love it. Roy Mack, dance creator for *Loose Ankles* and other feature pictures as well as many Technicolor Vitaphone Varieties, staged this novel production with unusual skill and imagery."

**JUDY'S NUMBER:** "The Land of Let's Pretend" (the Gumm Sisters).

**NOTES:** The short opens with the song, "My Pretty Bubble," sung by an unbilled Mae Questel, just a year prior to her debut as the unseen voice of cartoon character Betty Boop. (Questel went on to provide speaking and singing talent for everyone from Olive Oyl to Winky Dink.) The Gumm Sisters appear in the first showcase number of the film's "dream sequence"; thereafter, they function merely as stage dressing. Nonetheless, "Bubbles" gave Baby Gumm her first (surviving) film close-up. It provides the opportunity to see a sort of Munchkin Judy Garland, already in possession of piercing vocal projection and already reaching out to an audience, even in a choreographed gesture. Forty years later, one of Jimmie Gumm's only memories of the Vitaphone shorts was shared with Garland biographer Christopher Finch when she recalled the girls' appearance as the "moon maidens" in "Bubbles."

## "LA FIESTA DE SANTA BARBARA"

METRO-GOLDWYN-MAYER

**A Technicolor two-reel short subject, 19 minutes**

**Release: circa spring 1936**

**CAST:** Eduardo Durant's Fiesta Orchestra and his Spanish Troubadours with a Galaxy of Screen Stars, including Warner Baxter, Ralph Forbes, the Fanchonettes, Garland Sisters, Kirby & DeGage, Dude Ranch Wranglers. [Uncredited: Pete Smith (narration), Adrienne Ames, Binnie Barnes, Mary Carlisle, Leo Carrillo, Irvin S. Cobb, Chester Conklin, Gary Cooper, Andy Devine, Steffi Duna, Concha Frandinho, Maria Gambarelli, Ted Healy, Buster Keaton, Rosalind Keith, Klayton Kirby, Edmund Lowe, Ida Lupino, Harpo Marx, Joe Morrison, Cecilia Parker, Paul Porcasi, Gilbert Roland, Mary Stewart, Robert Taylor, Jim Thorpe, Toby Wing, Shirley Ross.]

**CREDITS:** Louis Lewyn (producer); Ray Rennahan (photography)

**JUDY'S NUMBER:** "La Cucaracha" (the Garland Sisters)

**NOTES:** Filmed on location in early August 1935, "La Fiesta de Santa Barbara" marked the last "formal" appearance of Judy with her sisters. A few days later, Susie left the act to marry musician Lee Kahn, and—as the Garland Sisters' performances had become more and more a showcase for Judy—Jimmie also decided to pursue a personal life rather than a career.

Although the Vitaphone Kiddies shorts had been photographed in primitive two-strip Technicolor, *La Fiesta de Santa Barbara* marked Judy's first appearance in full three-strip glory. The Garland Sisters are here beguiling Paul Porcasi and Concha Frandinho.

Introduced in the film by Leo Carrillo, the three girls are only provided with seventy seconds of footage, and they share their brief screen time with Buster Keaton, Andy Devine, a clowning Carrillo, a dancing Steffi Duna, a placid Concha Frandinho, an alternately joyous or tearful Paul Porcasi, a somnambulant burro, and several others. Sung "live" on camera, the four Garland choruses of "La Cucaracha" are interspersed with a special material list of city names: "Santa Barb'ra, Palo Alto/Tijuana, Caliente/Albuquerque, and Puente/San Diego . . ." with "Hoboken" as a final ringer. *La Fiesta de Santa Barbara* was a 1936 Academy Award nominee for Best Color Short Subject. Though produced independently by Louis Lewyn, the film was distributed by MGM, making it—by coincidence—Garland's first release for the company.

## "OPERA VS. JAZZ"

METRO-GOLDWYN-MAYER

**A one-reel exhibitors' short subject**

**RELEASE:** circa spring 1936

**CAST:** Judy Garland and Deanna [then Edna Mae] Durbin.

**NUMBER:** "Opera vs. Jazz"—This is possibly the same Roger Edens amalgam of songs performed three years later by Garland and Betty Jaynes in *Babes in Arms*.

**NOTES:** Never intended for commercial release or public exhibition, this musical short was purportedly created and photographed to test the Garland and Durbin screen appearances and appeal. Virtually nothing specific is known about it beyond a brief autobiographical quote offered by Judy in the early 1960s: "My first film assignment [at MGM] was an overall screen test with Deanna [Durbin], sort of on 'Jazz versus Opera.' I had an apple in my hand and a dirty face, and she was the Princess of Transylvania or some crazy thing. But I think the only people who ever saw the film were the studio executives."

In truth (or, at least, in legend) the audience was a bit larger, and the brief film was well-received at a spring 1936 MGM exhibitors' convention in Los Angeles. That crowd's response finally gave Metro the impetus to team the girls in a legitimate short subject, and the studio prepared *Every Sunday* for that purpose. By the time they began actual preproduction, however, Durbin's contract had lapsed. It remains a minor Hollywood historical mystery as to whether she was intentionally or unintentionally dropped by MGM, or if her departure was a paperwork slip-up on the part of the legal department.

Edna Mae (not yet Deanna) Durbin and Judy Garland around the time of their first screen teaming in an MGM exhibitors' short. They're brandishing head shots of two already-established Metro stars, both of them younger men: Freddie Bartholomew and Jackie Cooper.

ABOVE FROM LEFT: "Pop—you just have no soul," chides an affectionate daughter: Judy and Richard Powell. | Judy and Edna look on as "Pop" Richard Powell convinces the actor portraying Deanna's grandfather to try "a new routine." (The name of the actor now seems to be lost to history.) "Americana" was written for *Every Sunday* by Con Conrad and Herb Magidson, who'd turned out the first Academy Award-winning song, "The Continental," two years earlier. BELOW: In this trade ad, Metro promotes its girl, but doesn't reference by name her concurrent Twentieth Century Fox feature or the title of the one in which Deanna had just appeared for Universal.

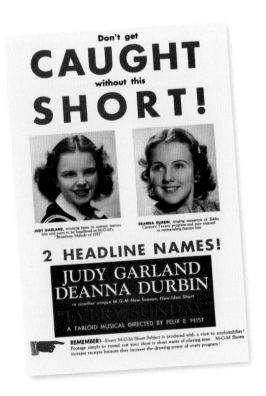

## "EVERY SUNDAY"

METRO-GOLDWYN-MAYER

**A one-reel short subject, 11 minutes**

**RELEASE: November 28, 1936**

**CAST:** Judy Garland (Judy Dale), Deanna Durbin (Edna Martin), Richard Powell (Judy's Father), Gwen Lee (Judy's Mother), Thomas Pogue (Mr. Barnfoggle), Paul Irving (Mr. Bixby)

**CREDITS:** "A Tabloid Musical." Jack Chertok (executive producer); George Sidney (producer); Felix E. Feist (director); Charles G. Clarke (photography); Mauri Grashin (screenplay)

**JUDY'S NUMBERS:** "Waltz With a Swing," "Americana," "Americana" finale reprise

**NOTES:** MGM's contract option for the services of Deanna [then still Edna Mae] Durbin was allowed to run out in late May 1936. By early June, she had been signed by Universal, where producer Joe Pasternak planned to cast her in his feature, *Three Smart Girls*. Pasternak later wrote that he'd been shown footage of both Judy and Deanna; this apparently was the *Opera vs. Jazz* exhibitor's short referenced on page 119. He wanted to hire Garland but was told that MGM was keeping her. So, surprised and delighted by Durbin as well, Pasternak brought her to Universal instead. (The subsequent Pasternak/Durbin films of the late 1930s literally saved that studio from bankruptcy.)

However, a clause in Durbin's MGM contract gave them the right to call on her services for up to sixty days following her termination, and although they'd let her contract lapse, Metro remained eager to act on the impression made by both girls at the exhibitors' conference. By June 30, Judy and Deanna had completed their *Every Sunday* musical prerecordings, and filming followed over a few days in July. (The short had originally been awkwardly titled *Every Other Thursday*.) Evidently, a retake policy was considered and/or implemented for some of its Garland footage; in an October interview, Judy noted that she had been "put in a two-reeler [sic] that isn't finished yet."

*Every Sunday* finally went into theaters a few weeks later. Neither Garland nor Durbin was especially thrilled with the final product. In 1940—and with no intended rancor—Judy self-deprecatingly wrote of both of them, "I wish I could burn that short that [Deanna] and I made together! Deanna wore fuzzy bangs, and she had a trick then of holding one arm out from her side, like a chicken with a broken wing. I was so pigeon-toed I tripped myself, and I had straight hair, nearly black, and cut short. They didn't put much makeup on me either, so my eyes looked about as big as a pig's!"

## "1937 CHRISTMAS TRAILER"

METRO-GOLDWYN-MAYER

**2 minutes**

**RELEASE DATE: December 1937**

**JUDY'S NUMBER:** "Silent Night"

**NOTES:** This very brief short, recorded and filmed November 6–9, 1937, is best summarized by an excerpt from a feature in *The Motion Picture and the Family*, December 16, 1937: "[Those] who attend motion pictures during Christmas week will hear and see [The St. Luke's Choristers] in a special Christmas trailer which has been made by Metro-Goldwyn-Mayer to carry their holiday greetings to the world. Little Judy Garland will sing 'Silent Night' with a choral background of boys' voices in four-part harmony. The scene is laid in a church, appropriately decorated for Christmas, and the boys appear in vestments. Thousands of copies of the trailer will be made and sent to practically every important theater in the world. . . . "

After working with the fifteen-year old Garland, Choristers' conductor William Ripley Dorr noted that "[Judy] told me she had sung in a church choir since she was very small and loved church music." Garland's *Silent Night* prerecording was later used in both the syndicated *Judge Hardy's Family* holiday radio program for 1939 and the 1940 *MGM Reporter Special Air Trailer for Christmas 1940*. In the late 1990s, Folger's Coffee utilized a colorized version of the Garland footage as its own TV commercial/ greeting for the holidays.

## "THE CAVALCADE OF THE ACADEMY AWARDS"

DISTRIBUTED BY WARNER BROS.

**A three-reel featurette, 30 minutes**

**RELEASE:** mid-1940

**CREDITS:** Frank Capra (director); Owen Crump (screenplay); Charles Rosher, Sr. (photography) Carey Wilson (commentary)

**NOTES:** As a sort of duo-promotion for the film industry and the twelfth anniversary of the Academy of Motion Picture Arts and Sciences, producer/director Frank Capra assembled this short subject to pay brief homage to Hollywood and lengthy tribute to Oscar winners, past and (especially) present. The featurette includes extensive footage both taken at, and in re-creation of, the ceremonies of February 29, 1940. On that occasion, Mickey Rooney presented Judy with her special miniature statuette for "the outstanding performance by a juvenile actress during the past year." Capra's excerpts from the event include those moments of honor. (Regrettably, he cuts away to a film clip of "Over the Rainbow" from *The Wizard of Oz* itself, just as Garland is about to sing it "live" for the Ambassador Hotel assemblage.)

FROM TOP: Choir director William Ripley Dorr was astounded at the low musical key in which his boys were expected to sing, until he heard Judy's voice and realized she was an alto. | Between takes of "Silent Night"

## "WILL ROGERS MEMORIAL FUND/ MEMORIAL HOSPITAL APPEAL"

METRO-GOLDWYN-MAYER

**A one-reel short subject, 8 minutes**

**RELEASE:** May 1940

**CAST:** Bette Davis, Judy Garland, Kay Kyser and His Orchestra

**JUDY'S NUMBER:** "If I Forget You"

**NOTES:** This was the fifth annual short subject produced to solicit funds from motion picture audiences of the day; their contributions benefited the Will Rogers Memorial Hospital and Fund, whose work (in different form) continues to the present. The 1940 appeal led off with Kay Kyser and His Kollege of Musical Knowledge in "Playmates" and segued to Judy and an off-camera chorus performing Irving Caesar's "If I Forget You." At its conclusion, Bette Davis made that year's plea for the financial support of those in attendance at the theaters.

## "MEET THE STARS"

A REPUBLIC SHORT SUBJECT

A LOS ANGELES EXAMINER BENEFIT (VOL. 1, NO. 4)

**9 minutes**

**RELEASE:** Spring 1941

**CAST:** Harriet Parsons (mistress of ceremonies), Mickey Rooney, Judy Garland, the Duncan Sisters, the Andrews Sisters, Milton Berle, Mary Martin, Abbott and Costello, Mary Beth Hughes, Reginald Gardiner, Constance Moore, Butch and Buddy, Buddy Pepper, Lorraine Krueger, Arthur Lake, Larry Simms, Bob Williams and Red Dust

**NOTES:** Apart from a one-sheet poster and contemporary newspaper ads, comparatively little is known about this one-reeler. The *Meet the Stars* series itself was overseen by producer Harriet Parsons, daughter of famed and feared Hollywood columnist Louella Parsons; it appears to have been compiled of newsreel-like footage, taken at various Southern California events and ceremonies. (Subsequent episodes of *Meet the Stars* celebrated the dedication of a Republic sound stage to the memory of silent screen star Mabel Normand and the visit of film performers to the United States naval base in San Diego.) Not unexpectedly, Rooney and Garland got top billing for their appearance in No. 4 of the series.

## "WE MUST HAVE MUSIC"

METRO-GOLDWYN-MAYER

**11 minutes**

**RELEASE:** Autumn 1941

**CAST:** Frank Whitbeck (narrator)

**JUDY'S NUMBER:** "We Must Have Music"

**NOTES:** Twice a year beginning in 1938, MGM produced a short subject that detailed behind-the-scenes activities and technical processes at the studio. Per narrator Frank Whitbeck: "The first 'Romance [of Celluloid]' gave audiences an insight into how film was made; the second showed how film was used and developed in the MGM laboratories. 'Power,' which was the title of the third, and *From the Ends of the Earth*, which concerned the property department, were the 1939 contributions. In 1940, fashions and the development and progress of the sound department were the subjects, and [in]

Already an international film star in 1941, Judy—in her "We Must Have Music" garb—graces the cover of a foreign fan magazine.

spring of 1941, the *Miracle of Sound* was released . . . *We Must Have Music* . . . reveals the inside workings of the music department. . . . The film will open with a complete musical production number featuring Judy Garland. We were fortunate in having this available. It was salvaged from excess footage of *Ziegfeld Girl*." (Unfortunately, only the first twenty seconds of the two-minute-plus routine actually made it into the short; the remainder of the Garland, Tony Martin, and chorus outtake remains lost.) *We Must Have Music* also includes scenes of conductor Herbert Stothart recording with the MGM Orchestra, Rise Stevens in a rendition of "America the Beautiful," and Busby Berkeley overseeing a *Babes on Broadway* "Hoe Down" rehearsal.

**ABOVE FROM LEFT:** Judy and Tony Martin share the honors; he has forever-after saluted her in his stage and café work when singing "You Stepped Out of a Dream" from the *Ziegfeld Girl* score. | At the conclusion of her song, Judy is referenced only by her first name in Frank Whitbeck's voice-over narration—the implication being that any moviegoer of 1941 would instantly recognize her as just "Judy."

## "ARMY-NAVY SCREEN MAGAZINE NO. 20"

THE [UNITED STATES] ARMY SIGNAL CORPS

**13 minutes**

**RELEASE:** 1944

**CAST:** Judy Garland, Betty Hutton, Lana Turner, Bob Hope (host), Ken Carpenter (announcer/narrator)

**JUDY'S NUMBER:** "Over the Rainbow"

**NOTES:** The *Army-Navy Screen Magazine* series was overseen and directed by Frank Capra for the Army Signal Corps from June 1943 until early 1946. The shorts were a composite of entertainment, World War II information and newsreel, and associated human interest features, specifically conceived and screened for service personnel as additions to the regular programming at military instillation motion picture theaters. Variety portions of Edition No. 20 were filmed on November 13, 1943, during prerecording of the Armed Forces Radio Service show, *Command Performance* (#92). Following Hutton, Turner, and badinage with Hope—and apart from his wrap-up verse and goodnight—Judy and her song were utilized as the finale of the program. (*Command Performance* was generally a half-hour show, and the dozen or so minutes excerpted here did not include footage of episode 92's other guests: Jimmy Durante and pop/gospel vocal group the Charioteers.)

# PART TWO ▷ JUST PUT HER NAME ON THE MARQUEE ▷ 1940-1944

▷ PART TWO

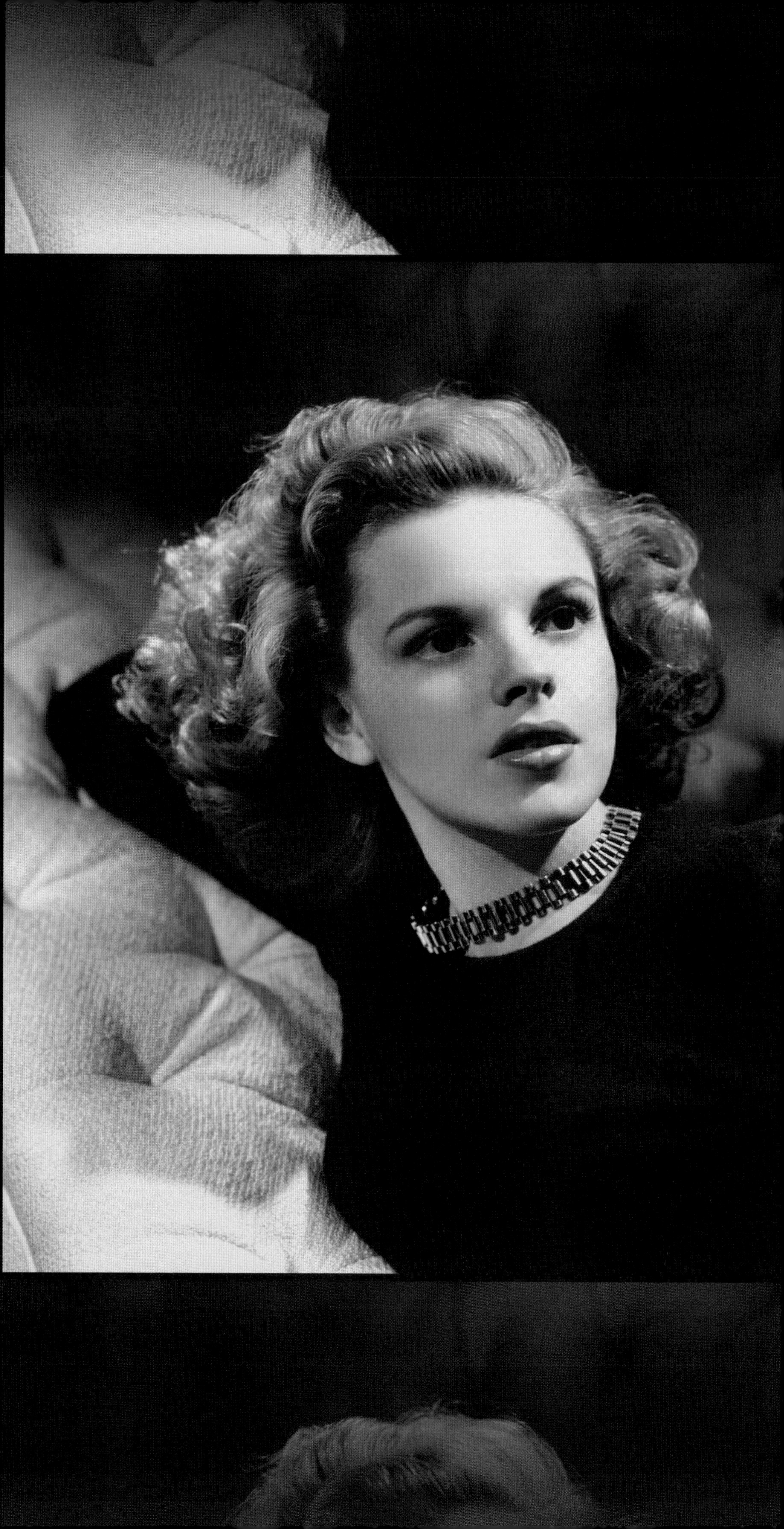

# JUST PUT HER name on THE marquee

1940-1944

Between February 1940 and June 1943, Judy Garland enjoyed (at least in the figurative sense) her most prolific film-making period. She completed leading roles in nine motion pictures, made a "special guest appearance" in a tenth, and was featured in several short subjects. After placing in the 1940 exhibitor's poll as one of the Top Ten Box Office Stars—referencing her films of 1939—she again made the list in 1941, thanks to the grosses of her movies during the preceding year.

The decade got off to shaky start though. After the completion (and even before the runaway success) of *Babes in Arms*, Arthur Freed hoped to reunite Garland and Mickey Rooney in a remake of the Broadway collegiate musical, *Good News*. Planning began as early as August 1939, and a script draft was finished by late October, but the property was then abruptly abandoned in favor of *Strike Up the Band*. Apart from its title song by George and Ira Gershwin, the new picture would boast an original story and score, and it went into immediate, enthusiastic preproduction.

Meanwhile, "Betsy Booth" was written back into the lives of "Judge Hardy's Family" in *Andy Hardy Meets Debutante*, the first of the six Rooney/Garland films released between 1940 and 1943. She appeared again in *Life Begins for Andy Hardy* (1941), and as Mickey's vis-à-vis in three major musicals—the aforementioned *Strike Up the Band* (1940), *Babes on Broadway* (1941), and *Girl Crazy* (1943). Finally, the duo was top-billed while playing themselves in MGM's all-star

*Thousands Cheer* (1943): although Rooney's introduction to Judy's song managed a new high in incomprehensible scripting: he referenced her as "a young lady I've been dying to meet for a long time." Mickey's status as the number-one box-office star of the country in 1939, 1940, and 1941 was a boost to Judy's own popularity, although she was well aware of his capacity to monopolize any film footage in which he appeared. She sagely, humorously told a contemporary interviewer, "When I'm in a picture with Mickey . . . I have to underplay my scenes; otherwise, I won't even show! Mickey is so dynamic that, to save myself from utter oblivion, I have to mumble my lines or do *something* to make my presence known. It's lots of fun to play with Mickey, but it's plenty hard trying to keep up with him." She appreciatively added, "We're just like brother and sister. We argue and discuss things. And we do have dates—for publicity."

Across those three years, there were also films designed as specific Garland

showcases: a dual role as mother and daughter in *Little Nellie Kelly* (1940), and three pictures in which she played fledgling entertainers: *Ziegfeld Girl* (1941), *For Me and My Gal* (1942), and *Presenting Lily Mars* (1943). The latter two vehicles enabled Judy to step out of juvenile parts and appear as a young woman opposite real leading men: Gene Kelly, George Murphy, and Van Heflin. Such an evolution was approved by contemporary critics, and one specifically noted, "Away from Mickey Rooney, Judy loses her ingénue tricks, and becomes a smart, poised, sophisticated leading lady."

During this era—indeed, throughout most of her film career—Garland was as popular with her coworkers as with audiences and critics. "Hers is an honest humility," enthused Arthur Freed, who produced fourteen of her twenty-seven MGM pictures: "She's a director's dream girl." In company with the ever-essential Roger Edens, Judy both inspired and made friends of such Metro newcomers as songwriters Hugh Martin and Ralph Blane, choreographer

Robert Alton, and dancer/dance director Charles "Chuck" Walters. And though she herself manifested concern over the type of dialogue specific to her films ("Let's face it: you have to say some pretty silly things in musicals"), scenarist and pal Fred Finklehoffe demurred and told Judy that she—among very few others—could rise above the "corn" and make the words work.

Meanwhile, Garland's movie musical repertoire continued to enjoy an additional, separate popularity. Of the twenty-nine tunes she waxed for Decca between 1940 and 1943, sixteen were selected from her actual (or intended) MGM songbook. These included numbers from *Girl Crazy*, for which she and Mickey sang the score in a souvenir album of six sides. Over the airwaves, Judy's vocals served as both a stateside plug for her new motion pictures and an around-the-globe welcome reminder of home for the men and women embroiled in World War II. Garland had the same impact with a similar catalog when she toured cross-country to sing in military service camps and participate in 1943's sixteen-city War Bond drive.

Such a workload began to take its toll. The completion of one of Judy's films frequently overlapped with wardrobe tests, rehearsals, and prerecordings for the next. Even when a film was "in the can," the reaction of sneak preview audiences—or any level of upper echelon studio discontent—could lead to retakes. The original finales of *Ziegfeld Girl*, *For Me and My Gal*, and *Presenting Lily Mars* were deleted in favor of new musical numbers and staging, as were individual songs in *Andy Hardy Meets Debutante*. By 1943, Garland, Rooney, Edens, and Freed had also become frustrated by the manic, on-set excesses—whether major or minor—of frequent coworker Busby Berkeley. (Judy had initially acquiesced to even the least of the director's shouted commands: "Eyes! Eyes! Open your eyes! I want to see your eyes!" But the result made for one of the very few affected expressions in her otherwise completely natural performances.)

Meanwhile, there were Garland's escalating health and personal problems. By 1942—and alternately aided or decimated by prescription medication—she had starved herself to the weight Metro demanded: a camera-thin ninety-five pounds. As a result, and coupled with overwork, she suffered her first nervous breakdown in January 1943. Judy's physical condition at that time was further exacerbated by the collapse of her marriage to David Rose; by a series of unhappy love affairs; and by the regimen required to maintain visibility on behalf of MGM in the glare of Hollywood's social limelight.

Little (if any) of these woes showed on screen. Some twenty years later, Shana Alexander enthused in *Life* magazine, "On film, the result was wonderful . . . [Judy] was about the nicest, prettiest, most talented minstrel girl a moviegoer could hope to see." By 1999, Garland's MGM compatriot Esther Williams could report more trenchantly: "That's what being an actress is all about—taking yourself out of your own difficulties to portray somebody else. All the women who were at MGM—Judy Garland is the classic example—were doing superlative work on the screen at the same time they were going through a great deal of turmoil and tragedy in their private lives. And by and large, they were going through it all by themselves."

The professional saving grace for Judy Garland was that her star had continued to rise. Her ability to carry such vehicles as *For Me and My Gal* and *Presenting Lily Mars* meant that she had made the transition (as few film youngsters ever did) from child star to "grown-up roles." Her declared hope was to continue the progression into adult dramatic parts and more substantial musicals.

Instead, at the end of 1943, MGM and Arthur Freed cast her once again as a teenager.

# Andy Hardy Meets Debutante

METRO-GOLDWYN-MAYER

### CAST:

| | |
|---|---|
| **Lewis Stone** | Judge Hardy |
| **Mickey Rooney** | Andy Hardy |
| **Cecilia Parker** | Marian Hardy |
| **Fay Holden** | Mrs. Hardy |
| **Judy Garland** | Betsy Booth |
| **Ann Rutherford** | Polly Benedict |
| **Diana Lewis** | Daphne Fowler |
| **George Breakston** | "Beezy" |
| **Sara Haden** | Aunt Milly |
| **Addison Richards** | Mr. Benedict |

### CREDITS:

**J. J. Cohn** (producer); **George B. Seitz** (director); **Annalee Whitmore** and **Thomas Seller** (screenplay); **Aurania Rouverol** (characters); **Sidney Wagner** and **Charles Lawton** (photography); **Nacio Herb Brown** and **Arthur Freed** (music and lyric to "Alone"); **Benny Davis, Milton Ager,** and **Lester Santley** (music and lyric to "I'm Nobody's Baby"); **David Snell** (musical score); **Roger Edens** (musical arrangements); **Leo Arnaud, Conrad Salinger, Robert Van Eps,** and **Wally Heglin** (orchestrations); **Cedric Gibbons** (art director), **Gabriel Scognamillo** (associate); **Edwin B. Willis** (set decorations); **Dolly Tree** (wardrobe); **Harold F. Kress** (editor)

### JUDY'S NUMBERS:

"Alone," "I'm Nobody's Baby."

Deleted: "All I Do is Dream of You,"
"Buds Won't Bud"

**RELEASE DATE:** July 5, 1940
**RUN TIME:** 89 minutes

## SYNOPSIS

To impress his fellow students at Carvel High School, Andy Hardy claims acquaintanceship with New York City's leading debutante, Daphne Fowler. As ever, the teen's boasting leads to trouble. Judge Hardy has legal business in Manhattan and decides to take along the entire family. In turn, Andy's friends Polly and Beezy challenge him to bring back a photograph of himself and Daphne for the school magazine. His efforts to meet the debutante lead to public embarrassment and debt, but he's once again saved by the intervention of New York City resident Betsy Booth (JG). She not only knows Daphne but arranges to take Andy to the socialite's debut, thus securing the necessary photo. Meanwhile, Betsy's song at the party wakens Andy to the realization that younger girls also have their charms. He returns, wiser and female-besotted, to Carvel.

# REVIEWS

"Best of the recent Hardy Family films. . . . Judy Garland, with a couple of songs and a good role, adds considerably to the entertainment quota of a sprightly, drop-your-worries movie."
— SYNDICATED COLUMNIST ROBBIN COONS

"Packed with amusing situations and plenty of laugh entertainment. . . . It will carry through the profitable biz of its predecessors. . . . JG is prominent and lovely [and] socks over two old tunes."
—VARIETY

"Mickey gets his first taste of having a scene stolen from under and all around him . . . that scene-stealing JG is the cutest package of oomph the screen has to offer. When Judy was singing 'I'm Nobody's Baby,' a couple of Andy Hardy prototypes seated alongside your movie reporter registered almost as much adoration as did the screen's million-dollar baby Casanova."
—BOSTON EVENING AMERICAN

"Mickey does the best work he has ever done as Andy Hardy. . . . Three girls clutter up his life; to me, Judy walks off with the feminine honors. Her characterization is a lovable one, and she makes the most of it."
—FAMILY CIRCLE

**BELOW:** "Judge Hardy's Family" and "Betsy Booth": Lewis Stone, Cecilia Parker, Fay Holden, and Sara Haden keep an eye on Mickey and Judy.

**CLOCKWISE FROM UPPER LEFT:** Judy prerecords "All I Do is Dream of You". | The number as filmed for (but deleted from) the picture. | William Newell appears as the insurance agent who investigates the loss of a $400 pearl shirt stud—Andy's latest transgression. | A deleted scene: Judy and Mickey Rooney look on as Gladys Blake plays "Goitrude . . . a domestic scientist from Brooklyn," who leaves the Hardys maid-less in New York.

ABOVE: In the penultimate party sequence, Judy's revives the 1921 hit, "I'm Nobody's Baby."
RIGHT: Sheet music touted the song's new association with Garland.

## NOTES

Two years after her first appearance in a "Judge Hardy's Family" picture, Judy's Betsy Booth reentered their lives while solving another raft of Andy's problems. If still a little girl in his eyes, she was nonetheless a sleeker, more sophisticated child, especially when taking charge after his customary missteps.

Garland and Rooney once again teamed on a professional level that bespoke their on and off-camera bond and comfort. She was given three song spots in the picture, although the first—a familiar Arthur Freed-Nacio Herb Brown standard, "All I Do is Dream of You"—was deleted prior to the film's release. Perhaps in compensation, her second number, "Buds Won't Bud," was then cut as well, replaced at the last moment by "Alone," another vintage Freed-Brown hit.

## What They Said

*"I was never happier than when I found out that I was going to play in a second Hardy film. [These movies are] about real people, and the Hardys in real life are real people. I didn't feel I was acting at all."* —JUDY GARLAND

*"The chemistry was so strong with Judy and me that I'd know exactly what she was going to say before she started—and the same applied for me. She knew exactly what I was going to say and how I was going to say it. Very few people have that kind of contact with each other. But I'm very happy to say that we had it."* —MICKEY ROONEY

*"Judy went along just like other little girls. [Then] in* Andy Hardy Meets Debutante, *there was a slight difference. 'That youngster is developing into a downright good looking young lady'— 'Say, why doesn't Andy fall for Judy; she's good enough for me'—'Judy's growing up.' These were a few of the comments whispered among the audience during the showing of the film."*

—CONTEMPORARY FAN MAGAZINE

OPPOSITE CLOCKWISE FROM TOP: Virtually all of Hollywood concurred that Rooney and Garland were an unbeatably talented team. | The debut of "Daphne Fowler": Diana Lewis and Judy between takes. Lewis was at that time newly married to MGM star William Powell. | May 10, 1940: Judy prerecords "All I Do is Dream of You" with conductor Georgie Stoll. ABOVE: Between takes of *Andy Hardy Meets Debutante*, Judy wrapped up assignments for her senior year of high school.

# Strike Up the Band

METRO-GOLDWYN-MAYER

### CAST:

**Mickey Rooney** ...................... *Jimmy Connors*

**Judy Garland** ............................. *Mary Holden*

**Paul Whiteman** ................................. *Himself*

**June Preisser** .......... *Barbara Frances Morgan*

**William Tracy** ......................... *Phillip Turner*

**Larry Nunn** ............................ *Willie Brewster*

**Margaret Early** ..................................... *Annie*

**Ann Shoemaker** ......................... *Mrs. Connors*

**Francis Pierlot** ............................... *Mr. Judd*

**Virginia Brissac** .................. *Mrs. May Holden*

### CREDITS:

**Arthur Freed** (producer); **Busby Berkeley** (director); **John Monks, Jr.** and **Fred Finklehoffe** (screenplay); **Ray June** (photography); **Roger Edens** (music and lyrics); **George Gershwin and Ira Gershwin** (music and lyric to "Strike Up the Band"); **Arthur Freed and Roger Edens** (music and lyric to "Our Love Affair"); **Georgie Stoll** (musical director); **Leo Arnaud and Conrad Salinger** (orchestrations); **Cedric Gibbons** (art director), **John S. Detlie** (associate); **Edwin B. Willis** (set decorations); **Dolly Tree and Gile Steele** (costumes); **Ben Lewis** (editor)

### JUDY'S NUMBERS:

*"Our Love Affair," "Do the La Conga," "Nobody,"* Nell of New Rochelle *(incorporating "Nell of New Rochelle," "She's More to Be Pitied Than Censured," "Heaven Will Protect the Working Girl," "Father, Dear Father, Come Home with Me Now,") "Drummer Boy",* Finale *(incorporating "Strike Up the Band" and reprises of "Our Love Affair" and "Drummer Boy").* Deleted: *"While Strolling Through the Park One Day," "Curse of an Aching Heart"*

**RELEASE DATE: September 27, 1940**
**RUN TIME: 120 minutes**

## SYNOPSIS

High school senior Jimmy Connors parlays his musical talent and expertise on the drums into the creation of an all-student swing orchestra, with Mary Holden (JG) as vocalist. The band enjoys a successful debut at a school dance, but the teens fail to enlist the principal's aid when requesting travel funds to compete in Paul Whiteman's national radio contest for young musicians. Determined to make the trip, the kids raise their own money by mounting a musical melodrama for the local Elks Club.

Meanwhile, Mary's crush on Jimmy is derailed when he's forcibly ensnared by blonde transfer student, Barbara Frances Morgan. When Barbara Frances's birthday party brings Whiteman and his orchestra to town, Jimmy, Mary, and their aggregation manage to audition for him on the spot. He agrees to include them on his upcoming broadcast, but the kids are thwarted again when one of their friends falls ill. Selflessly, they donate their mutual fund to arrange his emergency surgery. Barbara Frances' father admires their action and, at the last minute, arranges special railroad transportation to Chicago for the group. Mary and Jimmy are musically and romantically united, and the Connors band wins the Whiteman competition.

ABOVE: Makeup and hair test for a segment of "Nell of New Rochelle" OPPOSITE: Judy and Mickey "Do the La Conga." Director Busby Berkeley shot the first two minutes and forty-five seconds of this six minutes-plus number in one take.

## REVIEWS

"A lively, spectacular, splashy, made-to-order musical film. Stomping, jazzy, streamlined, it's America, 1940."

—LIBERTY

"It's *Babes in Arms* again, but bigger and better . . . safe and sane entertainment for everybody. Amazing Mickey Rooney struts, sings, plays the drums, and tears your heart out . . . Judy Garland, growing into a beauty, is more appealing than ever."  —SCREENLAND

"Lavishly mounted, fast-paced, and tuneful . . . solid entertainment every minute. The surprise performance is that of JG, who finally ceases to be a foil of Mickey's and pushes him for acting honors every inch of the picture. In addition to displaying acting talent which verges on being really great, she also makes a transition from childhood to maturity. She photographs maturely, dances sensationally, and sings divinely."  —MOVIE-RADIO GUIDE

"It's the same basic plot [as *Babes in Arms*]—but Metro probably figured it was good the first time, so why not try it again? Okay, Mr. Metro, do it a third time as long as you keep JG in it! To our way of thinking, Judy is just about the *ne plus ultra* of all time. The kid's got everything. She can sing a song like a trouper, she can peddle a line with the best of 'em, and she can do a Conga that'll positively astonish you."

—MODERN SCREEN

"Miss Garland has grown into a provocative seducer, and the boys will next be called upon to coin her a word that vies with It, Oomph, and Glamour. If there is a money prize for it, we offer mmm-geeyum! girl!"  —MOVIES

## NOTES

*Strike Up the Band* was the figurative sequel to *Babes in Arms*, although (if possible) it upped the ante in spirit, energy, and patriotism. The budget increased as well—to $851,000—but the picture's revenue also topped that of *Babes*, bringing MGM more than $3,472,000 in its initial release alone.

In the midst of *Band*'s five-month production schedule, from April until late August 1940, there were the customary script and song alterations. In a deleted, character-revelatory subplot, Tommy was to pawn his cherished drums for the funds to take Barbara Frances to the carnival. When he went to retrieve the drums, he was horrified to find it had been sold, but—typically—Mary had already bought it back for his birthday.

Roger Edens oversaw revisions and retakes of various script passages. He also wrote all of the new songs for the score. His "Drummer Boy" supplanted the intended use of the Louis Prima standard "Sing, Sing, Sing" for a pivotal slot in the story. Then Edens proposed a featured love ballad, which evolved into the Best Song Academy Award nominee, "Our Love Affair." The song climbed the *Billboard* charts three separate times in 1940; recordings by the orchestras of Tommy Dorsey, Glenn Miller, and Dick Jurgens peaked respectively at number five, eight, and ten.

Interestingly, *Strike Up the Band* marked Judy's first professional encounter with future husband Vincente Minnelli, new to MGM and serving a Freed-sponsored internship on the lot. Remembering a recent *Life* magazine feature that had used fruit puppets to represent musicians, Minnelli suggested utilizing the same approach to expand "Our Love Affair" into a unique production number. The concept and its execution (by the extraordinary George Pal) won raves.

The film was otherwise directed by Busby Berkeley, whose new success at MGM was being offset by his increasing on-set demands and tumultuous personal life.

The average audience celebrated Judy in *Strike Up the Band*, starting at the sneak previews. She was acclaimed as "very beauteous," "a swell actress," "a regular glamour girl," and the "*lovely* Judy Garland." Meanwhile, a handful of malcontents found the picture "noisy," "too loud," and "a little drawn out." Perhaps as a consequence of the comments like the latter, the lengthy *Nell of New Rochelle* musical melodrama was trimmed by three songs before *Strike Up the Band* was officially premiered.

OPPOSITE CLOCKWISE FROM TOP LEFT: Two of the deleted numbers from *Nell of New Rochelle*: the Garland/Rooney "While Strolling Through the Park One Day" and Judy's "Curse of An Aching Heart" | "Jimmy Connors & His Band" are sent off to the radio contest: (from left) Judy, Milton Kibbee, Virginia Brissac, Mickey, Francis Pierlot, Ann Shoemaker, George Lessey, and June Preisser. | Judy rehearses the score with composer/lyricist/arranger Roger Edens, her lifelong musical mentor. | Judy, Mickey, and cast members celebrate with director Busby Berkeley at his mother's on-set birthday party. | Mickey, Judy, and the renowned "King of Jazz," Paul Whiteman | Judy holds her namesake doll, marketed by Ideal in a replica of her *Strike Up the Band* finale dress. RIGHT: Judy and some of the gang: (from left) William Tracy, Leonard Sues, and Sidney Miller

## What They Said

*"We had to do a rumba and a Conga number in the picture, so of course we had to practice. We went to every nightclub where they had a rumba band, so we could dance and watch different couples do different steps. It worked out fine, too; we brought back six new ideas for steps in the picture."*

—JUDY GARLAND

*"Busby Berkeley did take shot after shot after shot. And you were never sure, after the first two or three, why. 'What are we doing this again for? What is it he wants? What is it we're not doing?' But he didn't take time to explain, he just kept doing what he wanted. And I guess he got it. Finally."*

—MGM CONTRACT DANCER
DOROTHY GILMORE RAYE

*"Buzz had his talents, but I thought he was a very cruel man. 'If you get tired, come to me,' he'd say [to Judy and Mickey]. Then he'd work the hell out of them. Very sincere!"*

—MGM ASSISTANT CHOREOGRAPHER
AND DANCER DONA MASSIN

**LEFT:** Garland and aggregation back up "Drummer Boy"; multi-talented Rooney actually played.

ABOVE: The film finale melded the title song and reprises of three Roger Edens originals. OPPOSITE, CLOCKWISE FROM LEFT: Girl talk between takes of "Nell of New Rochelle." June Preisser is in costume for her (ultimately deleted) solo, "I Just Can't Make My Eyes Behave." | Henry Rox, assistant professor of art at Mt. Holyoke College in Massachusetts, proudly shares one of his "Our Love Affair" fruit models with Judy and Mickey. | One of the film's reviews praised MGM "for at last developing a leading woman who didn't remind you of your mother."

# Little Nellie Kelly

METRO-GOLDWYN-MAYER

**CAST:**

Judy Garland.... *Nellie Kelly/Little Nellie Kelly*

George Murphy .............................. *Jerry Kelly*

Charles Winninger ............... *Michael Noonan*

Douglas McPhail ................... *Dennis Fogarty*

Arthur Shields ...................... *Timothy Fogarty*

Rita Page ................................. *Mary Fogarty*

Forrester Harvey ............................. *Moriarity*

James Burke .................... *Sergeant McGowan*

George Watts .................................... *Keevan*

**CREDITS:**

**Arthur Freed** *(producer);* **Norman Taurog** *(director);* **Jack McGowan** *(screenplay);* **George M. Cohan** *(original play);* **Ray June** *(photography);* **George M. Cohan** *(music and lyric to "Nellie Kelly, I Love You");* **Arthur Freed and Nacio Herb Brown** *(music and lyric to "Singin' in the Rain");* **Georgie Stoll** *(musical director);* **Roger Edens** *(musical adaptation);* **Cedric Gibbons** *(art director),* **Harry McAfee** *(associate);* **Edwin B. Willis** *(set decorations);* **Dolly Tree and Gile Steele** *(costumes);* **Fredrick Y. Smith** *(editor)*

**JUDY'S NUMBERS:**

*"A Pretty Girl Milking Her Cow" and reprise, "Saint Patrick Was a Gentleman," "It's a Great Day for the Irish," "Singin' in the Rain," "Nellie Kelly, I Love You" and reprise. Deleted; possibly never filmed: "Danny Boy"*

**RELEASE DATE: November 22, 1940**

**RUN TIME: 100 minutes**

## SYNOPSIS

Nellie Noonan (JG) is the pride of her eternally jobless, ne'er-do-well father, Michael Noonan. She's also the love of local lad Jerry Kelly. They marry against the wishes of Noonan, who vows never to speak to his new son-in-law. It's a promise he keeps as the three emigrate from Ireland to New York City as Jerry trains to become a police officer and as Nellie dies in childbirth.

Her daughter, "Little Nellie," (also JG) grows up loving both her father and grandfather, working to effect a reconciliation between them. As a teen, she catches the eye of Dennis Fogarty, son of fellow Irish immigrants. Jerry Kelly approves of the potential relationship, while Noonan rants and rails until both daughter and father finally stand up to the older man. He disappears, but when next seen, he's not only employed but delighted to shake hands with Jerry and stand in full support of Little Nellie.

**OPPOSITE, LEFT FROM TOP:** Judy accompanies "The Irish Three": Douglas McPhail, George Murphy, and Charles Winninger. | Douglas McPhail, Garland, Charles Winninger, and Arthur Shields, just prior to Roger Edens' exuberant "It's a Great Day for the Irish." | Kidding the fact that he was twenty years Judy's senior, George Murphy later noted, "I used to call her 'Grandma' when she was a little girl." **OPPOSITE, RIGHT:** Judy prerecorded "Danny Boy" for this spot in the film but instead sang George Murphy a chorus of "A Pretty Girl Milking Her Cow."

# REVIEWS

"If you like the simple things of life, you'll like *Little Nellie Kelly*. With a tribulation here, a laugh there, and a sprinkling of tears both here and there, the action proceeds unremarkably but pleasantly on its way. Judy gives her all and sings pleasingly when the script demands."—CHICAGO *TRIBUNE*

"It's a hit show because it has little Judy Garland."

—*THE HOLLYWOOD REPORTER*

"Judy turns in a dual characterization in which she presents sharply contrasting personalities. . . . Her deathbed scene, which will tug at the stoniest of hearts, definitely demonstrates that she is fully as competent as a dramatic actress as she is a vocalist."—*VARIETY*

"JG grows up—which is the big news about this one. It's not the sort of picture that you are likely to write letters home about, but it's good, clean fun . . . 'a family picture.' And in this classification, it is tops. It's pretty much hearts and flowers with a lot of brogue thrown around, but it holds up throughout because of Judy's splendid work."

—*MODERN SCREEN*

"The picture is too long, in this reviewer's opinion. Early scenes . . . seem drawn out. Highlights are songs by Miss Garland. The singing actress, who gains star billing, gives a very fine performance."

—LOS ANGELES *TIMES*

ABOVE: George Murphy was Judy's life-long champion: "She was the greatest all-around talent ever in show business"; RIGHT: McPhail & Chorus: "The boys are all mad about Nellie, the daughter of Officer Kelly!"

ABOVE LEFT: Preparing the stars for a take  ABOVE RIGHT AND OPPOSITE: It was a George M. Cohan musical, but Judy reprised producer/lyricist Arthur Freed's "Singin' in the Rain" as a highlight. BELOW FROM LEFT: Producer, star, and director: Arthur Freed, Judy, and Norman Taurog | Ethel Gumm Garland visits her daughter on the set. Judy has a *Strike Up the Band* still in her lap. | Director Norman Taurog, Roger Edens, and Judy relax outdoors between takes of "It's a Great Day for the Irish."

## NOTES

A lifelong admirer of the legendarily accomplished George M. Cohan, Arthur Freed bought the rights to Cohan's 1922 Broadway musical specifically for Judy. He retained only the *Little Nellie Kelly* title, one song, and the plot conceit that Nellie was the daughter of a policeman. It was Roger Edens's task to set additional numbers for the film. He once again managed to pay homage to his producer by creating a sparkling vocal arrangement of the 1929 Freed-Brown hit, "Singin' in the Rain," which Garland sang to a fare-thee-well. Several other traditional Irish and standard songs were considered. Perhaps best of all was Edens' own "It's a Great Day for the Irish" which thereafter became so associated with St. Patrick's Day that comparatively few people realize it was written for Judy Garland in 1940.

*Nellie Kelly* was in production for eight weeks, from the end of July until retakes were completed at the end of September. As Nellie's father (and Little Nellie's grandfather), Charles Winninger's character was softened just prior to principal photography. He was initially scripted to be caught in a speakeasy raid while his daughter lay dying in childbirth. Even so, when the picture was previewed, some in the audience felt the finished picture still contained "too much" of the actor and his irascible portrayal—and that the film itself was "much too long." Others bemoaned the fact that Judy was being allowed to grow up too quickly on the screen: "Don't let her play [another] married woman for a long time yet!" But the general tenor of their comments praised Judy, defining her performance as "magnificent" and noting that "she gets more beautiful in every picture."

Pros and cons aside, the final box office was an acknowledgement of the acumen of Freed, Edens, Garland, et al. On an estimated budget of $665,000, *Little Nellie Kelly* achieved film rentals of $2,046,000 in its first release.

NELLY - CHANGE #14
1940 - 17 YRS.
INT. POLICE BALL!

NELLY - CHANGE #2 OR 3
1919 - 19 YRS.
EXT. DECK OF SHIP
INT. EXT. LOG CABIN COTTAGE

NELLY - CHANGE #2 OR 3
1919 - 19 YRS.
EXT. DECK OF SHIP
INT. EXT. LOG CABIN COTTAGE

DIRECTOR TAUROG PRODUCTION 1133.
CAMERAMAN CAMERA 1
JUNE
DAY-NITE SOUND-SILENT DATE 7-30-40
X X
SCENE TAKE

DONLEY & DUGAN
SECOND FURN.

HATS-CAPS

NELLY - CHANGE #5
1924 - 24 YRS.
NELLY BECOMES CITIZEN

NELLY - CHANGE 9
1940 - 17 YRS.
BIRTHDAY PARTY

NELLY - CHANGE #2 OR 3
1919 - 19 YRS.
EXT. DECK OF SHIP
INT. EXT. LOG CABIN COTTAGE

## What They Said

*"I play my first grown-up dramatic character part in* Little Nellie Kelly; *I even die! And—this is a very important first in my life—I play my first grown-up love scene. I, who have said I was never embarrassed on the stage, in front of a mike, or a camera, take it all back now. George Murphy plays my sweetheart (and my father!). . . . And he was certainly the most perfect choice, for he is so kind and tender and understanding—and humorous, too. But just the same, after we made that love scene, I didn't know what to do or where to look. I'd just kind of go away . . . because I couldn't look at him! He kept kidding me, too, saying he felt like he was 'in Tennessee with my child bride!'"* —JUDY GARLAND

*"Judy's death scene was so emotional and effective that it wrung the hearts of all those watching. When it was finished, the set was completely empty, with the exception of Judy, the director, and myself. All those so-called hardbitten workers were so affected that they had to get away so that their sobs would not disturb the soundtrack."*

—GEORGE MURPHY

*"Norman Taurog can twine laurel with his holly this year for having taken a child wonder and turned her into an assured and artistically matured leading woman."*

—COLUMNIST JACK MOFFITT

*"Judy is the finest potential actress in America. Her ability is great and versatile."* —DIRECTOR NORMAN TAUROG

*"I once made a picture called* Little Nellie Kelly; *that was in about 1782 that I made that . . . And a friend of mine by the name of Roger Edens discovered a rather obscure, Irish folk song that fit the picture quite well. [So] we did it. And they released the picture. And the song became . . . an obscure, Irish folk song!"*

—JUDY GARLAND, REFLECTING ON THE GENESIS OF "A PRETTY GIRL MILKING HER COW" (1963)

**OPPOSITE:** Between mid-July and early September 1940, Judy tested or posed for reference photos in her wardrobe for the film. **ABOVE, FROM TOP:** *Little Nellie Kelly* provided Judy the opportunity for both a dual role and her only on-screen death scene. | George Murphy looks incredulous at the (however necessary) lack of glamour supplied Judy for her demise.

# Ziegfeld Girl

### CAST:

James Stewart .......................... *Gilbert Young*

Judy Garland ........................ *Susan Gallagher*

Hedy Lamarr ............................ *Sandra Kolter*

Lana Turner ............................. *Sheila Regan*

Tony Martin .............................. *Frank Merton*

Jackie Cooper............................. *Jerry Regan*

Ian Hunter .............................. *Geoffrey Collis*

Charles Winninger .......... *Ed "Pop" Gallagher*

Edward Everett Horton................. *Noble Sage*

Philip Dorn ................................ *Franz Kolter*

Al Shean .................................................... *Al*

Paul Kelly ............................... *John Slayton*

Eve Arden.................................. *Patsy Dixon*

Dan Dailey, Jr. ........................ *Jimmy Walters*

### CREDITS:

**Pandro S. Berman** *(producer)*; **Robert Z. Leonard** *(director)*; **Marguerite Roberts and Sonya Levien** *(screenplay)*; **Ray June** *(photography)*; **William Anthony McGuire** *(original story)*; **Nacio Herb Brown and Gus Kahn** *(music and lyric to "You Stepped Out of a Dream")*; **Roger Edens** *(music and lyric to "Minnie from Trinidad")*; **Harry Carroll and Joseph McCarthy** *(music and lyric to "I'm Always Chasing Rainbows")*; **Edward Gallagher and Al Shean** *(music and lyric to "Mr. Gallagher and Mr. Shean")*; **Georgie Stoll** *(musical director)*; **Herbert Stothart** *(musical score)*; **Leo Arnaud, George Bassman, and Conrad Salinger** *(orchestrations)*; **Busby Berkeley** *(dance director)*; **Cedric Gibbons** *(art director)*, **Daniel B. Cathcart** *(associate)*; **Edwin B. Willis** *(set decorations)*; **Adrian** *(costumes)*; **Blanche Sewell** *(editor)*

### JUDY'S NUMBERS:

*"Laugh? I Thought I'd Split My Sides," "You Stepped Out of a Dream," "I'm Always Chasing Rainbows" (both ballad and comedy versions, the latter with Charles Winninger), "Minnie from Trinidad," Finale (incorporating "Ziegfeld Girls," "You Gotta Pull Strings," and "You Never Looked So Beautiful Before"). Deleted: "We Must Have Music" (with Tony Martin), "I'm Always Chasing Rainbows" reprise*

**RELEASE DATE: April 25, 1941**
**RUN TIME: 134 minutes**

**RIGHT:** Lana Turner and Hedy Lamarr join Judy in her dressing room trailer. (Jacques Kapralik ad art for *Little Nellie Kelly* is visible on the vanity.) **OPPOSITE, FROM TOP:** The three Ziegfeld Girls in costume on the "Trinidad" set | Judy, Sergio Orta, and the "Minnie from Trinidad" ensemble. This was the "hot" number for which Judy had been lobbying Roger Edens since she was fourteen. | During a "Minnie from Trinidad" lull, Judy speaks with showgirl [Irma Wilson].

ABOVE: Diminutive chorus "pony" Susan Gallagher makes her *Follies* debut as set-dressing in the "You Stepped Out of a Dream" production number. **OPPOSITE FROM TOP:** To the mixed emotions of Charles Winninger, Jackie Cooper, Paul Kelly, and Edward Everett Horton, Judy's "I'm Always Chasing Rainbows" audition is championed by Lana Turner. | Jackie Cooper played Garland's onscreen boyfriend—a function he'd performed when they dated as young teens in 1936. | "Ed Gallagher & Co." (Charles Winninger and Judy) greet real/reel-life vaudevillian Al Shean backstage at the Harlem Opera House. | Winninger, Kelly, Horton, and Garland in the Ziegfeld offices. Both of these sequences were trimmed before the film was released.

## REVIEWS

"Lush and spectacular. . . . Whatever faults are to be found with the production will not be reflected in theater grosses. It is headed for really big money at the box office. Lana Turner perhaps shines brightest. . . . Judy Garland scores solidly, is growing up charmingly, and her singing is smartly utilized." —*THE HOLLYWOOD REPORTER*

"With its glamour and star-studded parade of talent, it's a cinch for top biz—a holdover attraction for the key spots. Smart casting provides vivid contrast . . . for [Ziegfeld's] showgirl ensembles. There's JG, youthful but veteran trouper, with showmanship, personality, and talent . . . [She] carries the sympathetic end most capably and delivers her vocal assignments in great style." —*VARIETY*

"Lavish musical spectacle is apt to overbalance the dramatics of this brilliantly produced picture. Lana Turner gets the acting honors . . . Hedy Lamarr is attractively pensive and languorous. A sparkling, vivacious characterization comes from JG." —*PICTUREGOER*

"We have not one cliché of the backstage movie plot, but three, served up in one gaudy, glittering dish complete with preposterous costumes, lavish settings, big production numbers and choruses by Tony Martin—to say nothing of corn on the side. Judy brightens the business no end." —COLUMNIST ROBBIN COONS

## SYNOPSIS

With a legendary penchant for spotting beauty and talent, Broadway producer Florenz Ziegfeld sends his deputy Noble Sage to offer three unknown girls the opportunity to participate in the chorus of his annual *Follies*. Susan Gallagher (JG) is plucked from a small-time vaudeville act and Sheila Regan from her post as a department store elevator operator. Sandra Kolter is discovered by accident when she accompanies her violinist husband Franz to the theater for his (unsuccessful) audition.

Over the next several seasons, Susan rises to stardom and finds young love with Sheila's brother, Jerry. Sandra catches the eye of married Ziegfeld tenor Frank Merton, yet remains faithful to her husband even though they have separated over his disapproval of her stage work. Sheila forsakes stalwart boyfriend Gil Young for encounters with Geoffrey Collis and other predatory stage-door millionaires. When Gil segues into bootlegging in an attempt to equal their financial appeal to the girl, he winds up in prison.

By the time he returns, Sheila's escapades have led to alcoholism and serious illness. She leaves her sickbed to attend the opening night of a new *Follies*, in which Susan and her father, Ed Gallagher (with partner Al Shean) make individual hits. Sandra has abandoned the show and proudly watches the production with her reconciled husband. The exertion of the evening is too much for Sheila. Suddenly stricken, she collapses on the lobby staircase while the performance—with its new crop of Ziegfeld Girls—continues in the theater.

## NOTES

*Ziegfeld Girl* had been in the works as a potential MGM project ever since the success of *The Great Ziegfeld* (1936). Over the next four years, virtually every female luminary under contract was rumored for the cast, including Joan Crawford, Margaret Sullavan, Eleanor Powell, and Virginia Bruce. (Frank Morgan was announced for a role as well.) But by 1940, it was "the next generation" of Metro maidens who found themselves glorified in the Ziegfeld manner. Hedy Lamarr lent statuesque beauty and compassion to the story; Judy, true to type and life, was the aspiring entertainer who made it to the top and provided much of the film's expected musical meaning and electricity. But the picture is most accurately summarized as a star turn for Lana Turner, portraying the Ziegfeld-girl-gone-beautifully-bad.

Her role, purportedly based in part on random character traits of showgirl Lillian Lorraine, was expanded as shooting went along, and Turner gave it her instinctive best. The male leads, meanwhile, from Jimmy Stewart to Tony Martin, Ian Hunter, Philip Dorn, and Jackie Cooper, were principally on hand to react to the women.

Although only one of a huge and all-star ensemble, Judy brought likable and necessary verve to the proceedings. Roger Edens finally wrote her the "torrid" song for which she'd been begging since "Dear Mr. Gable." "Minnie from Trinidad" enabled her to both kid and typify a tropical heroine. Conversely, the Garland rendition of "I'm Always Chasing Rainbows" gave that 1917 ballad a permanent revival.

Most of *Ziegfeld Girl* was completed between November 1940 and February 1941, including the "We Must Have Music" finale for Judy, Tony Martin, and company. Perhaps it failed to satisfactorily cap the picture for preview audiences; by late March 1941, it had been supplanted by "Ziegfeld Girls," written by Edens as a new framework for vintage clips from *The Great Ziegfeld*. In its final moments, a suddenly blonde Garland appeared in close shot; when the vision dissolved and the camera pulled back, her footage was supplanted by a more distant view of Virginia Bruce in the "wedding cake" finale of "A Pretty Girl is Like a Melody," also from *The Great Ziegfeld*. If audiences noticed, they didn't care. *Ziegfeld Girl* provided a much more than full measure of popular entertainment by 1941 standards.

**BELOW FROM LEFT:** "A dictionary's necessary—but not for talkin'. It's used for walkin' the Ziegfeld way . . ." But Judy's on break! | Despite having a few men in common, the Garland/Turner friendship and mutual devotion extended across three decades. | Three years after *Broadway Melody of 1938*, Judy is reunited—if only on-set—with dancer extraordinaire Eleanor Powell. **OPPOSITE:** Judy touts "the newest crop of Mr. Ziegfeld's girls" in the film finale.

## What They Said

"I had so much fun working with Lana Turner and Hedy Lamarr. But all during the picture, I had the same feeling I had the night I strolled over to meet Mickey Rooney's girlfriends. I was surrounded by beautiful women. Glamour to the right of me, glamour to the left of me, and not a drop for Judy."

—JUDY GARLAND

"She constantly put up against herself criteria that she could in no way measure up to. Therefore, she was constantly dissatisfied with herself. She was always looking at the long-stemmed American beauty which was synonymous with Metro-Goldwyn stardom. In other words, if you put yourself up against a girl like Elizabeth Taylor, you can be damn good looking and still look pretty ugly to yourself. [So] it was in her marrow; 'I'm ugly, I'm funny, I don't look good, I can't sing like. . . .' It wasn't so much an inferiority thing that she had as something that had been imposed on her by the environment that she lived in. Her reality was what I would call insanity."

—ARTIE SHAW (BANDLEADER AND JUDY'S BOYFRIEND IN 1940, WHO WENT ON TO MARRY LANA TURNER)

"I got a call; Mr. Mayer wanted to see me. He asked me to sit down and said, 'You're new on the lot. [But] we're going to have a big picture, and you're going to be in it. It's a good chance for you to get off the ground at this studio; you sing beautifully, and I think you'll be in with some pretty good people.' Pretty good?: Hedy Lamarr, Judy Garland, Lana Turner—now that's a real triangle! I was to sing a song by Gus Kahn and Nacio Herb Brown, 'You Stepped Out of a Dream.' We prerecorded it; my first time with a big forty-five-piece orchestra—what a thrill that was. And then to have the playback on the set... and sing it to those three girls, coming down the stairs. Well, the first time the director said, 'Camera; action,' I just stared at the three girls. I forgot to sing, although the voice was coming out of the playback machine. The director said, 'Wait a minute! We're rolling! You're supposed to be singing!'"

—TONY MARTIN

# Life Begins for Andy Hardy

METRO-GOLDWYN-MAYER

## CAST:

Lewis Stone ............................... Judge Hardy

Mickey Rooney ........................... Andy Hardy

Judy Garland ............................. Betsy Booth

Fay Holden ................................. Mrs. Hardy

Ann Rutherford ....................... Polly Benedict

Sara Haden ................................. Aunt Milly

Patricia Dane ........................... Jennitt Hicks

Ray McDonald ..................... Jimmy Frobisher

## CREDITS:

**Carey Wilson** (producer); **George B. Seitz** (director); **Agnes Christine Johnson** (screenplay); **Aurania Rouverol** (characters); **Lester White** (photography); **Georgie Stoll** (musical director); **Cedric Gibbons** (art director), **Harry McAfee** (associate); **Edwin B. Willis** (set decorations); **Kalloch** (gowns); **Elmo Veron** (editor)

## JUDY'S NUMBER:

"Happy Birthday to You" (a cappella, as a plot point). Deleted: "America (My Country 'Tis of Thee)." Deleted; possibly never filmed: "Easy to Love," "The Rosary," "Abide with Me"

**RELEASE DATE:** August 15, 1941

**RUN TIME:** 100 minutes

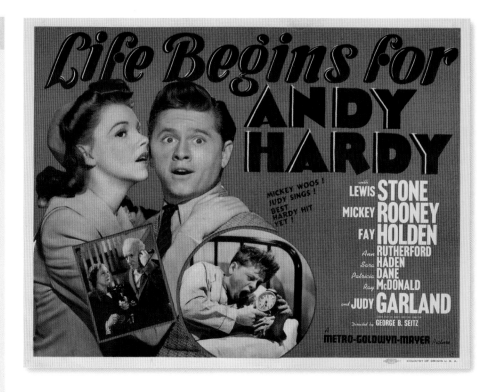

## SYNOPSIS

Newly graduated from high school, Andy Hardy seeks permission from his father to spend the summer working in New York City before starting college in the fall. Judge Hardy allows the trip but fears the lad will succumb to the city's excitement and opt for employment rather than further education. Stalwart Betsy Booth (JG)—now a Manhattan debutante herself—tries to help the stubborn Andy, who is practically destitute before finally getting a job in an office. Almost immediately, Andy falls prey to coworker Jennitt Hicks, not realizing that the girl is a divorcee (and, in Betsy's indignant parlance, "a wolfess!"). The teen's life is further complicated by the death of his NYC roommate, Jimmy Frobisher. Andy selflessly pawns his new car to pay for Frobisher's funeral. Meanwhile, the investigative Betsy contrives behind the scenes to make sure Andy discovers the truth about Jennitt. By story's end, Andy's back in Carvel, working to raise the funds to get his car out of hock in time to start his freshman year of college.

**OPPOSITE:** The face-off: Mickey and "wolfess" Patricia Dane versus Judy and Lewis Stone

# REVIEWS

"Another top-notch *Hardy* picture. Picture carries more serious tone than its predecessors, but is tightly knit, expertly directed, and excellently performed. In keeping with his growing up, Mickey Rooney assumes a more serious manner in presentation of the Andy character, without the various degrees of mugging that characterized earlier issues. Judy Garland clicks solidly in getting Mickey out of romantic trouble." —*VARIETY*

"One of the best [of the Hardys]. . . . JG announced her engagement to Dave Rose while making puppy love to Andy on the screen. She objected to playing the role, claiming audiences would not accept her as a sweet young thing of sixteen. She was wrong. She has never been more charmingly youthful." —*LIBERTY*

"It's better than any [of the *Hardy* pictures] which have gone before. . . . We are treated to another excellent performance by JG. . . . she's a lot of help to any motion picture." —TACOMA *TIMES*

"The opening drew a big audience. Those Hardys have grown into the heart of America; each new episode proves a bit of a classic of native family life, and everyone sees himself or his brothers and sisters or his parents right there on the screen. Fun is still there, but this time it is of a quieter sort. The philosophy of life is now more apparent. . . . Andy has three pretty girls . . . One is the appealing JG." —SEATTLE *POST-INTELLIGENCER*

ABOVE LEFT, TOP AND BOTTOM: Judy's "Betsy" is a maturing and sleek Manhattan sophisti-cate—at least in terms of hair, hat, makeup, and wardrobe. ABOVE RIGHT: In wardrobe not seen in the finished film, Betsy tries to corral Andy by phone. OPPOSITE LEFT COLUMN FROM TOP: Andy's financial and spiritual problems bring Judge Hardy to Manhattan, where he confides in Betsy. | Tommy Kelly assigns "Private Willis" (unidentified player, center) to "Judy duty" prior to her rendi-tion of "America" at the Haversford Military Academy. This moment and the subsequent song were both deleted from the release print. | Betsy returns to Carvel, just in time to escort Andy to New York for his summer of opportunity.

ABOVE FROM TOP: Judy, Ann Rutherford, and Mickey arrive in Andy Hardy's car for the film premiere at Grauman's Chinese Theatre. Mostly obscured in the background are Sara Haden, Fay Holden, and Lewis Stone. | In costume in her (for the moment) matching dressing room, Judy plays with pet dog Choo Choo.

## NOTES

Judy's final adventure with a *Hardy* picture was noteworthy for several reasons. In this, the series' eleventh entry, her Betsy Booth acquired additional teen "sophistication": some sassy slang, a chic wardrobe, and the necessary savvy to provide ballast for Andy's amorous ambitions and professional difficulties. The film was also notable in that all four of Garland's prerecorded songs were either cut from the release print or (in a couple of cases) possibly never filmed. It's been suggested that the deletions were implemented so as to not take the edge off *Babes on Broadway*, the major Garland-Rooney musical which followed the *Hardy* picture into theaters four months later. No authority confirms that theory, but the decision to drop Garland's vocals from *Life Begins for Andy Hardy* was certainly a precipitous one. While there was time to alter some of the film's promotional copy, a number of ads went into circulation proclaiming "Mickey Woos! Judy Sings!"

"Nothing doing... I'll starve before I borrow any money from you!"

Perhaps most interestingly, this edition of the universally acclaimed "family series" ran into trouble with the then-powerful National Legion of Decency. Andy had matured in the four years since his screen debut. As a result, he was now encountering adult issues. In the penultimate moments of *Life Begins*, he found himself invited into a divorcée's apartment for an evening of unspecified "fun." Earlier in the movie, Judge Hardy had quietly confronted his son with a man-to-man discussion about pre-marital fidelity. The Legion took these points into consideration and classified the picture as "unobjectionable for adults." Their clear implication, however, held that Andy & Co. were—at least in this installment—improper viewing for a young audience.

Ironically, the movie's August 1941 premiere had been a special, public event, involving the entire principal cast. Hundreds of cheering fans looked on as Los Angeles Mayor Fletcher Bowron honored Rooney, Garland, Stone, Holden, Rutherford, and Haden by unveiling a special plaque on the façade of Grauman's Chinese Theatre that proclaimed the Hardys "the first family of Hollywood."

## What They Said

*"The other day, I dropped in to watch [Judy] at work with Master Mickey Rooney; they were making their latest Andy Hardy picture, which pleased me to no end. She was in a pretty outdoor costume and hat, to make scenes supposedly in New York's Central Park. If you had been with me, you'd probably have had to agree that there is no more accomplished actress on the screen today than Judy. Her lines are delivered with such conviction, such striking, unactress-like ease. She must have a prodigious memory (so must Rooney, come to that), for they went on for a full five minutes, just talking in the park, and it sounded exactly as though they really had just met there for a little heart to heart chat."*

—W. H. MOORING, *PICTUREGOER* MAGAZINE

*"I was nineteen and married and portraying a fifteen-year-old [sic], love-sick kid. Brother, that really took some acting!"*

—JUDY GARLAND

**ABOVE:** Between sequences at the Hardy home, Judy poses on "Carvel Street," part of MGM's legendary backlot. **OPPOSITE, BELOW:** Stone, Garland, and Rooney—three of MGM's mainstays.

# Babes on Broadway

METRO-GOLDWYN-MAYER

## CAST:

Mickey Rooney .................... Tommy Williams

Judy Garland ............................ Penny Morris

Fay Bainter ....................................... "Jonesy"

Virginia Weidler .......................... Barbara Jo

Ray McDonald .......................... Ray Lambert

Richard Quine .................... Morton Hammond

Donald Meek ................................. Mr. Stone

Alexander Woollcott ......................... Himself

Luis Alberni .......................................... Nick

James Gleason ...................... Thornton Reed

## CREDITS:

**Arthur Freed** (producer); **Busby Berkeley** (director); **Fred Finklehoffe and Elaine Ryan** (screenplay); **Fred Finklehoffe** (original story); **Lester White** (photography); **E. Y. Harburg, Burton Lane, Ralph Freed, Roger Edens, and Harold J. Rome** (music and lyrics); **Georgie Stoll** (musical director); **Roger Edens** (musical adaptation); **Leo Arnaud, George Bassman, and Conrad Salinger** (orchestrations); **Cedric Gibbons** (art director), **Malcolm Brown** (associate); **Edwin B. Willis** (set decorations); **Kalloch and Gile Steele** (costumes); **Fredrick Y. Smith** (editor)

## JUDY'S NUMBERS:

"How About You?," "Hoe Down," "Chin Up! Cheerio! Carry On!," Ghost Theater sequence [incorporating "Mary's a Grand Old Name," "I've Got Rings on My Fingers," "La Marseillaise" (spoken), "The Yankee Doodle Boy,"] "Bombshell Over Brazil," "Blackout over Broadway," Minstrel Show Finale (incorporating "Minstrel Show," "F. D. R. Jones," "Waiting for the Robert E. Lee," "Babes on Broadway." Deleted: "The Convict's Return" (nonmusical sketch with Rooney)

**RELEASE DATE: December 31, 1941**

**RUN TIME: 121 minutes**

OPPOSITE TOP: Though his on-and-off-camera boundless energy could wear her down, Judy forever acknowledged Mickey as her favorite performing partner—or, graciously, "the genius who taught me everything I know." OPPOSITE BOTTOM FROM LEFT: Judy and Mickey share the picture's hit song, "How About You?" | "Three Balls of Fire" and the object of their affection—Rooney, Judy, Richard Quine, and Ray McDonald | Judy saves the day by convincing James Gleason to watch the "babes" in action. The man at center is Joe Yule, Sr., Mickey Rooney's real-life father.

## SYNOPSIS

Tommy Williams, Ray Lambert, and Morton Hammond are the "Three Balls of Fire," a small-time New York act that impresses "Jonesy," right-hand factotum to Broadway producer Thornton Reed. She initially fails in her attempts to get them an audition, but Tommy devises his own showcase: a fund-raising benefit to send underprivileged city children on a country vacation.

Vocalist Penny Morris (JG) and the kids' ringleader, Barbara Jo, gleefully aid Tommy, but complications arise when his ambition threatens to overwhelm him. For the sake of self-promotion, he considers exploiting a group of juvenile British war refugees. He's then prepared to abandon both the emigrants, and his efforts on behalf of the neighborhood youngsters, when he's offered the chance to perform out of town in a Thornton Reed revue. Penny brings him to his senses, and Jonesy donates one of Reed's old abandoned theaters so that the gang can put on their show as planned.

On opening night, they're routed after a single song by a police inspector; the place is not only abandoned, it's condemned. The audience leaves but refuses refunds, allowing the kids to have their trip to the country after all. At that moment, the beleaguered Reed arrives, in manic disbelief at activity in a theater he thought deserted. Penny sees her opportunity and convinces him to watch one number. Within moments, he's delightedly impressed and, ultimately, brings Tommy, Penny, and all to Broadway.

# 42 STREET
# BROADWAY

Believe it or not...it's Mickey Rooney and Judy Garland in a couple of their hilarious impersonations.

"It is hard to imagine a rank-and-file American audience for which [the film] will not have an irresistible appeal."

—*LOOK*

"Although little Judy Garland is a matron now, and Mickey Rooney is of draft age and engaged to be married, MGM hasn't hesitated to co-star the pair in another show of wholesome adolescence. . . . Anyone who enjoyed [their preceding musicals] will undoubtedly relish the further ingenuous brashness and breathless energy of *Babes on Broadway*."

—*NEWSWEEK*

"A big hunk of entertainment for the whole family is this refreshing musical. Rooney and Garland were never better . . . they run rampant in every scene."

—*HOLLYWOOD*

"They're back with a bang . . . the film is well done enough throughout to make it a grand musical. Highlights are the scenes of Mickey and Judy transported by imagination into imitations of famous stars."　　—*FAMILY CIRCLE*

"There is a love scene between Mickey and Judy that is one of the classics of the age. By far their best show to date . . . about the only thing to do is stand up and cheer. *Babes on Broadway* is enough to make anyone shout, 'Oh, baby!'"

—SEATTLE *POST-INTELLIGENCER*

**TOP:** A proud, perkily-illustrated (and accurate) trade paper boast by MGM **MIDDLE:** "Cyrano de Bergerac" meets George M. Cohan's leading lady, Fay Templeton. **OPPOSITE TOP:** Art imitates life: "Penny Morris" sings "Chin Up! Cheerio! Carry On!" on an international radio hook-up. Judy had introduced the song in similar fashion several months before. **OPPOSITE BOTTOM:** In the "Ghost Theatre" sequence, Judy sang "Mary's a Grand Old Name," imitated Sarah Bernhardt, and joined Mickey for "Yankee Doodle Boy."

## NOTES

For the third major Garland-Rooney musical, an original story and score were crafted to accommodate their increased ages and appeal. No longer teens whose ambitions extended to shows in the barn, they were now young adults in Manhattan, specifically auditioning for the New York stage. The (comparative) reality of their latest picture found Judy and Mickey's characters populating the Pitt-Astor Drugstore in the heart of Times Square which was, indeed, an actual hangout for performing hopefuls. Launching the film was a brief introduction from renowned radio commentator/arts critic Alexander Woollcott, which gave further heft to the reality of the babes' theatrical world. Finally, the duo got involved with the burgeoning World War situation, a plot point underscored when the United States moved into active participation in that desperate battle just three weeks prior to the film's premiere.

Abetting the leads were such worthy young players as Ray McDonald, Richard Quine, and Virginia Weidler. Weidler essayed a role intended for Shirley Temple, whose mother purportedly pulled her from the cast, fearing that the youngster wouldn't be able to hold her own against Garland and Rooney. Also seen in brief bits were stars-to-be Donna Reed and Margaret O'Brien. Meanwhile, Fay Bainter, James Gleason, and Donald Meek were among the "old-timers" whose veteran capabilities brightened the offering.

One of the film's major interludes was crafted by Roger Edens and Vincente Minnelli; their "Ghost Theater" sequence found Mickey and Judy in celebration of early stage luminaries. At Minnelli's suggestion, vaudeville headliner Elsie Janis was brought in to guide the kids in their approach to the vintage material. Among those represented were Sir Harry Lauder, Fay Templeton, Blanche Ring, Richard Mansfield, Sarah Bernhardt, and George M. Cohan. In a more contemporary number, Mickey impersonated current rage Carmen Miranda. The Brazilian singing sensation personally coached Rooney in his South American drag and presentation.

At least ten numbers or routines were suggested for and rejected from *Babes on Broadway*. One of these, which was actually filmed and then deleted, was "The Convict's Return," a tour de force/quick-change sketch for Rooney. "Ballad for Americans," introduced in Broadway's *Sing for Your Supper* (1939), was purchased for performance by Judy and Mickey but tabled until *Born to Sing* (1942), a vehicle that showcased Weidler, McDonald, and Freed Unit alumni Douglas McPhail and

FROM TOP: Mickey and Judy lead an MGM tour for newcomer Shirley Temple. At this point, it was planned that she would be cast with them in *Babes on Broadway*. | Louis B. Mayer (right) proudly escorts Lord and Lady Halifax to the set. | Mickey, Judy, Virginia Weidler, and Berkeley with Roger Edens, the creative power behind Arthur Freed's throne. | Behind-the-scenes multitasking—if only for the camera. | By 1941, Judy was an expert at touching up her own makeup.

Larry Nunn. But the elimination most to be regretted was a scripted (though never recorded) Garland solo of "The Man I Love." Of the retained score, both the stirring "Chin Up! Cheerio! Carry On!" and the frenetic "Hoe Down" had their adherents, but the picture's runaway song hit was the Oscar-nominated "How About You?"

*Babes on Broadway* opened at New York's Radio City Music Hall, and the jubilant Garland-Rooney energy and take-no-prisoners determination to achieve their goals imparted inspiration to a public in dire need of such encouragement. On an investment of $955,000, *Babes* grossed $3,859,000 in its initial run.

Costume, makeup, and hairstyle tests for *Babes on Broadway*, July 1941.

## What They Said

*"Babes on Broadway held over in twenty-one more of its first key-city engagements. This brings to thirty-seven total of extended engagements thus far. Business throughout the country averaging more than 200 percent [above] normal. In nine new openings,* Babes *is doing business ranging up to 369 percent of normal."*

—TELEGRAM FROM HOWARD DIETZ, DIRECTOR OF ADVERTISING AND PUBLICITY FOR LOEW'S, INC., TO HOWARD STRICKLING, MGM DIRECTOR OF PUBLICITY

*"She was such a delight to work with; I have the greatest respect in the world for her. To me, she and Mickey Rooney are the greatest. When it comes to talent, I don't think anyone has ever touched them. They just had an innate talent. You couldn't really describe it, and you don't know where they got it. It was just there. And you know that, a lot of time, they would never read a script beforehand. I would ask Judy, 'What is this [picture] about?' And she would say, 'I don't know; I never read the script.' She and Mickey would get on the set, and they would wing it. They'd ask the script girl, 'What's that next line?' And they were so quick that, after hearing it two or three times, they had it. And they were real tearjerkers, too; they could put you in any kind of mood they decided. Judy had great eyes; the rest of her face wasn't really much to look at—it was a kind of a cute face. But she could read a line and make you believe anything she ever said. And when she sang a song, no one's ever equaled her."* —MGM MAKEUP MAN WILLIAM TUTTLE

**BELOW FROM LEFT:** The deleted "Convict's Return" saw Rooney as Judy's father, butler, a prison warden, and escapee/boyfriend. | Broadway's legendary "Jonesy" turns over the old Duchess Theatre for the kids' benefit show. **OPPOSITE TOP:** Mickey and Judy wait for lighting and camera preparation during filming of "Hoe Down." **OPPOSITE BOTTOM:** The ensemble demonstrates "a pioneer square dance—but with a new deal"—and (per the dialogue) give it "lots of zombo!"

*"Long before* Meet Me in St. Louis *and* The Clock, *Vincente Minnelli and I were 'working together,' and I never knew it. After all, I just got a script, and it never said who had sat at a desk in one of the offices and planned what went into it. But when Vincente told me the numbers he had worked on, I realized that even then— before we really met—he understood me better than anyone else. The numbers he worked on always were my favorites."* —JUDY GARLAND (1945)

# For Me and My Gal

**CAST:**

Judy Garland..................................Jo Hayden

George Murphy ................ Jimmy K. Metcalfe

Gene Kelly..................................Harry Palmer

Marta Eggerth..............................Eve Minard

Ben Blue ....................................... Sid Simms

Richard Quine.........................Danny Hayden

Keenan Wynn ............................Eddie Melton

Horace (Stephen) McNally ........... Mr. Waring

Lucille Norman ............................Lily Duncan

Betty Welles..... member of Jimmy's company

Anne Rooney .... member of Jimmy's company

Ben Lessey......................... "Dough Boy Dan"

**CREDITS:**

**Arthur Freed** (producer); **Busby Berkeley** (director); **Richard Sherman, Fred Finklehoffe, and Sid Silvers** (screenplay); **Howard Emmett Rogers** (original story); **William Daniels** (photography); **George W. Meyer, Edgar Leslie, and E. Ray Goetz** (music and lyric to "For Me and My Gal"); **Georgie Stoll** (musical director); **Roger Edens** (musical adaptation); **Conrad Salinger, George Bassman, Leo Arnaud** (orchestrations); **Bobby Connolly** (dance director); **Cedric Gibbons** (art director), **Gabriel Scognamillo** (associate); **Edwin B. Willis** (set decorations), **Keogh Gleason** (associate); **Kalloch and Gile Steele** (costumes); **Ben Lewis** (editor)

**JUDY'S NUMBERS:**

"The Doll Shop," "Don't Leave Me, Daddy," "Oh, You Beautiful Doll," "By the Beautiful Sea," "For Me and My Gal," "When You Wore a Tulip," "After You've Gone," "'Till We Meet Again," "Ballin' the Jack," "How Ya Gonna Keep 'Em Down on the Farm?," "Where Do We Go From Here?," Y.M.C.A. Montage (incorporating "It's a Long Way to Tipperary," "Smiles," "Pack Up Your Troubles in Your Old Kit Bag and Smile, Smile, Smile"), "When Johnny Comes Marching Home," "For Me and My Gal" finale reprise. Deleted: "Three Cheers for the Yanks," "For Me and My Gal" original finale reprise (with Gene Kelly and George Murphy). Deleted; possibly never filmed: "Don't Bite the Hand That's Feeding You" (with Abe Dinovitch and Maude Erickson), "Smiles" (full version)

**RELEASE DATE:** October 21, 1942

**RUN TIME:** 104 minutes

OPPOSITE, CLOCKWISE FROM TOP LEFT: Entertaining the troops with "Pack Up Your Troubles in Your Old Kit Bag" | The original, deleted finale | "Palmer and Hayden"—a slow trek to The Big Time (the film's original title) | Judy and Marta Eggerth. The acclaimed classical vocalist and actress played "the other woman" in both this and Garland's next film, *Presenting Lily Mars*.

## SYNOPSIS

Harry Palmer is one of the most egotistical actors on the small-time vaudeville circuit. But even he's impressed by the talent of Jo Hayden (JG), a member of the troupe of Jimmy Metcalfe, Sid Simms, and Company. Palmer feigns humility to get Jo to try out a song-and-dance routine with him. He later ashamedly admits his ruse, and when the Metcalfe act is dissolved, Palmer and Hayden become a team.

Jo falls in love with Palmer, despite his crazed ambition and momentary dalliance with established singing star Eve Minard. But he eventually commits to Jo, and their happiness seems complete when they're booked to play New York's Palace Theatre, the vaudeville mecca. When World War I intervenes, Jo's beloved brother Danny is killed in action, and she's appalled to discover Palmer's latest machination: in order to avoid the draft long enough to fulfill the Palace engagement and marry Jo, he has purposely crippled his hand.

Jo abandons Palmer and becomes the singing sweetheart of the armed forces abroad. Unable to use a gun because of his injury, Palmer also goes over to entertain the troops, managing as well to heroically warn an ambulance brigade of an impending barrage. War's end finds him, Metcalfe, and Simms in the Palace audience, watching Jo's triumphant act. She's overwhelmed when she spots Palmer; he's propelled to the stage, and they reprise their theme song, in love and performing in the theater they'd dreamed of playing.

# REVIEWS

"There's something for everyone . . . It all adds up to strong audience appeal and big box office possibilities. It is entertainment for the masses, [and] the entertainment is prodigal, indeed."

—MOTION PICTURE DAILY

"Leo the Lion has something to really roar about in the instance of the current Judy Garland vehicle. The young star is enabled to shine with the full light of her versatile talents." —FILM DAILY

"Story is obvious, naïve, and sentimental. It's also genuine, affectionate, and lively. . . . The film's theme is so sincere, and the treatment is so warm, that it holds interest throughout and achieves a number of irresistibly touching moments. JG is a knock-out . . . selling a number of the songs persuasively, getting by neatly in the hoofing routines . . . and giving a tender, affecting dramatic performance. George Murphy is ingratiating, and Gene Kelly gives a vividly drawn portrayal." —VARIETY

"When you start picking the ten best entertainers in show business, you wouldn't be too far off the beam were you to head the list with JG . . . who will be around after 90 percent of the so-called stars of stage and screen have been relegated to a permanent dim-out. This reviewer has always felt that way about her ability, and after having seen For Me and My Gal, he has another 'exhibit A' to justify his judgment." —TACOMA TIMES

"JG has gone a long way . . . [and] has developed into an emotional actress of scope and power. But there's something about it all that bothered me. She's too thin, too finely drawn. Slow down, Judy!" —CHICAGO TRIBUNE

OPPOSITE, TOP LEFT: MGM used this still of Murphy, Garland, and Kelly for a colorized lobby card, even though it depicted the original—deleted—film finale. ABOVE: Rehearsing with Gene Kelly. In 1973, he asked if he could be the one to induct Judy into the *Entertainment Hall of Fame* over ABC-TV. Producer/writer Bernie Rothman remembers that, at the end of his prepared speech, Kelly "look[ed] up from his script and into the camera. He [could] barely get these last improvised words out. 'And you know, something, ladies and gentlemen, I miss her very, very much. . . . ' I've got his script. The words are smudged with teardrops."

## NOTES

MGM elevated Judy to "star" status on the studio roster in late 1938 by presenting her with a portable dressing room trailer on the set of *The Wizard of Oz*. But *For Me and My Gal* marked the first time she technically received star billing—i.e., her name listed above the title of a motion picture. This achievement was compounded by the fact that Garland's was the only name posted; MGM regarded her reputation as more than sufficient to bring in the cash customers.

The film also marked the screen debut of Gene Kelly, Broadway's *Pal Joey* (1940), whom Judy had admired on the stage and championed for *For Me and My Gal*. The originally assigned leading man, George Murphy, was then demoted to the role of (in his own words) "the schnook who never gets the girl." Kelly's off-camera charm, drive, and determination dovetailed beautifully with the anti-hero/opportunist characteristics of the picture's male protagonist. The scope of his success can be measured by the actor's subsequent decades of screen preeminence as dancer, actor, and (eventually) director/choreographer.

Preliminarily titled *The Big Time* and *Applause*, *For Me and My Gal* was first envisioned as a showcase for two females: a singer and a dancer. But Metro dramatic coach Stella Adler recommended conflating the roles for Judy, enabling her to play an adult for the first time in her screen career. The film's World War I background created instant empathy with an audience deep into the first year of World War II, but it was the public's ongoing appreciation for Garland that spurred a box office sensation.

*For Me and My Gal* hit its only real snag when first previewed. The original finale saw Garland, Kelly, Murphy, and Ben Blue performing together in vaudeville, and in the end, Kelly got the girl. The picture's initial audience was dissatisfied and found his character (a draft-dodging heel) reprehensible. Their comment cards agreed that Judy should have wound up onscreen as Murphy's romantic partner. As a result, MGM instituted a hasty series of rewrites and retakes, in which Kelly's "Harry" performed heroically in the French trenches; the musical finale was then reconfigured and reshot to spotlight his emotional reunion with Judy. In real life, Murphy was disgruntled at being dropped from the number, but subsequent audiences were happily fulfilled.

Among other deletions: "I'm Sorry I Made You Cry" and "Tell Me" performed by Murphy and Blue; Judy's rousing "Three Cheers for the Yanks"; and Marta Eggerth's brilliantly sung "The Spell of the Waltz." Eggerth fell victim to another sort of editing when the décolletage of her dress was hastily "blurred" in the filmed footage of "Do I Love You?" in order to minimize her cleavage.

At a final cost of $802,000, *For Me and My Gal* grossed more than $4.3 million

in its initial release. In London, it was the Empire Theatre's fourth greatest hit of 1943, playing to more than 69,500 customers in two weeks. Director Busby Berkeley always claimed it as his own personal favorite of the four dozen motion pictures with which he was involved. The title song, originally written in 1917, became one of Judy's preeminent standards. During her concerts in the 1950s and 1960s, she informally exhorted audiences to "Sing it with me, please!" Whatever the world-wide locale, they always knew the words.

OPPOSITE: Costume, makeup, hair, and hat tests for *For Me and My Gal* ABOVE: A pensive Judy during work on the finale

## What They Said

"Since this was a story about vaudeville and the struggles of a young couple to reach the top, we needed someone who knew the route, someone who knew about the hard work and heartaches that went with this sort of life. The obvious choice was [Busby Berkeley], who had lived this kind of story himself—it was his own background. Our only reservation in choosing him was that this was not simply a musical, but an emotional story with some pathos and drama. It also contained a great deal of music, and we were a little afraid he might concentrate on that rather than the story. But he didn't. He came up with a very warm and human picture."

—ARTHUR FREED

"I was under contract to David O. Selznick, and he loaned me to MGM, which was heaven—mainly so because I worked with Judy Garland. She pushed me and helped me through For Me and My Gal, which was the first picture I did. I was constantly being thrown by the piecemeal way in which pictures were being made. I knew nothing about playing to the camera, and I didn't even know whether I was being shot close, medium, or long—or about the intricate business of hitting all the marks laid out on the studio floor for the movement of the actors. My film-acting techniques weren't very good; as a matter of fact, I think they were pretty bad . . . but I could see there was some kind of cinema know-how. I quickly learned that with Judy. She was so good. I sort of followed her around on those little vaudeville routines we did. And I owe her an eternal debt. They previewed the picture in Riverside, and I was appalled at the sight of myself blown up twenty times. I had an awful feeling I was a tremendous flop, but when I came outside, executives started pumping my hand, and Judy came up and kissed me. I went home thinking they were just being nice, until the picture opened in New York and did well." —GENE KELLY

"New York Infirmary for Women and Children benefit plus press preview tonight [drew] packed house with enthusiastic reception. Frequent applause toward end of picture indicated inspirational quality went over big. Regular opening this morning combined with community sing in Times Square at midnight, followed by midnight show for theater old-timers and Broadway stage celebrities."

—REPORT TO ARTHUR FREED FROM MGM DIRECTOR OF PUBLICITY HOWARD STRICKLING ABOUT THE FILM'S LAUNCH AND PREMIERE

"Astor Theatre reporting new all-time house record . . . Gal topped every weekend gross since theater opened its motion picture policy more than eighteen years ago. Receipts exceed every type engagement, including reserved seat policy."

—NEW YORK BOX OFFICE REPORT TO HOWARD STRICKLING FROM HOWARD DIETZ, DIRECTOR OF ADVERTISING AND PUBLICITY FOR LOEW'S, INC.

OPPOSITE: Judy in her "Ballin' the Jack" costume; *Time* magazine appreciatively championed her "race horse legs." **ABOVE FROM LEFT:** Lucille Norman, Judy, and George Murphy between takes of "Oh, You Beautiful Doll" | Directions from all sides for the title song sequence | Flirting with the camera, preparatory to the filming of "After You've Gone"

# Presenting Lily Mars

METRO-GOLDWYN-MAYER

**CAST:**

Judy Garland................................Lily Mars

**Van Heflin** ..............................John Thornway

**Fay Bainter**............................Mrs. Thornway

**Richard Carlson**.............................Owen Vail

**Spring Byington**..........................Mrs. Mars

**Marta Eggerth**..........................Isobel Rekay

**Connie Gilchrist**..............................Frankie

**Leonid Kinskey**.......................................Leo

**Patricia Barker**...................................Poppy

**Janet Chapman**....................................Violet

**CREDITS:**

**Joseph Pasternak** (producer); **Norman Taurog** (director); **Richard Connell and Gladys Lehman** (screenplay); **Booth Tarkington** (original author); **Joseph Ruttenberg** (photography); **Walter Jurmann, Paul Francis Webster, E. Y. Harburg, Burton Lane, and Roger Edens** (music and lyrics); **George Stoll** (musical director); **Roger Edens** (musical adaptation); **Ernst Matray and Charles Walters** (dance directors); **Cedric Gibbons** (art director), **Harry McAfee** (associate); **Edwin B. Willis** (set decorations), **Richard Pefferle** (associate); **Shoup** (gowns); **Albert Akst** (editor)

**JUDY'S NUMBERS:**

*"Tom, Tom, the Piper's Son," "Every Little Movement (Has a Meaning All Its Own)," "When I Look at You" and "Caro Mona" (parody) "A Russian Rhapsody" (fragment), "Where There's Music" finale (incorporating the title song and "Three O'Clock in the Morning"), "Broadway Rhythm." Deleted: "Paging Mr. Greenback," "Where There's Music" verse and the following numbers from that medley: "St. Louis Blues" (with Judy Carol), "It's a Long Way to Tipperary," "In the Shade of the Old Apple Tree," "Don't Sit Under the Apple Tree" (danced with Charles Walters)*

**RELEASE DATE:** April 29, 1943

**RUN TIME:** 104 minutes

## SYNOPSIS

Stage-struck Lily Mars (JG) longs to leave Indiana for Broadway. She sees her chance when producer John Thornway returns to their hometown with his current success and current leading lady, Isobel Rekay. Thornway is unimpressed with Lily, but the girl hitchhikes to New York, crashes a Thornway/Rekay rehearsal, and the quickly smitten producer adds her to the show's chorus.

Recognizing Thornway's interest in Lily, the volatile Isobel walks out of the starring role in his new production. Thornway instead casts it with Lily, but at the last minute, he realizes the girl is not yet seasoned enough to carry a show. With her mother, brother, and sisters traveling to Manhattan to see her as a musical star, Lily is slated instead for a bit part in the final scene. But she rises to the occasion, and by the following season, Lily Mars is both Mrs. John Thornway and the headliner of her own Broadway musical.

TOP: The revamped finale: Tommy Dorsey and his aggregation (top) accompany Judy, Charles (Chuck) Walters and company in "Broadway Rhythm." BOTTOM FROM LEFT: Van Heflin suggests that Judy leave his Indiana home. | "Tom, Tom, the Piper's Son": "Lily" crashes a party and is trapped into singing with the band. | "We love you best of all the stars—we're proud of you, Miss Lily Mars!" The family surprises "Lily" before opening night. *From left:* Annabelle Logan, Janet Chapman, Patricia Barker, Douglas Croft, and Spring Byington.

"Rating: Excellent. Brilliant entertainment with lilting music, a charming love interest—and costars Judy Garland and Van Heflin, supported by a nearly flawless cast. Smart direction, dialogue, and costuming—against a background of lavish production—are blended harmoniously in this box office bell-ringer."
—*MOTION PICTURE HERALD*

"A most entertaining picture . . . music, drama, and comedy in beautifully balanced doses. JG gets a fine chance to display her talents . . . and rollicks through a series of hilarious situations, mixed with touching dramatic moments." —*MOVIE RADIO GUIDE*

"If ever there was a shining example of 'young lady stampedes to fame,' it's Judy, who proves herself capable of the heavy assignment given her."
—*PHOTOPLAY*

"The kind of movie Hollywood turns out now and then when it has a lot of money and talent to use up and isn't sure what to do with them. It has a couple of swell moments, [including] 'Every Little Movement,' or later when Lily is being groomed for a role for which she is not ready." —*COMMONWEALTH*

"It has a quiet charm but threatens to break away from all tradition by making its characters, at odd moments, talk like adult-minded people. JG is a sweet girl, and she sings charmingly. She is getting more angular as she grows up but should be quite an actress if she learns some of the lessons that are vaguely hinted at." —LONDON *NEWS CHRONICLE*

Only in the movies: Bob Crosby and orchestra accompany an impromptu supper club number by new-to-New-York "Lily Mars".

## NOTES

Based on Booth Tarkington's novel, *Presenting Lily Mars* was originally intended as a darker dramatic vehicle for Lana Turner. But producer Joe Pasternak, newly arrived at MGM after launching the career of Deanna Durbin at Universal, had wanted to work with Judy for at least six years. The *Lily* storyline was thus revamped as a gentler musical, and Pasternak surrounded Garland with a top-drawer cast, including Academy Award-winning actor Van Heflin—her first leading man who wasn't a song-and-dance vaudevillian.

Expert dramatic practitioners Fay Bainter, Spring Byington, and Richard Carlson lent immeasurable entertainment value; Marta Eggerth reprised her *For Me and My Gal* persona as "the other woman." Eggerth not only sang beautifully, but provided Judy with a wicked opportunity to satirize the accented, classical, and "classy" vocalese of a European diva. Though limited to just a few scenes, Connie Gilchrist played for warmth as an aging ex-actress turned theater scrubwoman, partnering Judy for one of the film's highlights, a low key duet of "Every Little Movement." Bob Crosby and His Orchestra lent additional marquee value, and the whole picture wrapped up with Garland and a mammoth chorus in their timely, patriotic plea for war bond sales, "Paging Mr. Greenback." Given such line readings, it's interesting to note that with uncharacteristic MGM economy, the finale was photographed in front of one of the *Babes in Arms* backdrops.

The entire picture was permeated with an intentionally modest charm—perhaps too much so for some of the Metro honchos. Just prior to *Lily*'s release, it was decided to replace "Mr. Greenback" with a lavish, lengthy, massively staged medley. Roger Edens assembled eight minutes of song, introduced by and intermingled with "Where There's Music," an outtake tune from Metro's *The Big Store* (1941). Charles "Chuck" Walters, new to MGM, was brought in to stage the number and partner Judy in dance; Tommy Dorsey and His Orchestra—at the studio for *Girl Crazy*—popped up (literally, on a hydraulic set piece) to accompany the Freed-Brown classic, "Broadway Rhythm."

Chronologically sandwiched between *For Me and My Gal* and *Girl Crazy*—not to mention the all-star, Technicolor *Thousands Cheer*—*Lily Mars* was scarcely among the major Garland vehicles. But its lack of pretension and combination of talent made it highly palatable to audiences of the day. Additionally, Judy never looked better on the screen than she did in late 1942 and early 1943. She was at an ideal weight for *Lily Mars*, and her make-up, hair styles, and Howard Shoup's contemporary wardrobe were unusually flattering and appropriate.

"Now get out — as you came in — over the wall!"

Judy GARLAND
VAN HEFLIN
*Presenting* LILY MARS

**OPPOSITE AND LEFT:** Van Heflin was perhaps Judy's first leading *man*—separate and apart from the vaudevillian/theatrical characters typified by Rooney and Kelly.

## What They Said

*"Judy is the finest girl actress of my whole experience. She possesses sweetness, charm, humor, and is both a sparkling comedienne and a moving dramatic actress."*

—DIRECTOR NORMAN TAUROG

*"Lily Mars [was] small in intention, deliberately so. It [was] a happy venture. But before it was ready for release, I learned to my astonishment that several people, who call themselves friends of the star, had arranged to see a rough-cut, without my knowledge or consent. If I had known, I would have absolutely and uncompromisingly forbidden it. No one likes to show a half-done job. These people ran to Judy with wails of pain and distress, all aimed in my general direction. Very few of us, let alone actresses of [twenty], are granitic enough to stand up under this kind of thing. I don't blame Judy for feeling that perhaps this new producer from a lot that specialized in inexpensive pictures had let her down. [Then] Louis B. Mayer called me into his office. With great tact and discretion, he let me know that I was no longer at a studio where expense mattered. Perhaps, he suggested, if I looked at the picture again, I might find I'd like to re-do the finale, stage it as lavishly as I might imagine. It would be quite all right with him. Well, I had my honest doubts. To plunge [Lily Mars] into a sequence of enormous opulence would, I thought, throw the whole story out of key. But I was new at the studio. I am also never as hard-headed as to insist on my way or no way. We shot a new finale. Spent a fortune on it."*

—PRODUCER JOE PASTERNAK

*"Judy had no confidence in her dancing at all: 'I can't do this!' And she'd kid it, you know . . . and we'd all fall apart! But we didn't have a lot of time to spend on the number, and I had to kind of coax her into it—make her feel comfortable. So I finally asked her, 'Judy, who do you admire as a dancer? Who is your favorite female dancer?' And, at that time, she said, 'Oh, Renee de Marco!' And I said, 'All right. From now on, you're doing an impersonation of Renee.' And then it just was beautiful. She was not a dancer, per se, but she could make herself look dandy!"*

—CHOREOGRAPHER/DANCE PARTNER CHARLES WALTERS

*"MGM killed her, absolutely. All of us at* Girl Crazy *were on layoff for a month—on full salary—while she was doing retakes on* Presenting Lily Mars. *Two pictures at once. And that wasn't the only time they did that to her."* —ACTOR GIL STRATTON

**OPPOSITE:** "Gowns by Shoup" was the screen credit, but his modern daywear was equally becoming to Judy. (Some of these creations, modeled here for fashion layouts, weren't worn in the finished film.)

CLOCKWISE FROM TOP LEFT: Former date and *Ziegfeld Girl* costar Jackie Cooper drops by to chat. | "The Mars Sisters" (Janet Chapman, Annabelle Logan, Patricia Barker) visit the Garland dressing room. | Crosby, Garland, Heflin, and coworkers on the nightclub set. | As the camera rolls, Van Heflin escorts Judy to her New York "incubator . . . a sort of young folks' home." | Judy goes sound-stage hopping and reunites with Gene Kelly, garbed and on one of the sets for his *DuBarry Was a Lady*. OPPOSITE: Then as now, movie making was often an ongoing "hurry up and wait" existence.

# Thousands Cheer

METRO-GOLDWYN-MAYER

## CAST:

Kathryn Grayson ..................... *Kathryn Jones*

Gene Kelly................................. *Eddy Marsh*

Mary Astor ............................. *Hyllary Jones*

John Boles.................. *Colonel William Jones*

Ben Blue ............................. *Chuck Polansky*

Frances Rafferty ..................... *Marie Corbino*

Mary Elliott ...........................................*Helen*

Frank Jenks ............................... *Sgt. Koslack*

Frank Sully...............................................*Alan*

Dick Simmons................. *Captain Fred Avery*

### GUEST STARS:

*Mickey Rooney, Judy Garland, Red Skelton, Eleanor Powell, Ann Sothern, Lucille Ball, Virginia O'Brien, Frank Morgan, Lena Horne, Marsha Hunt, Marilyn Maxwell, Donna Reed, Margaret O'Brien, June Allyson, Gloria DeHaven, John Conte, Sara Haden, Don Loper, Maxine Barrat, Kay Kyser and His Orchestra, Bob Crosby and His Orchestra, Benny Carter and His Band, Jose Iturbi*

## CREDITS:

**Joseph Pasternak** *(producer);* **George Sidney** *(director);* **Paul Jarrico and Richard Collins** *(screenplay and story);* **George Folsey** *(photography);* **Ferde Grofé and Harold Adamson** *(music and lyric to "Daybreak");* **Lew Brown, Ralph Freed, and Burton Lane** *(music and lyric to "I Dug a Ditch");* **Walter Jurmann and Paul Francis Webster** *(music and lyric to "Three Letters in the Mail Box");* **Earl Brent, E. Y. Harburg** *(music and lyric to "Let There Be Music");* **Dmitri Shostakovitch, Harold Rome, and E. Y. Harburg** *(music and lyric to "United Nations");* **Herbert Stothart** *(musical director and score);* **Cedric Gibbons** *(art director),* **Daniel B. Cathcart** *(associate);* **Edwin B. Willis** *(set decorations),* **Jacques Mersereau** *(associate);* **Irene** *(costumes);* **George Boemler** *(editor)*

### JUDY'S NUMBER:

*"The Joint is Really Jumpin' Down at Carnegie Hall"*

**RELEASE DATE: September 13, 1943**
**RUN TIME: 126 minutes**

## REVIEWS

"Gorgeous and pretentious, really two shows in one package." *—DAILY VARIETY*

"A surefire smash hit. . . . The mammoth camp show is climaxed by the great delivery of a song by Judy Garland." *—HOLLYWOOD REPORTER*

"Miss Garland sings one song . . . and the juniors will be telling each other about that number for months." *—MOTION PICTURE DAILY*

## SYNOPSIS

Aspiring singer Kathryn Jones holds dear a two-fold plan of getting her career off the ground and reuniting her estranged parents, Colonel William and Hyllary Jones. Meanwhile, Eddy Marsh is a new army camp inductee—a reluctant and rebellious private who was formerly an ace circus aerialist. He is at first resentful of Kathryn, the daughter of one of his commanding officers. When they fall in love, their own romance is played out against the concern of her mother and father, who face an evolving reconciliation of their own.

Just prior to the departure of soldiers and officers for overseas duty, Kathryn produces an all-star entertainment for the servicemen, utilizing many of MGM's top names. Mickey Rooney serves as master of ceremonies, and the penultimate number showcases Judy Garland, coaxing classical pianist Jose Iturbi to accompany her in a boogie woogie song. At the finale of the show, Eddy is reunited with his circus family and performs with them for the occasion.

ABOVE: MGM's boast of possessing "More Stars Than There Are in the Heavens" seems very much for real in this conglomeration of caricatures by the great Al Hirschfeld.

## NOTES

By 1943, the major Hollywood studios were deep into their own contributions to the war effort. Each in turn produced an all-star musical movie to rally public morale; *Thousands Cheer* was the Metro-Goldwyn-Mayer offering. Unlike most such films—which scattered their performers across two hours of extraneous plot—*Thousands Cheer* marshaled its resources for the last quarter of the feature. More than a dozen musical and comedy types from the lot joined forces with "name" bands and orchestras to present a mammoth camp show, featuring Mickey Rooney as performing emcee. In her first Technicolor appearance since *The Wizard of Oz*, Judy was accompanied at the piano by classical musician/conductor Jose Iturbi in the Roger Edens number, "The Joint is Really Jumpin' Down at Carnegie Hall." Because Edens had appropriated a jazz "fill" from a Hugh Martin–Ralph Blane song for the "Carnegie Hall" composition, he insisted they take credit with him for its creation. The concept of all-American girl Garland, coaxing Iturbi to let down his figurative "long hair" and "get in the groove," was enough to make their number the penultimate routine in the program—another measure of Judy's growing Metro preeminence and public popularity.

**ABOVE:** The northwest corner of Broadway and 45th Street was enlivened by a special Hirschfeld marquee when *Thousands Cheer* premiered in New York. **OPPOSITE:** In 1998, Carnegie Hall celebrated Judy and her music in two sold-out, all-star concerts. The film clip of this number led off the first night.

## What They Said

"I must tell how George Sidney, my director; Roger Edens, our musical director; and I approached Jose Iturbi when we wanted him to play a boogie-woogie piano for Judy. We were all so very skeptical, afraid he might regard us as tasteless philistines. Still, it was an engaging idea; our boys in the service did like boogie, and with Judy singing, it would be wonderful. 'You'd have to be very diplomatic,' George said. 'Very,' Roger added. . . . So Jose came to see me. I told him how the camp shows were very informal, and what we had found the boys liked to hear. And finally I let it out that I would like him and Judy to do a boogie number together. 'When do I start?' he said." —PRODUCER JOE PASTERNAK

# Girl Crazy

METRO-GOLDWYN-MAYER

## CAST:

| | |
|---|---|
| Mickey Rooney | Danny Churchill, Jr. |
| Judy Garland | Ginger Gray |
| Gil Stratton | Bud Livermore |
| Robert E. Strickland | Henry Lathrop |
| "Rags" Ragland | "Rags" |
| June Allyson | Specialty |
| Nancy Walker | Polly Williams |
| Guy Kibbee | Dean Phineas Armour |
| Frances Rafferty | Marjorie Tait |
| Henry O'Neill | Mr. Churchill, Sr. |

## CREDITS:

Arthur Freed (producer); Norman Taurog (director); Fred F. Finklehoffe (screenplay); Guy Bolton and Jack McGowan (original play); William Daniels and Robert Planck (photography); George Gershwin and Ira Gershwin (music and lyrics); Georgie Stoll (musical director); Roger Edens (musical adaptation); Conrad Salinger, Axel Stordahl, and Sy Oliver (orchestrations); Hugh Martin, Ralph Blane (vocal arrangements); Charles Walters (dance director); Busby Berkeley (dance director of "I Got Rhythm"); Cedric Gibbons (art director); Edwin B. Willis (set decorations), Mac Alper (associate); Irene (costumes), Sharaff (associate); Albert Akst (editor)

## JUDY'S NUMBERS:

"Bidin' My Time," "Could You Use Me?," "Embraceable You," "But Not for Me," "I Got Rhythm." Deleted; possibly never filmed: "Bronco Busters" (with Mickey Rooney and Nancy Walker)

**RELEASE DATE: November 1943**
**RUN TIME: 100 minutes**

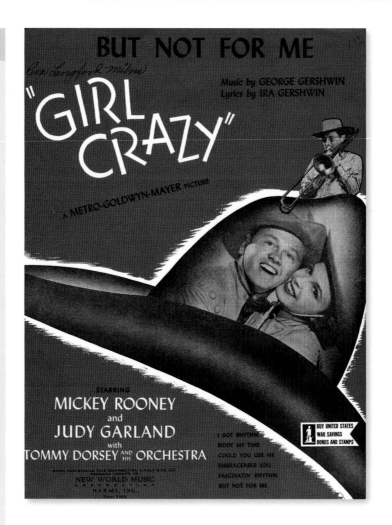

## SYNOPSIS

Yale refugee Danny Churchill, Jr. would rather spend time partying in New York City with beautiful girls than tending to his classes on the New Haven campus. After a headline-making night on the town, Danny is sent out west by his father to enroll at the non-coeducational Cody College of Mines and Agriculture in Arizona. There's not a girl within miles of the place, except for Ginger Gray (JG), granddaughter of Dean Phineas Armour. Danny is instantly smitten, but Ginger's not impressed, and the young man's disdain for the school doesn't help his suit.

Eventually, the two fall in love and almost immediately join forces to save the college when the state legislature threatens to shut it down. The duo creates a Wild West Rodeo to attract publicity and potential enrollees. It's an immediate sensation, but the festivities almost end their relationship when Danny is forced to bypass Ginger and crown the more-newsworthy governor's daughter, Marjorie Tait, "Queen of the Rodeo." But love endures, and the school is saved when the boys-only Cody is flooded with hundreds of applications—from girls.

Mickey later wrote, "I always loved Judy without ever being *in* love with her. . . . No one [else] has ever given so much of herself for her profession to everybody in the world."

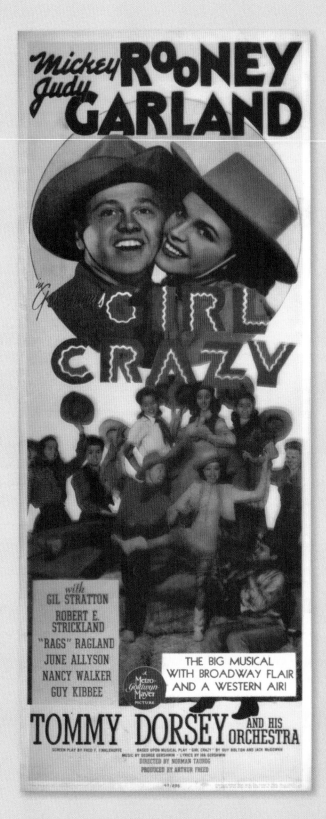

## REVIEWS

"Recipe for a highly successful attraction: Take Mickey Rooney and Judy Garland, mix well with brisk tempo and comedy, sprinkle with light love story, add attractive girls, apply George Gershwin music, garnish with production numbers, and top off with Tommy Dorsey's Orchestra. What with paper shortage and the like, this review could end here." —MOTION PICTURE DAILY

"Smash entertainment. *Girl Crazy* has every element of popular appeal. . . . Picture should be a natural at the box office, of type attractive to every class audience. [The] two stars are in top form and spark film with their personalities. They're engagingly effective. . . . Judy adds dancing to her talents in a clever number with Charles Walters."

—DAILY VARIETY

"Judy's dancing routines are outstanding. Wonder why Fred Astaire doesn't try to capture her for one of his partners. She's expert enough, Heaven knows, and her singing of those Gershwin tunes is so 'boo'ful.'"—LOS ANGELES *EXAMINER*

"Dance direction by Charles Walters sends JG through some of the most engaging steps she has performed for the cameras. . . . When a team like Rooney and Garland wrap up an entertainment, it is expert wrapping."

—HOLLYWOOD REPORTER

**OPPOSITE, COUNTERCLOCKWISE FROM TOP:** From left: a script girl, Rooney, the Freed Unit's musical supervisor Lela Simone, and Judy ride the studio sound truck in Palm Springs. | In a deleted scene, Judy imitated the governor so that Mickey could rehearse the plea he planned to make to the genuine article. | Another deleted scene: "Ginger" and "Danny" are a hit with the real governor, but his secretary (Sarah Edwards) disapproves of their celebratory moment.

## NOTES

Although its plot was much revised from that of the original 1930 Broadway show, the film version of *Girl Crazy* kept what was important: music and lyrics by George and Ira Gershwin. It was the fourth and final major Garland-Rooney musical, and it completed an interesting arc of transition in the screen roles the two entertainers had played together. Where she had pined for him in *Babes in Arms* and *Strike Up the Band* (not to mention all three of their Andy Hardy teamings), Mickey did more of the chasing in *Babes on Broadway*. By the time of *Girl Crazy*, he was totally in pursuit, and Judy finally got to be both the understandable object of desire and—at least initially—dismissive of his attentions.

*Girl Crazy* proved to be more problematic than any of their past vehicles. Busby Berkeley's personal demons had worsened, and neither the now-adult Judy and Mickey, nor Roger Edens or Arthur Freed, were prepared to submit to his combative, dictatorial methods. Berkeley's extended production concepts for "I Got Rhythm" were detrimental to Edens' vocal layout for the number and sent *Girl Crazy* immediately over-budget in its first weeks of filming in January 1943. His relentless rehearsals and overtime hours taxed the now-exhausted Rooney and ever-more-frail Garland. Barely a month into production, Freed was forced to shut down the picture until he could bring in Norman Taurog to replace Berkeley as director. Chuck Walters and Jack Donohue took over musical staging for the film.

During the layoff, an underweight Judy was confined to bed for three weeks; later on, both she and Mickey missed days of work. But the picture was completed by mid-May and included some of the best numbers of Garland's career. Walters again partnered her for much of "Embraceable You," and she otherwise had an entire male corps to accompany her in the routine he provided.

William Daniels' camera work made an enormous contribution, especially in "But Not for Me." Mickey's versatility was exemplified by both a lengthy piano solo with Tommy Dorsey and His Orchestra and a series of impressions of radio announcers and sports figures. Though few performers had much of a chance when Garland and Rooney were shining, *Girl Crazy* also provided happy appearances by newcomers June Allyson, Nancy Walker, and Frances Rafferty, as well as familiar favorites Guy Kibbee and Rags Ragland.

The picture came in at a cost of $1.4 million—over budget by $323,000, with at least a third of that amount attributable to Berkeley and the shut down. But *Girl Crazy*'s initial take topped the box office for both *Babes in Arms* and *Strike Up the Band*: $3,770,000.

LEFT: Judy and the Cody College student body on a camp out, each of them "Bidin' My Time."

## What They Said

"I came out from New York to do my role in Best Foot Forward for MGM—only to be told that Tommy Dix was going to play the part. Very dejected, I was called into Arthur Freed's office, and he told me, 'I'm going to put you into the next Judy-Mickey [picture] in place of Ray McDonald,' who'd gone off to the war. Well, he was a dancer; I was a singer. But they said that was okay . . . and [then] I watched the music being doled out. I ended up with four bars of 'Embraceable You'! And when I went to the sneak preview, all my funny lines were gone, too. In place after place, there was a dissolve or a cut or a fade-out, so I'm not in the picture very much, despite the billing. I ran into Al Akst, the editor, at the Brown Derby, and he explained, 'In a picture with Mickey Rooney, no other young guy is going to get the laughs!' But the moments with Judy made it all worthwhile. I just sat and watched the filming on 'But Not for Me' for two and a half days . . . something you ought to have paid admission to see."—GIL STRATTON

"Buzz was a great, great genius. And it paid off. But I guess a lot of people resented him, because he was really, really a devil. Hah! He knew what he wanted, and he wouldn't settle for anything less. He didn't care if the person had a broken leg, or whether they were half-dying. He said, 'No! I wanna get this shot! Move that camera in there, and move your bloomin' behind! Get it going!' This is the way he thought. He just wanted to get his shot, get it over with, and go home."—ANN MILLER

"They wanted me to stage and dance with Judy in 'Embraceable You.' By that time, I was asking for scripts; I wanted to know what the characters were, what their flavor was, and how to get [that into the number] . . . the smoothness of sliding in and out surreptitiously, so it wasn't a 'bump'—you stop the book and do a number. I think being conscious of that helped get me into directing, because Arthur said one day, 'Chuck, you think like a director, and I think one day you'll be a director.' And I said, 'Oh, Arthur, you've got to be kidding!' I was a rotten actor; I never thought I'd be a director! It never entered my mind."—CHARLES WALTERS

" . . . unquestionably to me, the two greatest talents—you must know this—were Judy and Mickey. Once, Louis B. Mayer looked at me (very dramatically, as only he could) and said 'Do you know that this whole studio is in the hands of two young girls?' One was someone I felt would never be ready for a film. 'The other is Judy Garland,' he said. I said, 'Oh, now you're talking. That's the greatest we'll have this century. She's as great as Yvette Guilbert must have been.' And he said, 'You're too young to have seen Yvette Guilbert.' I said, 'I didn't say I saw her. I merely know who she was and what she did.'"—MGM DRAMA COACH LILLIAN BURNS SIDNEY

The Tommy Dorsey Orchestra falls in behind, while the Busby Berkeley girls and boys wait for their cue.

# Meet Me in St. Louis

## METRO-GOLDWYN-MAYER

### CAST:

Judy Garland.............................Esther Smith

Margaret O'Brien ..................."Tootie" Smith

Mary Astor .........................Mrs. Anna Smith

Lucille Bremer............................Rose Smith

Leon Ames........................Mr. Alonzo Smith

Tom Drake ...................................John Truett

Marjorie Main ...................................... Katie

Harry Davenport...............................Grandpa

June Lockhart..........................Lucille Ballard

Henry Daniels, Jr. ................... Lon Smith, Jr.

Robert Sully .........................Warren Sheffield

Joan Carroll.............................. Agnes Smith

### CREDITS:

**Arthur Freed** *(producer);* **Vincente Minnelli** *(director);* **Irving Brecher and Fred F. Finklehoffe** *(screenplay);* **Sally Benson** *(original author);* **George Folsey** *(photography);* **Hugh Martin and Ralph Blane** *(music and lyrics to "The Trolley Song," "The Boy Next Door," "Skip to My Lou," "Have Yourself a Merry Little Christmas");* **Georgie Stoll** *(musical director);* **Roger Edens** *(musical adaptation);* **Conrad Salinger** *(orchestrations);* **Charles Walters** *(dance director);* **Cedric Gibbons, Lemuel Ayers, and Jack Martin Smith** *(art directors);* **Edwin B. Willis** *(set decorations),* **Paul Huldschinsky** *(associate);* **Sharaff** *(costumes);* **Albert Akst** *(editor)*

### JUDY'S NUMBERS:

"Meet Me in St. Louis", "The Boy Next Door," "Skip to My Lou," "Under the Bamboo Tree," "Over the Bannister," "The Trolley Song," "Goodbye, My Lady Love," "Under the Anheuser Bush," "Hiawatha," "Little Brown Jug," "Home, Sweet Home," "Auld Lang Syne," "Have Yourself a Merry Little Christmas." Deleted: "Boys and Girls Like You and Me"

**RELEASE DATE: November 22, 1944**
**(World Premiere in St. Louis)**
**RUN TIME: 113 minutes**

**OPPOSITE:** When first shown Irene Sharaff's attempts at 1903 costume-design realism, producer Arthur Freed agonized, "How can you have a star with no cleavage?"

## SYNOPSIS

A look at one year in the life of the Smiths, 5135 Kensington Avenue, begins in summer 1903. Mr. Alonzo Smith practices law; Mrs. Anna Smith and Katie the cook oversee the household. Grandpa Prophater enjoys his hat and gun collection, while oldest son Lon prepares for his freshman year at Princeton. Oldest daughter Rose moons over collegiate Warren Sheffield in far-off New York. Her little sisters, Agnes and "Tootie," are preoccupied with pets, dolls, and pranks. And high school junior Esther Smith (JG) is smitten with the new boy next door, John Truett.

The family's adventures include burgeoning expectations for the following summer and the Louisiana Purchase Exposition of 1904. Along the way, Agnes and Tootie create havoc on Halloween; Esther beats up John when she mistakenly thinks he hit Tootie; and the ever-affected Rose flirts with an older colonel. But all of these otherwise earth-shattering concerns are dwarfed when Mr. Smith announces that he's being transferred, and that the whole family will have to move to New York. Everyone is decimated by the news but determined to do what's required—until Tootie finally breaks down on Christmas Eve, and Mr. Smith realizes what St. Louis means to his family. Summer 1904 finds the Smiths still happily ensconced at 5135 Kensington Avenue and en route, en masse, to the World's Fair.

"There is no difficulty in describing [the film:] a completely delightful, homey, warmly human entertainment which has captured a nostalgic charm rarely if ever equaled on screen. . . . . In addition to its intrinsic fine quality, it has Judy Garland and Margaret O'Brien . . . all any picture needs for a box office gold rush. JG is delightful, plays her role with easy conviction, and is in exceptionally good voice." —HOLLYWOOD REPORTER

"Substantially produced . . . in superb Technicolor, the film captures interestingly and entertainingly a period in American life. Under expert direction . . . [the film] is acted most capably. Miss Garland is more charming than ever. Margaret O'Brien almost makes away with the film." —INDEPENDENT FILM JOURNAL

"Freed and Minnelli have contrived a charming attraction, magnificently mounted and produced. Like good showmen, they also remembered to keep it commercial. The attraction has four song numbers. Accelerating in popularity, of course, is 'The Trolley Song,' sung in best Garland by Judy. It is probably inevitable that little Margaret packages the picture neatly under her own label. She is practically resistant-proof, but, anyway, this reviewer didn't even try. He's a goner on Miss Garland, too, but that's a professional romance hardly new." —MOTION PICTURE DAILY

"With five out of sixteen of the first-run films on Broadway musicals, it is high time to do some . . . comparing, with a standard of excellence in mind. By any gauge, Meet Me in St. Louis would stand at the head of the list. Indeed, [it] ranks high with the musicals of all time." —THE NEW YORK TIMES

## NOTES

Whether considering contemporary success or historical resonance, *Meet Me in St. Louis* vies with *A Star is Born* (and perhaps *Easter Parade*) as second to *The Wizard of Oz* in terms of importance to the overall Garland film career. There were challenges along the way, but it turned out to be a charmed production. Continuing his pursuit of vehicles for Judy, Arthur Freed brought Sally Benson's "Kensington Stories" from the pages of the *New Yorker* to MGM and planned to musicalize the autobiographical memories about turn-of-the-century Midwestern life. To augment four or five traditional melodies, Hugh Martin (with Ralph Blane) wrote three new songs, all of which became standards. And despite wartime restrictions, the studio agreed to invest more than $100,000 in the creation of a "St. Louis Street" as setting and ambiance. Meanwhile, there were preproduction problems in staff and casting. A comparative novice with just two pictures to his credit, Vincente Minnelli came in to direct only after George Cukor went off to World War II. Robert Walker, Van Johnson, Gil Stratton, and Fred Brady were rumored to play "boy next door" John Truett before Tom Drake was assigned the part.

History has made much of the fact that Judy didn't want to do the picture, feeling it would be a mistake to regress from Jo Hayden and Lily Mars to once again appear as a teenager. Her dissatisfaction with the project can be traced even more pointedly to the early, meandering *St. Louis* scripts. As originally scripted, Esther Smith and her actions were alternately coy, simpering, or one-dimensional. Necessary adjustments were made to the scenario. Garland eventually learned to trust newcomer Minnelli and cope with his penchant for detail and "virtual" direction: "Vincente talks fast, and then he gets excited and stutters and doesn't finish his sentences—just says with a wave of his arm, 'Well, you know what I mean.'"

*Meet Me in St. Louis* rehearsed, prerecorded, and filmed between November 1943 and April 1944. Its schedule was plagued by absenteeism. Judy's penchant

**FROM LEFT:** An entire prelude sequence to "Lon's going-away party" was filmed for and dropped from *Meet Me in St. Louis* prior to its premiere. It began when Henry Daniels, Jr., and Judy offered an appreciative cup of punch to the baggage man (Victor Kilian), who was trundling the boy's college trunk to the train station. | "Esther" then helped her mother (Mary Astor) prepare for an evening out. | Family approval—and affection—were everywhere apparent as mother, father, and grandfather prepared to depart. *From left:* Harry Davenport, Lucille Bremer, Mary Astor, Margaret O'Brien, Joan Carroll, Henry Daniels, Jr., Leon Ames, and Judy.

for tardy arrivals and illness was matched or surpassed by the lengthy ailments that beset Mary Astor, Harry Davenport, Joan Carroll, and seven-year-old Margaret O'Brien, whose mother briefly pulled her out of the picture for a "rest"—and salary renegotiation. But the finished product painted a glowing portrait of what American family life could or should have been like, whether in 1903–04 or the present. Wherever shown throughout a war-torn world, the film was an uplifting reminder of what the resolution of the conflict would protect. The ensemble approach in no way deflected praise from the star of the movie. Columnist Hedda Hopper put it most squarely and succinctly: "It will be a long time before anyone equals Judy's performance and quality in *St. Louis*." Garland ever after cited the picture as one of her own personal favorites.

Not surprisingly, the film had its world premiere in St. Louis, on November 22, 1944. Ever-creative Howard Dietz originally suggested it first be screened on a show boat cruise from New Orleans up the Mississippi, with Judy on board to entertain and a full dress ball upon arrival in Missouri. *Meet Me in St. Louis* placed seventh on the 1944 "ten best" list of the National Board of Review. It was nominated for four Academy Awards: Best Screenplay, Best Color Cinematography, Best Score, and Best Song. The tune that earned the film its Best Song nomination, "The Trolley Song," latter produced hit records for the Pied Pipers (charting for fourteen weeks to number two), Judy (charting for eight weeks to number four), the King Sisters, Guy Lombardo, and Vaughn Monroe.

On a budget of $1.7 million, *St. Louis* grossed $7.5 million and provided MGM with its biggest box-office bonanza since *Ben-Hur* (1926). In 1994, *Meet Me in St. Louis* was added to the list of the National Film Registry for preservation in the Library of Congress.

LEFT: "Tootie" declaims, "I can do the cakewalk if Esther does it with me!"—and they do, "Under the Bamboo Tree." RIGHT: "Over the Bannister" is the romantic peak of the evening, as well as an amalgam of superlative direction, photography, lighting, and make-up in its visual presentation of Judy Garland.

## What They Said

"Because of my photographic memory, I was known on the lot as the one-take girl—two at the most. Nobody directed me very much; I just went out there and did what came naturally. So I hadn't reckoned on Vincente Minnelli. He made me do that first scene in St. Louis [eleven] times! I couldn't believe my ears. I was baffled and scared cross-eyed. When I went to my dressing room for lunch, I told my maid something dreadful had happened between my last picture and this one; I'd lost all my talent. I cried all over my makeup, and she almost had to push me back on that set. But then on the first try, it went off smooth as cream. Suddenly, I knew what he had wanted all along; I saw that if I was ever going to be any good, I had to let go of myself and be whatever character I was portraying. Vincente drove the whole cast, and in the end, I was more pleased with Meet Me in St. Louis than with anything else I had done up to that time." —JUDY GARLAND

"She's the most responsive actress I've ever worked with. When we have rehearsed a scene, I have only to say, 'Judy, I wish you could do it more . . .' and before I have finished, I know by her eyes she understands. And when we do the scene, then it has just the essence that I wanted for it." —VINCENTE MINNELLI

"The thing that was very touching to me was Judy's reaction to Margaret [O'Brien's] mother and aunt, who were always on the set. And they were pushing and pushing; I mean, she didn't even get to sit down. They wanted her in everybody's sight. And one time Judy stayed on the set and sat with three or four of us, talking . . . about Margaret, her age, and what she was doing. And Judy was quiet for a minute, and then she looked up and she said, 'You know, that little girl is not having any life. And I've been there, and I know what I'm talking about.'"

—MGM CONTRACT DANCER DOROTHY GILMORE RAYE

"She did treat me like her little sister, and I enjoyed looking up to her. She never gave me any advice as an actress, because she treated me sort of as an equal. And she was the type of person who didn't forget working with you. She always said hello, and we'd look back and laugh about funny incidents that happened on the set. [During St. Louis], I had lost my two front teeth, so they had some false teeth for me—like a little bridge. And in one scene, I was talking to Judy, and my teeth flew across the room and hit her in the head. And we always laughed about that. I think what made the movie a classic is that everybody got along like that, and everybody liked each other. So we really were a happy family, and it had to be that way for the movie to be successful. So Judy felt very at home in that movie. And she was very, very sweet to me." —MARGARET O'BRIEN

"I thought Judy was one of the best actresses I've ever come across—both technique-wise and innately—and just fabulous, all the way from comedy to tragedy. There are few parts she had that you can really get any idea of that. But she was marvelous with comedy . . . terribly sophisticated. She had a very brittle type of humor that you would expect to find on people who had been around for years and years, like [John] Barrymore. It's a sophistication you don't find in average people; it's the genius type of sophistication. And this when she was twenty-one." —TOM DRAKE

"Larry [Parks] and I used to go to parties where Judy would get up and sing, and invariably someone would ask her to do 'Boys and Girls Like You and Me.' The lyric is lovely, and the tune is simply ravishing. When I asked Judy about it, she said Rodgers and Hammerstein had written it for Oklahoma!, but it had been cut. Later, she had sung it in Meet Me in St. Louis, and it had been taken out again. Not long afterwards . . . in Take Me Out to the Ball Game, Frank Sinatra and I went for a walk on a pier, and he sang it to me. Then they cut it out of that picture!" —BETTY GARRETT

OPPOSITE BOTTOM FROM LEFT: A St. Louis music store provided a logical location—and window—to promote the picture. | One series of promotional photos showed a suddenly bang-less Judy with Margaret O'Brien and Tom Drake.

*"If MGM could have put Judy in every single movie they made, they would have!"*

So spoke actress June Allyson as she looked back on many years of association with Judy Garland—both as Metro-Goldwyn-Mayer cohort and lifelong "gal pal." Of course, it's the kind of statement that reads as outright hyperbole. But at the moment she made it in 1996, there was no mistaking Allyson's passion and sincerity, personally reflecting on the professional admiration and esteem in which Judy was held at MGM. When one then looks at the titles of films that were discussed, rumored, or wish-listed for Judy Garland across more than thirty-one years of motion-picture history (only fifteen of which she spent at Metro), it seems there's a good deal of heft to Allyson's words.

Granted, many of these properties were bandied about by syndicated columnists or referenced in the trade papers of the day (primarily *Daily Variety* and *Hollywood Reporter*). There were scores of entertainment reporters who had space to fill multiple times per week, whether their work was regarded as serious journalism or gossip mongering. Thus, any news was fair game, and publicists, agents, and managers worked beyond overtime to "plant" whatever they could on behalf of their employers.

It's also important to note that the major studios—especially during the 1930s and 1940s—released dozens of movies every year. As a result, almost any idea, story, scenario, article, book, play, song, biography, or news item was considered possible motion picture fodder, especially if a company could associate it with a star already under contract. In the process, countless properties were investigated, negotiated, acquired, announced, developed, put aside, revitalized, dropped, begun, revised, or canceled.

Given Judy's combination of talent and box office acumen—and the hold she never lost on the hearts of the general public—it's not surprising to see the scope of possible films for which she was (on some level, at some point) discussed or under consideration. And beyond the obvious issues of overbooking and conflicting schedules, there were specific, valid reasons that a number of the projects never materialized for her. Paramount among these were her three pregnancies, her own health issues, the desire MGM had to keep her (and her film profits) for themselves, and the manipulations of husbands and managers—who, it seems, frequently put their own ambitions and egos ahead of whatever might have been good for Garland.

More than a hundred motion pictures are referenced in the following pages. Some seem incomprehensible as Garland movies; others would appear to be so right for her that their omission from Judy's filmography is regrettable. And while one can't even pretend that the following list is complete, it may well inspire further research and serve as a good foundation on which to build.

**NOTES:** As carefully as could be determined, the following citations are presented in chronological order, and a specific year is referenced whenever possible. Additionally, several of these properties came much closer than others to fruition as vehicles for Judy Garland; their entries are more extensive.

**NP** = Never Produced.

## The 1930s

### THE UNEXPECTED FATHER
**(Universal, 1932):**
Garland—then still Frances Gumm—was considered for the role played by Cora Sue Collins in this Slim Summerville/ ZaSu Pitts feature.

### BABES IN HOLLYWOOD
**(MGM, 1934):**
As noted in the Los Angeles *Times* on February 13: "Immediately upon the completion of their present stage engagement, Jane, Frances, and Jimmie Gumm will appear in [this] two-reel picture." **NP**

### THE GREAT ZIEGFELD
**(Universal, 1935; produced and released by MGM, 1936):**
The Garland Sisters were signed to appear in this Universal biopic in early 1935. When the nearly bankrupt studio sold the property to MGM in March, the trio was dropped from the picture.

### PADDY O'DAY
**(Fox, 1935):**
Judy was submitted for a cameo role in this Jane Withers feature.

### OUR GANG FOLLIES OF 1936
**(Hal Roach, 1935):**
MGM agreed to loan Judy to Roach for this two-reel musical, as the picture was to be released under Metro's aegis. The studio pulled her from the cast at the last minute.

### THIS TIME IT'S LOVE
**(MGM, 1935/36):**
In October 1935, Judy's father wrote to friends in Lancaster, CA, and mentioned this as the title of Judy's first feature under her new MGM contract. She was to play a supporting role opposite Buddy Ebsen; the picture would star Robert Montgomery and Jessie Matthews. **NP**

### BORN TO DANCE
**(MGM, 1936):**
Signed to write the songs for *Born to Dance*, Cole Porter made the following entry in his diary on March 10, 1936: "[At MGM,] I heard to my great joy that the picture will be played by Allan Jones opposite Eleanor Powell, Sid Silvers opposite Una Merkel, Buddy Ebsen opposite Judy Garland, and Frances Langford to play the jilted society girl." By the time the movie was produced, Jimmy Stewart had replaced Jones, Bruce had moved into the part of the society girl, Langford appeared as a production singer, and the only child's role was filled by five-year-old Juanita Quigley.

### CORN-HUSKING MUSICAL
**(working title; Twentieth Century Fox, 1937):**
A proposed sequel to *Pigskin Parade*, in which Judy would reprise her role of "Sairy Dodd." **NP**

### ROSALIE
**(MGM, 1937):**
According to MGM Music Department paperwork, Judy did an ultimately-unused prerecording of the song "Who Knows?" for the film on August 27, 1937.

### GONE WITH THE WIND
**(Selznick Pictures International, 1939):**
A November 26, 1937 memo from producer David O. Selznick notes his interest in testing Judy for the role of Carreen O'Hara, Scarlett's youngest sister. In 1939, the part went to Ann Rutherford.

### THE SARAH BERNHARDT STORY
**(MGM, circa 1937/38):**
Judy would have played the young Bernhardt. **NP**

### THE FANNY BRICE STORY
**(MGM, circa 1937/38):**
Judy would have played the young Brice. **NP** but please see *The Fanny Brice Story* under the 1950s on page 216.

### MOLLY, BLESS HER
**(MGM, circa 1938):**

A biopic about MGM's late and cherished character actress Marie Dressler, starring Sophie Tucker. Judy would have played Dressler as a child. **NP**

### THE CAPTURED SHADOW
**(MGM, circa 1938):**

An F. Scott Fitzgerald screenplay (based on his *Saturday Evening Post* story of December 29, 1928) to star Judy, Mickey Rooney, and Freddie Bartholomew. **NP**

### AMERICAN SYMPHONY
**(circa 1938): NP**

### WONDER CHILD
**(circa 1938): NP**

### TOPSY & EVA
**(MGM, circa 1938/39):**

Mervyn LeRoy planned to produce this as a vehicle for Judy and Betty Jaynes. It was mentioned again as a Technicolor costarring project for Judy and Shirley Temple when the latter was briefly under contract to Metro in 1941. It was referenced again for Judy (with no indicated costar) both in the late 1940s and to follow her participation in *Show Boat* in 1951. **NP**

### LOOKING AFTER SANDY
**(MGM, 1939):**

A drama with songs, based upon the 1914 novel by Margaret Turnbull. Judy was to play a teenage orphan who wins the hearts of a large American family; she would costar with Freddie Bartholomew. **NP**

### SUSAN AND GOD
**(MGM, 1939):**

A film adaptation of the 1937 Broadway play, with Garland as the daughter of Greer Garson and Fredric March. When ultimately produced in 1940, the picture was cast with March, Joan Crawford, and Rita Quigley.

### HIGH SCHOOL (MGM, 1939):

With Mickey Rooney. **NP**; it's possible that this might have been a working title for what became *Strike Up the Band*, but no contemporary information suggests it.

### DEAR OLD BROADWAY
**(MGM, 1939):**

With Mickey Rooney, in which he and Judy were to celebrate the past greats of the theater. **NP**

### BROADWAY MELODY OF 1939/
### BROADWAY MELODY OF 1940
**(MGM, 1939):**

Released in 1940 with Eleanor Powell, Fred Astaire, and George Murphy. It's uncertain as to whether Garland was envisioned for a specific role or would have appeared as an added attraction/"special guest star."

**FROM TOP:** Though Judy and Sophie Tucker worked together in two 1937 feature films, their pairing in the unproduced *Molly, Bless Her* never happened—nor did Judy's appearance in the title role of a 1950s Tucker biopic. | Judy and Freddie Bartholomew at the premiere of *Marie Antoinette* (July 8, 1938). They were rumored to be paired onscreen in the late 1930s in *The Captured Shadow* and *Looking After Sandy* but only made *Listen, Darling* together. | Mother and daughter? Judy visits Greer Garson on the set of 1939's *Pride and Prejudice*. They were then tentatively penciled-in as two of the stars of *Susan and God*.

# The 1940s

**THE YOUNGEST PROFESSION**
**(MGM, 1940):**

With Walter Pidgeon as her father, Judy was to lead a pack of teenagers who collect celebrity autographs. When produced in 1943, the film roles were filled by Edward Arnold and Virginia Weidler.

**THERE THEY GROW**
**(MGM, 1940):**

Described as "a sort of *Babes on Sound-Stages*," costarring Mickey Rooney; to be directed by Norman Taurog. **NP**

**NO, NO, NANETTE**
**(MGM, 1940):**

An adaptation of the 1925 Broadway musical, costarring Mickey Rooney. A much revised version of the show was filmed as *Tea for Two* and released by Warner Bros. in 1950. It starred Doris Day and Gordon MacRae.

**NATIONAL VELVET**
**(MGM, circa 1940):**

Irish horse-racing drama, eventually produced by MGM with Elizabeth Taylor in 1944.

**GOOD NEWS**
**(MGM, 1940):**

A film adaptation of the 1927 Broadway musical, reuniting the cast of *Babes in Arms*: Judy, Mickey Rooney, Betty Jaynes, Douglas McPhail, and June Preisser. (It was planned to interpolate the new song, "Our Love Affair," into the *Good News* score; this was ultimately heard instead in *Strike Up the Band*.) The project was reconsidered in 1943 for Judy, Rooney, and Desi Arnaz, and finally produced in 1947 with June Allyson and Peter Lawford.

**FUNNY FACE**
**(MGM, 1940):**

With Mickey Rooney—an adaptation of the 1927 Broadway musical that starred Fred and Adele Astaire. **NP**; in 1957, Paramount produced a movie musical that utilized this title and several songs from the score; the storyline was completely different from that of the stage show.

**POT O'GOLD**
**(United Artists, 1940):**

Producer James Roosevelt and director George Marshall hoped to borrow Judy for this independent motion picture in which she'd play opposite James Stewart. Released in 1941 with Stewart and Paulette Goddard.

**LADY BE GOOD**
**(MGM, 1940):**

With Mickey Rooney. Released in 1941 with Ann Sothern and Robert Young.

**THOUSANDS CHEER**
**(MGM, 1940):**

Touted as "Judy's first glamour role" but not produced until 1943 when Kathryn Grayson played the lead. (Garland prominently figured in the all-star, army camp show finale.)

**KATHLEEN**
**(MGM, 1940):**

Produced in 1941 for Shirley Temple.

**THE BIG TIME**
**(MGM, 1940):**

Costarring Jimmy Stewart, Lana Turner, Walter Pidgeon, and Rags Ragland. *The Big Time* was one of the working titles for Judy's *For Me and My Gal* (1942), but this seems to be an entirely different project. **NP**

**THE CORPORAL'S COUSIN KATIE**
**(MGM, 1941):**

With George Murphy. **NP**

**EIGHT GIRLS AND A HORSE**
**(MGM, 1941):**

With Kathryn Grayson, to be produced by Edgar Selwyn. **NP**

**CLAUDIA**
**(David O. Selznick, 1941):**

Judy wanted to play the title role in the film adaptation of this successful Broadway play by Rose Franken. When the vehicle was brought to the screen in 1943 by Twentieth Century Fox, Dorothy McGuire recreated her stage triumph in that part.

**PANAMA HATTIE**
**(MGM, 1941):**

With Ann Sothern, Mickey Rooney, Jack Oakie, and Shirley Temple. Released in 1942 with Sothern, Red Skelton, Lena Horne, Rags Ragland, Ben Blue, and Marsha Hunt.

**VERY WARM FOR MAY**
**(MGM, 1941):**

Judy, Ray McDonald, and Marta Eggerth were to be teamed in this screen adaptation of the 1939 Broadway musical, produced by Arthur Freed. In 1944, Jack Cummings produced it as a less faithful version of the show, retitled *Broadway Rhythm*. It starred George Murphy, Ginny Simms, and Gloria DeHaven.

**FEELING LIKE A MILLION**
**(MGM, circa 1941):**

Built around the song of the same title (used in *Broadway Melody of 1938*); Tony Martin was cited as potential costar. **NP**

### BABES IN HOLLYWOOD
**(MGM, 1941):**

Per the contemporary press blurb, "a 'local color' story of all the youngsters who come to Hollywood in hopes of making it." With Mickey Rooney. **NP**

### DRAGON SEED
**(MGM, 1942):**

A planned adaptation of the contemporary Pearl S. Buck novel about the Japanese invasion of a Chinese village. When expressing her desire to do the film, Judy gleefully noted, "I wouldn't look like Mickey Rooney's girlfriend!" Produced in 1944, starring Katharine Hepburn.

### JUMBO
**(MGM, early 1940s):**

A screen adaptation of the 1935 Broadway musical, costarring Mickey Rooney; reconsidered in 1948 and 1950 for Judy and Frank Sinatra. In every instance, Jimmy Durante was slated to recreate his stage role. (Finally produced in 1962 with Durante, Doris Day, and Stephen Boyd.)

### THE STORY OF GABY DES LYS
**(MGM, 1943):**

A biopic of the French actress and dancer, developed for Judy by Arthur Freed. **NP**

### THE MOON VINE
**(MGM, 1943):**

A 1943 Broadway play, suggested as a film for Judy by Arthur Freed.

### ANCHORS AWEIGH
**(MGM, circa 1943):**

With Gene Kelly. Produced in 1945 with Kelly, Kathryn Grayson, and Frank Sinatra.

### THE BELLE OF NEW YORK
**(MGM, 1943):**

With Fred Astaire and a new score by Richard Rodgers & Oscar Hammerstein II; to be directed by Rouben Mamoulian and adapted from the 1897 Broadway stage play. Early scripts were written for the project by Chester Erskine (1943; including a modern-day prologue/epilogue), Irving Brecher (1944, 1945, 1946, 1947), and Sally Benson (1947). By then, the score was scheduled to be written by Harry Warren and Johnny Mercer and include two of their Garland numbers deleted from *The Harvey Girls:* "My Intuition" and "Hayride." During the period of Astaire's retirement (circa 1946–1947), Arthur Freed planned to make the picture with Judy and either Van Johnson or Peter Lawford. *The Belle of New York* was finally produced with Astaire opposite Vera Ellen in 1951; the Mercer/Warren score included no discarded *Harvey Girls* material.

### VALLEY OF DECISION
**(MGM, circa 1944):**

With Peter Lawford. Produced in 1945 with Greer Garson and Gregory Peck.

### SHOW BOAT
**(MGM, 1944):**

With Garland as Magnolia, opposite either Gene Kelly or James Melton; reconsidered in 1945 with Garland opposite Kelly and, in support, Gloria DeHaven, Walter Huston, and Agnes Moorehead. Reconsidered in 1949, with Garland as Julie and a supporting cast to include Frank Morgan and either Mario Lanza or Howard Keel. By early 1950, the project was very much in preproduction. The role of Julie had been expanded for Garland (by, among others, scenarist John Lee Mahin). In addition to new dramatic scenes, she was slotted to offer a reprise of "Ol' Man River" and the interpolated "Why Was I Born?" as well as "Can't Help Lovin' Dat Man" and "Bill." The proposed

FROM LEFT, OPPOSITE: Virginia Weidler reenacts her starring role in *The Youngest Profession* while visiting Judy on the set of *Girl Crazy* (1943). Weidler's film had been suggested for Garland three years earlier. | Over the years, *Jumbo* was rumored to be in the works for Judy, Jimmy Durante, and either Mickey Rooney or Frank Sinatra. She and "Schnozzola" are shown here during a 1945 radio rehearsal. | At least eight feature films (and one suggested full-length cartoon) would have coupled the voices of Garland and Sinatra between 1943 and the mid-1960s. The two preeminent singers are shown here while preparing for a 1946 broadcast with Phil Silvers; he would later star in Broadway's *Do Re Mi* (1960), which had been developed as a Garland screen vehicle a decade earlier.

finale of the picture involved the entire cast in reprise of: Why Do I Love You?" On September 29, 1950, Jane Powell was scheduled to complete *Royal Wedding*, which meant that Judy's current MGM suspension would no longer be in effect. Producer Arthur Freed and director George Sidney requested that she report to them as of that day for conferences and preliminary work on *Show Boat*. Instead, MGM canceled Garland's contract, and she left MGM. *Show Boat* was released in 1951 with Ava Gardner as Julie (dubbed by Annette Warren), Kathryn Grayson as Magnolia, and Howard Keel, Joe E. Brown, Agnes Moorehead, and Marge and Gower Champion.

## YOLANDA AND THE THIEF
### (MGM, 1944):
With Fred Astaire. Produced in 1945 with Astaire and Lucille Bremer; Judy had been convinced to do *The Harvey Girls* instead.

## WEEKEND AT THE WALDORF
### (MGM, 1944):
Judy was among those discussed to head-up the all-star cast for this remake of *Grand Hotel* (1932). As released in 1945, the film starred Lana Turner, Ginger Rogers, Walter Pidgeon, and Van Johnson.

## SARATOGA TRUNK
### (Warner Bros., circa 1944):
Rumored as a loan-out to Warner Bros. for Judy. Later made at that studio with Gary Cooper and Ingrid Bergman for release in 1946.

## THE RAZOR'S EDGE
### (Twentieth Century Fox, 1945):
Fox's Darryl F. Zanuck wanted to borrow Judy for the dramatic role of Sophie—an idea endorsed by director George Cukor. (Garland herself thought the part would provide a welcome challenge.) But by the time the film adaptation of the W. Somerset Maugham novel went into production, a loan out couldn't be arranged, Cukor had been supplanted by Edmund Goulding, and Anne Baxter was cast in the role of Sophie instead. Fox released the picture in 1946.

## FOREVER
### (MGM, 1946):
With Tyrone Power, from the novella by Mildred Cram. Later rumored for Judy opposite Gregory Peck, with songs by Rodgers & Hammerstein. **NP**

## TAKE ME OUT TO THE BALL GAME
(MGM, 1946):

Garland was Arthur Freed's suggestion for the film's leading lady, replacing Kathryn Grayson, who had been suggested by Gene Kelly in a conscious effort to reunite the two of them with Frank Sinatra. (This would echo the trio's earlier success in *Anchors Aweigh*). But by the time filming began, Esther Williams was playing the female lead. MGM released *Take Me Out to the Ball Game* in 1949; its original working title had been *In the Good Old Summertime*.

## YOUNG BESS
(MGM, mid-1940s):

A biographical treatment of the early life of Elizabeth I, to costar Judy and James Mason. Eventually produced with Jean Simmons and Stewart Granger and released in 1953.

## THE SHOCKING MISS PILGRIM
(Twentieth Century Fox, 1946):

Garland was the first choice to star in this original musical comedy. When Fox was again unable to borrow her from MGM, the role went to Betty Grable; the film was released in 1947.

## CIMARRON
(MGM, 1946):

Judy and Gene Kelly were considered to head the cast of this musical remake of the 1931 Academy Award-winning Best Picture, originally based on an Edna Ferber novel. Ultimately, Metro waited until 1960 to release a second (non-musical) version of *Cimarron*, starring Glenn Ford, Maria Schell, and Anne Baxter.

## ROMANCE ON THE HIGH SEAS
(Warner Bros., 1947):

Jack Warner hoped to borrow Judy for the role in this picture that finally went to Doris Day. (Along the way, the part was also discussed for Betty Hutton, Hutton's sister Marian, and Lauren Bacall.) The finished film was a 1948 Warner Bros. release.

## PRIDE AND PREJUDICE
(MGM, 1947):

A musicalization of the Jane Austen novel, which MGM planned to film on location in England. With direction by Vincente Minnelli and a screenplay by Sidney Sheldon, Judy would have costarred with Peter Lawford, Kathryn Grayson, June Allyson, and Lucille Bremer. **NP**

## FINIAN'S RAINBOW
(MGM, 1947):

Arthur Freed hoped to acquire film rights to the 1947 Broadway musical for Garland and Gene Kelly, with Mickey Rooney as Og the Leprechaun and Barry Fitzgerald as Finian. Several years later, it was rumored that the property would be produced instead as a feature-length cartoon, with Garland singing opposite Frank Sinatra. The show finally came to the screen as a live-action Warner Bros. release in 1968, starring Fred Astaire, Petula Clark, Tommy Steele, and Don Francks.

## ROBERTA
(MGM, 1948):

An intended remake of the 1935 RKO musical film, starring Judy with Gene Kelly, Frank Sinatra, and Betty Garrett. Produced as *Lovely to Look At* (1952) with Kathryn Grayson, Howard Keel, Red Skelton, and Ann Miller.

## PEG O'MY HEART
(MGM, 1948):

Once finished with his role in MGM's *A Date with Judy*, Robert Stack was supposed to join Garland for this remake of the 1922 and 1933 films of a 1912 Broadway success. (The original play and first film had starred Laurette Taylor; the second film was built around Marion Davies.) **NP**

## UNTITLED OUTTAKES PROJECT
(MGM, circa 1948/49):

A collection of musical numbers that had been deleted before release from the studio's motion pictures was assembled as a potential feature film by George Murphy. Shown privately. **NP**

## CABBAGES & KINGS
(MGM, 1948):

With Fred Astaire, as a follow-up to *Easter Parade*. **NP**

## MISS LIBERTY
(MGM, 1949):

A proposed film musical of the unsuccessful Irving Berlin/Moss Hart/Robert Sherwood Broadway show. **NP**

## THE U.S.O. STORY
**(RKO, 1950):**

Judy was proposed as the headliner of an all-star cast, gathered to both celebrate and tell the back story of the performers who had been sent around the world to entertain servicemen and women under the aegis of the United Service Organizations.

## ANNA & THE KING OF SIAM
**(Twentieth Century Fox, 1950):**

A proposed musicalization of the 1946 Twentieth Century Fox film, with songs by Rodgers & Hammerstein. Retitled *The King and I*, the project was ultimately produced on Broadway in 1951 as a vehicle for Gertrude Lawrence, with Yul Brynner in his breakthrough role as "The King."

## THE DUCHESS OF IDAHO
**(MGM, 1950):**

Judy was considered for a guest appearance in this Esther Williams/Van Johnson musical; one possible routine would have teamed her with Fred Astaire and Eleanor Powell for a dance specialty. In the end, Powell worked alone, as did additional guest Lena Horne.

## GIVE A GIRL A BREAK
**(MGM, 1950):**

Judy and Gene Kelly were discussed as a possible team for this backstage saga. When produced in 1953, the film starred Marge and Gower Champion, Debbie Reynolds, and Bob Fosse.

## STRICTLY DISHONORABLE
**(MGM, 1950):**

Judy was discussed as possible casting opposite Ezio Pinza in this heavily revised remake of a 1931 Universal release. By the time the film went into production, she had left MGM, and the role of Isabelle Perry was played by Janet Leigh. Released in 1951.

## UNTITLED WESTERN
**(Paramount, 1950):**

This vehicle was conceptualized as a showcase for Judy, her frequent radio costar Bing Crosby, and contemporary film/TV/radio sensation William Boyd "as" Hopalong Cassidy. **NP**

## CAUSE FOR ALARM
**(MGM, 1951):**

According to legend, producer Tom Lewis wanted Judy for this drama. In retaliation, Mrs. Tom Lewis retained a lawyer who accused her husband of discrimination because he didn't cast his wife in the part. In the end, the role in question was played by Loretta Young—Mrs. Tom Lewis.

## KISS ME, KATE
**(Independent British production, 1951):**

Judy's stage success at the London Palladium led to rumors that she would star in a British-made film version of Cole Porter's triumphant 1948 Broadway musical. Ultimately, the motion picture was produced by MGM in Hollywood in 1953 and starred Howard Keel, Kathryn Grayson, and Ann Miller.

## FAMOUS
**(Paramount, 1951):**

Another suggested teaming with Bing Crosby. The property was ultimately cast with Crosby and Jane Wyman, retitled *Just for You*, and released in 1952.

## THE JANE FROMAN STORY
**(Twentieth Century Fox, circa 1951):**

A biopic of the beloved singer, this property was retitled *With a Song in My Heart* and cast with Susan Hayward (1953).

## BLOODHOUNDS OF BROADWAY
**(Twentieth Century Fox, 1951):**

Producer George Jessel planned this as a vehicle for Judy and Scott Brady. Released in 1952, the finished product teamed Brady with Mitzi Gaynor.

## THE JUDY GARLAND STORY
**(an independent production from Louis B. Mayer, 1952):**

Judy's Palace Theatre comeback led to much renewed interest in her future film plans. Mayer, who'd left MGM in 1951, set himself up as an independent producer and wanted to cast Garland in her own life story. **NP**

## PAINT YOUR WAGON
**(an independent production from Louis B. Mayer, circa 1952):**

One of two properties Mayer took with him when he departed MGM, *Paint Your Wagon* had been a successful Broadway musical in 1951. He envisioned Garland as its cinematic lead, while hoping for Gary Cooper to play the principal male role. *Paint Your Wagon* was finally produced by Paramount and released in 1969, a dozen years after Mayer's death. It starred Lee Marvin, Clint Eastwood, and Jean Seberg.

## THE STUBBORN WOOD
**(circa 1951/52):**

Screen rights for this 1948 novel by Emily Harvin were held by Paul Henreid, who wanted to do the film with Judy. She would have played a woman whose husband has her committed to an asylum to get her out of his life. **NP**

FROM LEFT: Frequent radio costars Judy and Bing Crosby never worked on a film together, although they were rumored for everything from a 1950 western to a 1962 Broadway adaptation. Here they visit June Allyson on the set of MGM's *Her Highness and the Bellboy* (1945); Allyson later would star in *Good News*, a vehicle first intended for Judy. But their appearance together as sisters in a musical *Pride and Prejudice* didn't material- ize. | In June 1952, The Friars' Club celebrated Judy's theatrical comeback. Offers for her screen return at that time included *Bloodhounds of Broadway*, which was to be produced by long-time cohort George Jessel.

### DO RE MI
#### (Columbia, circa 1952):

Scenarist Garson Kanin suggested Judy as the star of his original story about a young recording artist. Per Kanin: "Surround her with the passé mugs, Edward G. Robinson, George Raft, etc., give her a snappy romantic leading boy, and then spice it up with specialty appearances by top recording artists such as Eddie Fisher, Jo Stafford, Peggy Lee, Joni James, etc." The property was later reconceived as a Broadway musical, which opened in December 1960 and starred Phil Silvers and Nancy Walker. Nancy Dussault was cast in a considera- bly revamped version of the Garland role.

### 14 FIFTH AVENUE
#### (MGM, circa 1952):

This screenplay by Sally Benson may have been the same property as *Meet Me in New York*, a sequel to *Meet Me in St. Louis*. **NP**

### BRIGADOON
#### (MGM, circa 1952):

Judy would have been reunited with Gene Kelly in this Arthur Freed/Vincente Minnelli film adaptation of the 1947 Broadway hit. The role was later rumored for Kathryn Grayson before being finally cast with Cyd Charisse. The picture was released in 1954.

### SOME OF THESE DAYS
#### (circa 1953):

The story of entertainer Sophie Tucker, "the last of the red hot mamas." Judy was Tucker's choice to play the role. **NP**

### THE GIRL IN PINK TIGHTS
#### (Twentieth Century Fox, 1953):

Judy was suggested for this remake of Betty Grable's *Coney Island*, opposite Frank Sinatra. The role was later rejected by Marilyn Monroe and considered for Sheree North before the film was canceled. **NP**

### THE FANNY BRICE STORY
#### (mid-1950s):

Producer Ray Stark originally planned to make a musical film about his celebrated mother-in-law and suggested Garland for the role. (Brice had died in 1951.) Isobel Lennart later adapted her screenplay to accommodate the story as a stage musical, and Stark cast Barbra Streisand as Brice in *Funny Girl* (1964). The show became a Columbia motion picture in 1968.

### THE HELEN MORGAN STORY
#### (Warner Bros., mid-1950s):

Jack Warner wanted Judy to play the title role in this musical biography, but she rejected the script: "There'll be no more sad endings for me." The part then went to Ann Blyth, opposite Paul Newman. Though a soprano like Morgan, Blyth had her singing voice dubbed throughout the picture by pop recording star Gogi Grant. According to Blyth, Grant possessed the kind of Garland sound that Jack Warner was determined to have for the film. It was released in 1957.

## BUTTERFIELD 8
### (MGM, mid-1950s):

From the novel by John O'Hara; per Sid Luft, Garland was considered for a film drama of the story. It was later played by Elizabeth Taylor, who won a 1960 Best Actress Academy Award for her efforts.

## CAROUSEL
### (Twentieth Century Fox, circa 1955):

Garland and Frank Sinatra were discussed as a potential screen team for this film version of the 1945 Broadway musical. He was ultimately cast opposite Shirley Jones, but left the production to be replaced by Gordon MacRae.

## THE THREE FACES OF EVE
### (Twentieth Century Fox, 1956):

Scenarist Nunnally Johnson actively pursued Judy for the role which later won Joanne Woodward a Best Actress Academy Award for 1957.

## ALICE ADAMS
### (RKO, 1956):

A musical version of the 1935 Katharine Hepburn picture that was reconceived for Garland. Eager to have Judy for the project, letters of intent and preliminary contracts were drawn up by the studio, but they refused to take on Sid Luft as the film's producer. **NP**

## BORN IN WEDLOCK
### (1956):

Judy and Sid Luft held the screen rights for this Margaret Echard novel for many years. At one point, it was announced that they would make the film in England, with Dirk Bogarde playing opposite Garland. Luft also announced plans to produce the story on stage, starring an unknown, and then film the vehicle with Judy. Tentatively retitled *Gaiety Girl*, the property told the story of a young widow whose uncertain stage career is interrupted when she meets a lonely lawyer. He provides a home for her and her two daughters, scandalizing the small Southern town in which he lives. **NP**

## CARELESS LOVE
### (mid-1950s):

A movie musical based on the song "Frankie & Johnny." **NP**

## MANHATTAN TOWER
### (Paramount [?], 1956):

A suggested movie musical expansion of Gordon Jenkins' concept record album, starring Judy, Bing Crosby, and Bob Hope. **NP**

## SPRING REUNION
### (United Artists, 1957):

The role suggested for Judy was later played by Betty Hutton.

## ALL ABOUT EVE
### (Twentieth Century Fox, 1957):

This screen musicalization of the classic Joe Mankiewicz script was planned with Garland in the Bette Davis role and Peggy King as Eve. Cole Porter was suggested as composer/lyricist. **NP**, although the property was later mounted as the 1970 Broadway musical *Applause*, which starred Lauren Bacall and featured a score by Charles Strouse and Lee Adams.

## SOUTH PACIFIC
### (Twentieth Century Fox, 1958):

Early in the planning stages for a film adaptation of the 1949 Broadway success, Judy was discussed for the Mary Martin role, and Mario Lanza was mentioned as a candidate to play opposite her. The movie was ultimately made with Mitzi Gaynor and Rossano Brazzi; Brazzi's songs were dubbed by Giorgio Tozzi.

# The 1960s

## A TREE GROWS IN BROOKLYN
### (Twentieth Century Fox, 1961):

A film version of the 1951 Broadway musical, rumored for Judy at different times between the late 1950s and early 1960s. The list of potential costars alternated between Frank Sinatra, Polly Bergen, Robert Goulet, and Marilyn Monroe, but in any of the variations, Garland was always cast as "Aunt Cissy," the role sung on stage by Shirley Booth. **NP**

## BY THE BEAUTIFUL SEA
### (MGM, 1961):

A film version of the 1954 Broadway musical, rumored for Judy at different times between the late 1950s and early 1960s. She would have played the role sung onstage by Shirley Booth; Bing Crosby was set to costar in the picture. The project was envisioned as a film reunion of sorts, with Chuck Walters as director and Roger Edens as producer. **NP**

## IRMA LA DOUCE
### (United Artists, 1963):

In 1961, director Billy Wilder envisioned Judy as the star of the screen version of this 1960 Broadway musical. He planned to rewrite the title role of a dancing Parisian prostitute into a singing Parisian prostitute. (Elizabeth Seal did the part on stage.) By the time the film came to the screen two years later, all the songs had been dropped from the script—and Irma was played by Shirley MacLaine, opposite Jack Lemmon.

## A HANDFUL OF DUST
### (Independent British production, circa 1962/63):

Judy and David Niven were possible casting for this screen adaptation of a story by Evelyn Waugh. The property wasn't actually filmed until 1988.

## LAURETTE
### (circa 1962):

A biopic about legendary stage actress Laurette Taylor. Both George Cukor and Taylor's daughter, Marguerite Courtney, championed Garland for the role. Discussions about the project continued throughout the 1960s. **NP**

## GYPSY
### (Warner Bros., 1962):

The creators of the 1959 stage musical were purportedly delighted when they heard the screen version of the show might star Judy Garland. Instead, the role done so brilliantly on Broadway by Ethel Merman was performed in the film by Rosalind Russell.

## IT'S A MAD, MAD, MAD, MAD WORLD
### (United Artists, 1963):

It was rumored that Judy would be one of several dozen stars who were to make cameo appearances in this Stanley Kramer production.

## SAY IT WITH MUSIC
### (MGM, 1963):

The intended grand finale of several careers, this feature was initially announced as a lavish Irving Berlin MGM musical, to be produced by Arthur Freed, directed by Vincente Minnelli, and supervised by Roger Edens. At first, Judy was slated to costar opposite Frank Sinatra; they would play specific (or implied) versions of Berlin and his wife, Ellin. But the songwriter railed against a retelling of his life story and preferred to write new music and lyrics for an original scenario. Sinatra bowed out, and Garland was then penciled in for a guest appearance, possibly in a duet medley with Ethel Merman. Subsequently, six years and at least six screenwriters failed to produce a workable script for the project. It was completely flushed in 1969 when new studio head James Aubrey decided that the renewed 1960s box-office potential for screen musicals had come to an end. (By that point, Edens was long off the picture, as was Minnelli. The latter had been replaced by Blake Edwards, whose fiancée Julie Andrews had joined the cast.) **NP**

## THE UNSINKABLE MOLLY BROWN
### (MGM, 1964):

Judy originally campaigned to do this Meredith Willson musical on the London stage in early 1961, and her agreement to do the show was predicated on the condition that MGM later star her in the motion picture. Ultimately, the part was played on screen by Debbie Reynolds, although it had been earlier slated for Shirley Jones and Shirley MacLaine.

## NEW YORK TOWN
### (1963):

Garland was mentioned as a potential "special guest" in this Rosalind Russell/Jane Wyman/Troy Donahue/Sandra Dee vehicle, and she was scheduled to sing two songs: "Why Was I Born" and "Chicago Can't Touch New York." **NP**, although Russell and Dee later teamed for the 1967 Universal film, *Rosie*.

## LITTLE ME
### (Embassy Pictures, circa 1963/64):

According to contemporary trade papers, Garland wanted to play female lead "Belle Poitrine" in a film version of the 1962 Neil Simon/Cy Coleman/Carolyn Leigh stage musical. The property was later announced as a motion picture which would star Donald O'Connor as the men in Belle's life. (Those roles had been done on Broadway by Sid Caesar). **NP**

## THIS PROPERTY IS CONDEMNED
### (Paramount, 1966):

Adapted from a one-act play by Tennessee Williams; Judy was discussed for the role of Natalie Wood's mother, ultimately played by Kate Reid.

## THE NIGHT OF THE GENERALS
### (Columbia, 1967):

Circa 1965–66, producer Sam Spiegel considered Garland for a cameo role in this World War II suspense thriller.

## LITTLE BIG MAN
### (National General Pictures, 1970):

Circa 1965–66, Garland was mentioned in Hollywood columns as possible casting in this Stuart Millar production. They had worked together on *I Could Go On Singing*.

## THE GRADUATE
### (Embassy Pictures/United Artists, 1967):

Director Mike Nichols was a Garland friend and admirer, which may be the reason her name turns up in the casting history of this classic comedy. The role of Mrs. Robinson—for which Nichols also considered Doris Day and Patricia Neal (and about which he was approached by Joan Crawford and Ava Gardner)—was finally played by Anne Bancroft.

## THE AIMEE SEMPLE MCPHERSON STORY
### (1967):

In March 1967, Garland told columnist Radie Harris that she wanted to do a biopic about the famous evangelist and her relationship with her mother—the latter role to be cast with Bette Davis. **NP**, although Davis would later play that part in a 1976 *Hallmark Hall of Fame* teleplay with Faye Dunaway as Aimee.

## PIAF
### (circa 1967/68):

George Cukor would have directed this biopic starring Garland as the classic French chanteuse. For some of the musical numbers, Cukor planned to film Garland in actual concert, performing excerpts from the Piaf songbook. **NP**, although Piaf's story was later told in *La Vie en Rose* (2007), which won a Best Actress Academy Award for Marion Cotillard as Piaf.

## MAME
### (Warner Bros., 1974):

In early 1968, Judy lobbied to appear in the Broadway company of this Jerry Herman musical after its original star, Angela Lansbury, left to take the show on tour. The producers' concerns about Garland's health and stability precluded Judy's employment, although at least twice in 1967 there had been press statements about her desire to do the movie as well. "The field's still wide open," she told a Hartford interviewer, and added, "The role's the kind that contains a tremendous excitement to me as a performer." When *Mame* came to the screen in 1974, she was played by Lucille Ball.

## THE JUDY GARLAND STORY
### (Embassy Pictures, 1968):

Boston newspaperman Ken Mayer championed Judy during the last year of her life and approached producer Joseph E. Levine about producing her screen biography. **NP**, although later TV movies told at least parts of the Garland saga: *Rainbow* (NBC, 1978) and the Emmy-Award winning *Life with Judy Garland: Me and My Shadows* (ABC, 2001).

## A DAY IN THE LIFE OF JUDY GARLAND
### (1969):

A proposed film documentary which planned to follow Judy through a performance day, preparing for and then delivering a concert. **NP**, although similar footage, taken during Garland's March 1969 appearances in Malmo and Copenhagen, was poorly cobbled together for an unsuccessful TV documentary, *The Last Performance,* and shown abroad after her death.

**FROM TOP:** Faye Emerson, Sonja Henie, Judy, and Ginger Rogers surround Edith Piaf after the latter performed in New York in autumn 1950. As late as 1968, there were discussions about Garland's appearance as Piaf in a film biography. | Here with Judy in 1957, Rosalind Russell later starred in the 1962 screen adaptation of *Gypsy*. Several of the show's Broadway creators envisioned "Mama Rose" as an ideal role for Garland. | Roddy McDowall and CBS executive James Aubrey join Lucille Ball in congratulating Judy after the first taping for her TV series (June 24, 1963). A decade later, Lucy would bring the musical *Mame* to the screen; it was a show Garland had longed to do, both on stage and film.

# PART THREE

# METRO'S GREATEST ASSET

## 1945-1950

O ver the last seven years of Judy Garland's tenure at MGM, she starred or guest-starred in ten motion pictures. All but one showed excellent profit, and seven of them were financial blockbusters.

The first of these turned out to be (in initial release) the highest grossing of all her Metro films. If twenty-one-year-old Judy Garland had to play a teenager one more time, she couldn't have found a better vehicle in which to do it than *Meet Me in St. Louis*. Director Vincente Minnelli genuinely admired her; in fact, months prior to his work on *St. Louis*, he had told the picture's songwriter Hugh Martin that he thought "the little Garland girl" had the greatest potential of MGM's entire star roster. When the ambitious Minnelli was provided the opportunity, he was quick to cast his professional lot with Judy.

He was next on hand to oversee the photography of her sketch in *Ziegfeld Follies*, an extravaganza conceived to celebrate MGM's twentieth anniversary. Garland's sequence was completed in late July 1944 after ten days of rehearsal, one day of prerecording, and three days of filming. It was the first footage she shot after *St. Louis*, and there was a startling contrast between high school junior "Esther Smith" (who extolled "The Boy Next Door") and the Tallulah-esque "Great Lady" (who extolled "Madame Cremantante"—and foreshadowed rap music in the process).

In the last months of 1944, Minnelli also guided Judy through her first straight dramatic vehicle. Off-camera, *The Clock* was notable in that Garland was always willing (sometimes on her own, sometimes with Vincente, and sometimes with favored makeup artist and surrogate mother Dottie Ponedel) to rescue costar Robert Walker from his nocturnal drinking depressions, brought on by a pending divorce from actress/wife Jennifer Jones. After completing *The Clock*, as well as George Sidney's full-scale musical *The Harvey Girls*, Garland married Minnelli in June 1945. When they returned from their honeymoon, he oversaw her scenes in the Jerome Kern biopic *Till the Clouds Roll By*, and she then retired to await the birth of their child. The future seemed to hold nothing but promise; the financial success enjoyed by *St. Louis* and *The Clock* once again placed Judy Garland in the United States Top Ten Box Office Stars (for 1945), and she was similarly ranked in Canada.

When she resumed work in late 1946 though, Judy's professional and personal confidence was shattered by *The Pirate*. That ambitious, odd property countered much of the professional good Minnelli had done for her in the preceding three years; it was almost as if the studio had forgotten how to make a Judy Garland musical. In its final version, the film was twenty-five minutes old before

she sang. Almost another hour passed before she sang again, and no matter how much Judy had longed to expand her performance range, the overall characterizations imposed by Minnelli on both her and Gene Kelly worked against every audience expectation.

Fortunately, the director's dark concept of light-hearted entertainment was dropped (as was he) from Garland's subsequent release. *Easter Parade* was guided by a masterful Charles Walters. It was Judy's only screen teaming with Fred Astaire, and their rapport made timeless magic of the Irving Berlin score. As recently as 2008, the duo was lavishly admired by Astaire biographer Joseph Epstein: "The most memorable number is 'A Couple of Swells.' Everything here works to the highest power. This is also the only dance in all his thirty-three movie-musical roles in which Astaire may have been outshone by a partner; next to Judy Garland, he seems for the first time not quite the main attraction. The two ended up holding each other, quite properly, in the highest regard as fellow professionals. As a great showman himself, Astaire was fully aware of Miss Garland's own immense showmanship, and he later claimed that working with her was a piece of great, good luck and one of the best things to happen to his career. Had

Garland and Astaire gone on to make . . . other movies, their impress as a team might have been stronger on the American consciousness, and the Fred and Ginger [Rogers] duo might have been somewhat eclipsed by the Judy and Fred duo."

The box-office bonanza enjoyed by *Easter Parade* raised Judy to a unique level of stardom circa 1948. As one journalist opined, she was the studio's most valuable asset—and no one was more aware of this than MGM. They delightedly began to plan the two elaborate vehicles per year that Garland was required by contract to make for them through 1951. Unfortunately, *The Pirate* had begun a pattern that was to continue. Judy would manage one film with comparative ease, and the money would pour into Metro. But while launching or working on the next, she would collapse in a morass of medication, marital misery, and insecurity. The long years of overwork had physically broken her; the failure of a second marriage took a heavy emotional toll. In 1948, she completed a guest appearance in *Words and Music* but had to be replaced in *The Barkleys of Broadway*. In 1949, she triumphed in *In the Good Old Summertime* but was dropped from *Annie Get Your Gun*. In 1950, under duress, she completed *Summer Stock* but was suspended from *Royal Wedding* when she canceled an inessential rehearsal. Two days later, on June 19, she broke a bathroom glass and made an ineffectual slash across

her throat. The subsequent international headlines were brandished on a Pearl Harbor level.

By that dismal point, political factions within the studio were working against her as well. Dore Schary had taken over as MGM production head in 1948. Though he was Judy's friend of a decade, and she had consoled him during his earlier years of professional uncertainty, Judy saw that he was now capable of only confrontation and "typical cold executive speech. . . . If he had said anything, one *word* that was friendly, or reminiscent of our earlier days, it could have made such a difference. [But] Dore was a stranger."

In the new, television-conscious, budget-cutting Hollywood, it's true that Judy's inability to robotically churn out product meant she was no longer *reliably* cost-effective. But those who knew her were aware of the years-old foundation of her prescription drug problems, exhaustion, and studio overwork. "If she could stand up, they'd photograph her," was the later condemnatory declaration of producer/director/writer Joe Mankiewicz, who'd watched MGM ignore Judy's need for help in the early and mid-1940s. Producer Freed, normally prone to verbal convolution, would look back at Garland's final years at Metro and manage a sorrowful summary that could have referenced any of the three films in which she was replaced: "We finally had to take her out of the picture. But none of us *wanted* to."

On September 29, 1950—virtually

fifteen years to the day after she'd first signed with MGM—the studio canceled Judy Garland's contract. (Hearing the news, a wary Ava Gardner turned to fellow star Stewart Granger and wonderingly, wryly, and rhetorically offered, "If they'll do that to Judy, imagine what they'll do to *us*.") Metro's move wasn't merely black villainy; Garland's doctors had encouraged the decision, and there was no denying that Judy herself was "too tired to think about how I felt, or what I was going to do. I was sick. I was hungry. And if I thought about it hard enough, I realized my marriage with Vincente was about over. The future wasn't too bright—no marriage, no money, no contract."

But she could—and did, quite quickly—take heart. The press, if uneven, was permeated with real encouragement. Bing Crosby instantly offered her radio work. Over the preceding six years, her movie songs had remained best-sellers, circulated on studio recordings of *Meet Me in St. Louis* and *The Harvey Girls* by Decca, and on six of the new "MGM Records" albums, edited from the actual soundtracks of the final pictures she made at Metro. Finally, on the date Judy was dropped from the studio roster, *Summer Stock* was playing in theaters across the United States to superlative business—and movie audiences were applauding her "Get Happy" number as if it were a live performance.

It seemed there would be life after Metro-Goldwyn-Mayer.

# The Clock

**METRO-GOLDWYN-MAYER**

**CAST:**

Judy Garland ............................ *Alice Maybery*

Robert Walker .................... *Corporal Joe Allen*

James Gleason.................................. *Al Henry*

Keenan Wynn ................................ *The Drunk*

Marshall Thompson.................................. *Bill*

Lucile Gleason............................ *Mrs. Al Henry*

Ruth Brady ............................................ *Helen*

Moyna MacGill ............... *Woman in Restaurant*

**CREDITS:**

**Arthur Freed** (*producer*); **Vincente Minnelli** (*director*); **Robert Nathan** and **Joseph Schrank** (*screenplay*); **Paul Gallico** and **Pauline Gallico** (*story*); **George Folsey** (*photography*); **George Bassman** (*musical score*); **Cedric Gibbons** and **William Ferrari** (*art directors*); **Edwin B. Willis** (*set decoration*), **Mac Alper** (*associate*); **Irene** (*costumes*), **Marion Herwood Keyes** (*associate*); **George White** (*editor*)

**RELEASE DATE: May 3, 1945**

**RUN TIME: 91 minutes**

## SYNOPSIS

Corporal Joe Allen has a forty-eight hour leave in New York City before shipping out to war. He's overwhelmed by the town until a chance meeting in Pennsylvania Station introduces him to office worker Alice Maybery (JG). Almost against her will, she's drawn into accompanying him around Manhattan, but by evening they are unaccountably attracted to each other. The two become even closer when circumstance dictates that they take over the delivery route of injured milkman Al Henry. After breakfast with Al and his wife, Alice and Joe begin to fully acknowledge their own emotions but are suddenly separated in the rush hour subway crowd. After hours of panic and searching, they're reunited by chance and determined to marry before he has to leave the next morning. Blood tests, bureaucratic red tape, and a hasty, sterile ceremony lead to regret, until the couple finds solace in an empty church. After their one night as husband and wife, Alice Maybery Allen sends her husband off to war with the firm and shared conviction that he'll return to her.

OPPOSITE: Walker, in the midst of a divorce action brought by wife Jennifer Jones, was bolstered by Judy throughout their weeks on *The Clock*.

# REVIEWS

"Vincente Minnelli has made a love story of great charm out of the most ordinary materials. . . . Robert Walker and Judy Garland make their story a very real experience. At times, Mr. Walker gets dangerously near being a shade too wide-eyed. But Miss Garland seems always right."

—*NEW MOVIES*
(NATIONAL BOARD OF REVIEW)

"A poignant story has been made into a screenplay filled with a lot of little things that add up to something big. *The Clock* will tingle at the box office in all situations. Highly credible performances are given by JG, Walker, and James Gleason."

—*VARIETY*

"A few exceptional moments, but it is pretty slow-moving and rather dull, due mostly to over-direction . . . entirely too much on the arty side."

—*HOLLYWOOD REPORTER*

"A songless JG, but one who will amaze you with her sensitive portrayal. She is at all times believable and proves her right to graduate from her familiar musical roles. Impressive film fare." —*MOVIES*

"Unquestionably a 'director's picture' with the brilliant touches of Minnelli at times outshining the story itself. Judy, with nary a song except the one in her heart, comes into her own as a dramatic actress of depth and charm. Robert Walker gives one of the best performances we've glimpsed." —*PHOTOPLAY*

Producer Arthur Freed on his star: "Judy's a natural actress—because you believe her. She has a great deal of wisdom, and there's not a mean bone in her body. I've never known her to do a mean thing to anybody."

CLOCKWISE FROM TOP LEFT: Walker and Garland kibbitz with cameraman George Folsey and Metro passerby Peter Lawford. | Judy bundles up on the set between takes. | Judy and Robert Walker take direction in cake-eating from Vincente Minnelli. The corresponding scene was cut from the finished film. | As the director would see it, from aloft on a camera boom or from the overhead scaffolding or catwalks.

## NOTES

On Judy's behalf, Arthur Freed searched for at least two years for a property in which she could play a straight dramatic role. He found it in *The Clock*, a two-page story idea by Paul and Pauline Gallico, which Robert Nathan developed into a full screenplay. The United States War Department approved an early draft script on May 5, 1944, and they would approve the final picture on February 27, 1945. But between those two dates, the simple project hit so many snags that at one point it was very nearly abandoned.

Early on, there were dissensions about the film title, and co-scenarist Joseph Schrank suggested *Don't Ever Lose Me* or *Never Lose Me* as alternatives. Casting was unusually complex for a film with just a handful of principal characters. Felix Bressart ("too European"), Donald Meek, Irving Bacon, and Hume Cronyn were considered for milkman Al Henry until James Gleason got the part. His wife, Lucile, was then cast as Mrs. Al Henry, though Connie Gilchrist had been preliminarily announced for that role. Audrey Totter and Louis Jean Heydt were confirmed as "roommate Helen" and her boyfriend Bill; they were supplanted by Ruth Brady and Marshall Thompson. Behind the camera, photographer Joseph Ruttenberg had to leave for another project and was replaced by George Folsey. Director Jack Conway fell ill, and successor Fred Zinnemann failed to mesh with either Judy or the script, and he was dismissed. At that point, Freed shut down the picture, until Judy convinced Vincente Minnelli to take it over.

As new director, Minnelli instituted many of the final casting choices. He encouraged extensive improvisation in the acting and dialogue, specifically in a café scene in which Keenan Wynn played an obnoxious drunk, and in the breakfast scene shared by Garland, Robert Walker, and the Gleasons. Stops, starts, and changeover in personnel notwithstanding, the film was completed between August and late November 1944.

The resulting picture won much praise and some dissension. Even a song-less Judy drew the customers though. On a $1.3 million budget, *The Clock* grossed more than $2.8 million in the United States alone during its first release. Titled *Under the Clock* for its United Kingdom engagements, it played to nearly 63,000 patrons in two weeks at the Empire Theatre in London.

OPPOSITE: Making movie magic: a treadmill provides the illusion that Joe is chasing after Alice's bus. RIGHT, FROM TOP: Alice mulls her choices for the evening: a date with her steady, Freddy—or a continuation of her encounter with Joe. (Photographed during Fred Zinnemann's stint on the film.) | A chance encounter with milkman Al Henry leads to an all-night delivery "run" for Alice and Joe.

# What They Said

*"I'm a little nervous about it. I told Bob Walker perhaps the picture should be retitled* Without a Song. *Then people will know what they're getting! But the girl is just my age, and the way Robert Nathan wrote the script, she thinks just like me. The same thing happens to her that is happening to young girls all over the world today. [So]* The Clock *is something special. I hope theatergoers will like it, because I've worked harder than ever before to do a good job, the best I know how."*

—JUDY GARLAND

*"I wrote Alice not as an imaginary character, but as Judy—I wrote Judy and her talk and her ways right into the picture. It was a pleasure, because she's the girl all writers write about. Meet Judy, and you've met the ideal heroine. [She has] a quick, eager mind, and delicious humor, and as sensitive a spirit as I've ever met."*

—ROBERT NATHAN

**OPPOSITE, CLOCKWISE FROM TOP LEFT:** A Central Park encounter from the discarded footage shot under Fred Zinnemann | U.S.O. receptionist Geraldine Wall can't help Alice find a soldier whose last name she doesn't even know. | Mr. and Mrs. Joe Allen share their parting moments with a little boy at Penn Station. | Minnelli's "pantomime" scene of the couple's first morning as newlyweds replaced random dialogue about ordering breakfast, grab shots of congratulatory telegrams from their families, and the sight of Alice rinsing out Joe's handkerchiefs in the sink.

*"They shot* The Clock *for a couple of weeks with another director and had decided to scrap it. So Judy came to see me . . . and she asked me if I would take it over. So I saw the stuff they had shot and read the script; it read beautifully, but it didn't 'play.' I decided that the only thing [to do] was to make New York one of the characters—the third character. Everything I could remember about New York [went into it]. And it was one of my best experiences, because [although] there was a great deal of improvisation, nobody bothered us; they were so happy to have it done! I've always had enough freedom. The studio never interfered, really, with what I wanted to do, but* The Clock *was unique. There was a big scene at the end, after Judy and Robert Walker had gotten married. It was very noble and had about three and a half, four pages of dialogue. They asked me what I intended to do with that, and I didn't know. But when we got to it. . . I decided to do it all in pantomime, because I thought that was all that was necessary to show that it was a good marriage [and] deserved to endure. He was going away to war, and I gave his speech to Judy, because it was more fitting to come from the girl. More gallant. [That film] was a marvelous experience."*

—VINCENTE MINNELLI

*"We showed* The Clock *in a ward of thirty-five burned men. The feeling that went through the air during the picture was like a field of electrical energy. Each man there, some scarred for life, lived that story in their souls as it unfolded before them. They felt the romance . . . as if it were themselves and the ones they love. Had they been men of tears, many would have cried at the closing scene of farewell, but as they were beyond outward emotions, what they felt was only mirrored in the lights of their eyes."*

—LETTER TO MGM FROM A WORLD WAR II HOSPITAL COMMANDANT

# The Harvey Girls

## CAST:

Judy Garland ............................ *Susan Bradley*

John Hodiak .................................... *Ned Trent*

Ray Bolger .................................. *Chris Maule*

Angela Lansbury ....................................... *Em*

Preston Foster ..................... *Judge Sam Purvis*

Virginia O'Brien ...................................... *Alma*

Kenny Baker .......................... *Terry O'Halloran*

Marjorie Main ......................... *Sonora Cassidy*

Chill Wills ................................. *H. H. Hartsey*

Selena Royle .................................... *Miss Bliss*

Cyd Charisse ...................... *Deborah Andrews*

Ruth Brady ............................................. *Ethel*

Jack Lambert ............................. *Marty Peters*

## CREDITS:

**Arthur Freed** *(producer);* **Roger Edens** *(associate producer);* **George Sidney** *(director);* **Edmund Beloin, Nathaniel Curtis, Harry Crane, James O'Hanlon,** and **Samson Raphaelson** *(screenplay);* **Samuel Hopkins Adams** *(original author);* **Eleanore Griffin** and **William Rankin** *(story);* **Kay Van Riper** *(additional dialogue);* **George Folsey** *(photography);* **Johnny Mercer** and **Harry Warren** *(music and lyrics);* **Lennie Hayton** *(musical director);* **Conrad Salinger** *(orchestrations);* **Robert Alton** *(dance director);* **Cedric Gibbons** and **William Ferrari** *(art directors);* **Edwin B. Willis** *(set decoration),* **Mildred Griffiths** *(associate);* **Helen Rose** and **Valles** *(costumes);* **Albert Akst** *(editor)*

## JUDY'S NUMBERS:

*"In the Valley (Where the Evening Sun Goes Down)," "On the Atchison, Topeka, and the Santa Fe," "The Train Must Be Fed," "It's a Great Big World," "Turkey in the Straw" (Harvey Dance Tonight), "Swing Your Partner Round and Round." Deleted: "March of the Doagies" and reprise, "My Intuition." Deleted; possibly never filmed: "In the Valley (Where the Evening Sun Goes Down)" and reprise, "Hayride"*

**RELEASE DATE:** January 1946

**RUN TIME:** 105 minutes

## SYNOPSIS

In 1890, Ohio-bred Susan Bradley (JG) entrains for Sandrock, New Mexico, in response to a matrimonial ad and a series of beautiful letters from "H. H. Hartsey, Esq." Upon her arrival, she learns that her intended is a middle-aged man, and that the correspondence was jokingly written for him by Ned Trent, owner of the Alhambra saloon and dance hall. Susan volubly condemns Trent but remains in Sandrock to join forces with the clean-cut female employees of the town's first restaurant—one of the famous Harvey House chain that brought civilization and tablecloths to travelers and the American West.

Crooked Judge Sam Purvis, Trent's inamorata Em, and her fellow saloon girls all square off against the Harvey faction, while Susan and Trent slowly fall in love. Many of the other waitresses find romance as well, specifically Alma with blacksmith Chris Maule, Deborah Andrews with pianist Terry O'Halloran, and cook Sonora Cassidy with H. H. Hartsey himself.

In a final desperate move, Purvis and his henchmen burn the Harvey House to the ground, but Trent turns the Alhambra over to the restaurant staff and their customers. He sends Em and the dance hall girls away on the train to Flagstaff and plans to stay in Sandrock with Susan. But she thinks he's left town as well, so she's on the same train. Selflessly, Em sets her straight, pulls the emergency cord, and puts Susan off the rear platform. At that moment, Trent comes galloping over the horizon on horseback to retrieve her.

OPPOSITE: Garland and Hodiak shared an on-location duet in "My Intuition," cut from the film before release. BELOW: The film plot as summarized in one photo: good (Judy Garland and John Hodiak, right) vs evil (Angela Lansbury and Preston Foster, left).

## REVIEWS

"[It's] in the *Oklahoma!* idiom—in fact, *The Harvey Girls* would have made an even better legit musical. Hodiak is curious casting in a musical of this nature. Miss Garland, however, makes much of it believable and most of it acceptable. The story, obviously, is one of those things, but under the lush Metro production auspices, along with the color, the fine scoring, director George Sidney's megging, and the rest of it, the film more than sustains itself."  —*VARIETY*

"JG is starred and excellent, but other players contribute many of the picture's high spots. Angela Lansbury comes close to walking off with things as a lush dance-hall queen."  —*LOOK*

"If you are an admirer of the spunky but girlish Judy, you should be well pleased with her performance. Besides being a trim little trouper, she is becoming our No. 1 exponent of transportation tunes."  —*FAMILY CIRCLE*

"JG sings, dances, and acts as capably as ever. The now-famous 'On the Atchison, Topeka, and the Santa Fe' is presented in one of the best and most tuneful scenes ever filmed, with everyone on screen—including the train—getting into the act."  —*HOLLYWOOD CITIZEN NEWS*

"JG is emaciated to a Frank Sinatra degree [and] needs a few square meals."  —SEATTLE *POST-INTELLIGENCER*

## NOTES

The success of Broadway's *Oklahoma!* (1943) spurred Roger Edens and Arthur Freed to devise a similarly "Americana"—themed musical, and they found their property in *The Harvey Girls*, which MGM had planned and then abandoned in 1942 as a Lana Turner drama. Early cast discussions for the revamped, song-and-dance version of the saga included Gene Kelly or William Johnson opposite pop singer Ginny Simms, who was then dating Metro studio head Louis B. Mayer. Quickly, however, the property grew important enough to warrant Judy Garland and Clark Gable as its tentative leads. Gable proved to be unnecessary to such a vehicle (the role went instead to John Hodiak), and Judy wound up once again with solo star billing above the movie title. In a part at first envisioned for either Lucille Ball or Ann Sothern, nineteen-year-old Angela Lansbury played Em, the traditional Wild West dance hall harlot.

*The Harvey Girls* was adapted from both factual and fictional tales of the respectable young women recruited for the wait staffs of the Fred Harvey chain of restaurants in the late 1800s. In attempting to emulate a full-blown, three-hour Broadway musical such as *Oklahoma!*, Freed encouraged the film's scenarists and composer Harry Warren and lyricist Johnny Mercer to overwrite. As a result, the rousing Western anthem, "March of the Doagies," was photographed (with two different endings and a reprise) and subsequently dropped from the picture, as was the Garland-Hodiak duet, "My Intuition." Another jaunty production number, "Hayride," apparently never made it past rehearsal and prerecording. Major and minor sections of plot were also lost at various stages of production in an effort to consolidate the expansive story, which involved ten principal characters and five love stories.

The picture was plagued by other challenges as well. Even in those late days of World War II, Kenny Baker and John Hodiak were in danger of being drafted. An increasingly visible pregnancy meant that Virginia O'Brien virtually disappeared, without explanation, midway through the movie plot. Hodiak, Preston Foster, and Ray Bolger each suffered on-set injuries, and the death of President Franklin Delano Roosevelt on April 12, 1945, shattered Judy and the entire film unit.

Eventually, production ran on for more than five months, finishing in early June 1945. By that time, *The Harvey Girls* featured number, "On the Atchison, Topeka, and the Santa Fe," was already a huge success; it would later win the 1946 Academy Award for Best Song. Lyricist Mercer had the hit recording of "Atchison," which remained on the *Billboard* charts for nineteen weeks—eight of them at number one as the best selling disc in the country. Bing Crosby, Tommy Dorsey, Judy, and Tommy Tucker enjoyed hit records with the song as well, peaking on the chart, respectively, at numbers three, six, ten, and ten.

On a budget of $2.5 million, *The Harvey Girls* grossed $5.1 million in its initial release. It scored the biggest non-holiday opening in history at Broadway's Capitol Theatre. In London, it was the fourth most popular Empire Theatre film of 1946, playing to more than 66,000 people in two weeks.

OPPOSITE: Judy, John Hodiak, and a publicity shoot set-piece.

## What They Said

*"This is a fine picture for me. I hate guns, and I'm scared to death of horses. When I even come near a bunch of horses, they nudge each other and say, 'This is going to be fun.' Then they snort and stamp their feet and do everything that's bad!"* —JUDY GARLAND

*"Judy's health wasn't of the greatest; she didn't have the greatest stamina to go on. We lined up the 'Atchison, Topeka' number for days and days— it ran eight or nine minutes. But we did Judy's section in two shots. And she came down after lunch, and she saw the rehearsal once. And she said, 'I'm ready.' And that was it; she just walked right on and did it. She had that kind of talent. She had the most precision, I think, of any actress I've ever worked with."* —GEORGE SIDNEY

*"She just worked and worked and worked. Judy never had vacations; she had breakdowns."* —RAY BOLGER

*"I'd been under contract for Ziegfeld Follies for Arthur Freed, and I had done a little dancing. But I was also studying dramatics. And Arthur had Robert Lewis come out—a director from New York, a wonderful man—to direct my screen test. And when George Sidney happened to see that, he put me into* The Harvey Girls, *which was really my first speaking role. Judy was fun and charming and good-natured. We shot so many numbers back on Lot Three, which no longer exists; it's now a housing development. But we had the Harvey Girls' restaurant set up there, and the train, and the whole town. We were always out on that back lot!"*

—CYD CHARISSE (1993)

*"The best! All of the best people who were working with Judy and all of the singing actors at MGM in those days— Kay Thompson, Roger Edens, Gene Kelly, Stanley Donen—all of those people I knew as a young player. And for some reason, they took me under their wing; I became very friendly with Kay and Roger. Everything they did in musicals in those days, a lot of it spilled onto me. I learned so much from them . . . [and] Judy. They weren't teaching her; she, of course, was a given, a jewel, an inimitable performer already, having come up through Andy Hardy and everything else. And I was there, thank God—this English kid! It was an amazing musical education, which stayed with me all my life."* —ANGELA LANSBURY (2010)

"Judy was a rare treat to watch—and I would have to say my favorite of all the stars I worked with. Most of the stars, between the actual shooting, would go to their dressing rooms and be very quiet. And she did this pretty much all the time, too. But when they would call her on set—once she started—she was prepared, she was natural, she was real, no matter what she did. She was a perfect performer. I don't recall having to do many takes because of Judy. And, of course, I always felt that she had more talent than almost anybody else I had the joy of working with. And I thought she had dramatic talents that were not exactly ever touched— and that she could have gone on and become a dramatic actress."

—MGM CONTRACT DANCER
DOROTHY GILMORE RAYE

FROM SPREAD LEFT: On the train to Sandrock, "Susan Bradley" meets the "Harvey Girls"— among them Ruth Brady, Virginia O'Brien, Marjorie Main, and Cyd Charisse. | "In the Valley," the original underscoring for the wedding finale, was replaced by "On the Atchison, Topeka, and the Santa Fe" when that song became a national hit. From left: Morris Ankrum, Judy, John Hodiak, Cyd Charisse, and Kenny Baker. | Garland is helped down off the luggage cart, from which she belted out the final phrases of the eight-minute production number, "On the Atchison, Topeka, and the Santa Fe." | Judy and makeup girl/confidante Dottie Ponedel. After multiple sclerosis forced Ponedel's early retirement, Judy maintained their friendship during hours of phone calls and visits to Dottie's home.

# Ziegfeld Follies

METRO-GOLDWYN-MAYER

**CAST:**

Fred Astaire, Lucille Ball, Lucille Bremer, Fanny Brice, Judy Garland, Kathryn Grayson, Lena Horne, Gene Kelly, James Melton, Victor Moore, Red Skelton, Esther Williams, William Powell, Edward Arnold, Marion Bell, Cyd Charisse, Hume Cronyn, William Frawley, Robert Lewis, Virginia O'Brien, Keenan Wynn

**CREDITS:**

Arthur Freed *(producer)*; Vincente Minnelli *(director)*; George Folsey and Charles Rosher *(photography)*; Harry Warren and Arthur Freed, George and Ira Gershwin, Ralph Blane and Hugh Martin, Kay Thompson, and Roger Edens *(music and lyrics)*; Lennie Hayton *(musical director)*; Roger Edens *(musical adaptation)*; Conrad Salinger and Wally Heglin *(orchestrations)*; Robert Alton *(dance director)*; Cedric Gibbons, Merrill Pye, and Jack Martin Smith *(art directors)*; Edwin B. Willis *(set decoration)*, Mac Alper *(associate)*; Helen Rose *(costumes)*; Albert Akst *(editor)*

**JUDY'S NUMBER:**

*"The Interview" (incorporating "Madame Crematante"). Never recorded: "I Love You More in Technicolor Than I Do in Black and White" (song with Mickey Rooney, preceded by a sketch with Rooney, James Craig, Van Johnson, and John Hodiak)*

**RELEASE DATE:** March 22, 1946
**RUN TIME:** 115 minutes

## SYNOPSIS

William Powell, recreating his title role from MGM's *The Great Ziegfeld* (1936), looks down from heaven and imagines the kind of all-star revue he could produce with the talent available in the mid-1940s. Thereafter, the film becomes a showcase for most of Metro's star roster. Judy's segment, "A Great Lady Has 'An Interview,'" was scripted as a rhymed patter/song-and-dance press conference between a sixteen-member male corps and a grandiose screen actress. In the course of their syncopated, faux-sophisticated questions-and-answers, the topic turns to the "glamorous, amorous, ham-orous" woman's next screen vehicle, *Madame Cremantante*, which will be a "monumental, biographical tribute" to the inventor of the safety pin.

ABOVE LEFT: *Ziegfeld Follies* color stationery—
Hirschfeld caricatures of the cast.

## REVIEWS

"Even a critic can pick his favorites in
this show of shows, and the Judy Garland
appearance is this journal's *piece de
resistance*. It is wackily and wonderfully
delightful. It is sparklingly inventive in
its situations."  —*HOLLYWOOD REVIEW*

"JG lets her beautiful auburn hair down
as far as it will go in a devastatingly funny
burlesque."  —NEW YORK *DAILY NEWS*

"The Garland routine is flamboyantly dull."
—NEW YORK *POST*

"Taking best numbers first, my vote
goes to JG [for] a genuinely bright and
amusing satire."  —BOSTON *HERALD*

"It seemed to me that JG's husband,
Vincente Minnelli, made a highly regrettable
selection of material for his wife. Her skit
seemed to me to be unsuited to her talents,
lengthy, and pointless."  —CHICAGO *TRIBUNE*

ABOVE: In Garland's support, the *Ziegfeld Follies* chorus boys appeared as "gentlemen of the press," quizzing a "glamorous, amorous, ham-orous" lady of the screen about her next picture. In time, she coyly reveals it to be "a monumental, biographical tribute to Madame Crematante—the "monumental, biographical woman" who invented . . . the safety pin. OPPOSITE: Garland is positioned on a traditional movie-set slant board, designed to provide support and relaxation for a performer without doing too much wrinkle damage to her costume. Judy's new makeup mainstay, Dottie Ponedel, is seen smiling at left.

A plotless, all-star revue, *Ziegfeld Follies* was envisioned as the screen equivalent of the lavish stage spectacles produced by Florenz Ziegfeld between 1907 and 1931. Arthur Freed had been mulling the prospect of such a film since 1939, and when preproduction finally began four years later, he reviewed countless song, dance, and comedy ideas. More than a dozen of these involved Judy, the most interesting of which would have teamed her with Fred Astaire for "The Babbitt and the Bromide," a Gershwin number originally introduced by the dancer and his sister Adele in Broadway's 1927 *Funny Face*. Ultimately, Astaire was paired with Gene Kelly for that routine in *Ziegfeld Follies*.

Many of the other suggestions for Garland included Mickey Rooney. In early 1943, consultant John Murray Anderson offered that the duo should open the film in a backstage setting. They'd be seen prior to "the show," peeking at the audience from the wings before being beckoned to the traditional curtain "peephole" by Fanny Brice. Finally, in April 1944, the Los Angeles *Times* confirmed a Hugh Martin-Ralph Blane song as the film's Garland-Rooney duet. Mickey was drafted before actual work could begin on "I Love You More in Technicolor Than I Do in Black and White," which suddenly left Garland without a slot in the picture.

Roger Edens and Kay Thompson sprang into action. They'd structured a *Follies* mélange of satirical patter, song, and dance for actress Greer Garson, in which she would lay comedic waste to her own grand screen image. "A Great Lady Has an Interview" was summarily rejected by the star, purportedly at the insistence of her husband and her mother. So, in Garson's stead, Thompson and Edens quickly taught the routine to Judy; Chuck Walters provided the staging, and Vincente Minnelli oversaw the actual filming.

The final result worked well for some audiences and confused others. In truth, the material didn't really fit Judy, for she was indeed the kind of pin-up girl and movie star that the lyric claimed she wasn't. In terms of dry, wry sophistication, and syncopated, flash song-and-dance, however, it was a dynamic and dazzling departure. Again devoid of the irony of the casting, both Lana Turner and Ann Miller performed variations of Judy's "Interview" material on television a decade and more later.

*Ziegfeld Follies* was in sporadic production from January until autumn 1944. After its November sneak preview, at least six sequences were dropped from the picture, with four later added. The final production cost topped $3.2 million. Early plans to make the *Follies* a bi-annual attraction were scuttled after such expense and complication. There was a Boston world premiere as a "reserved seat" road show in August 1945, and the film finally went into general release eight months later. Although its participants were billed in alphabetical order on the screen and in prepared promotional copy, the film's star roster was often rearranged by local theater owners across the country so that the ads they placed would best appeal to their audiences. As a result, Judy's name often came out on top. *Ziegfeld Follies* grossed more than $ 5.3 million in its original release; in London, it was the Empire's biggest hit of 1946, playing to nearly 112,000 patrons in three weeks.

Ironically, by the time the picture was officially launched in April 1946, Judy's most frequent screen partner had returned from active military duty. Columnist Hedda Hopper noted this fact in her report about a *Follies* screening: "It's a joy having Mickey Rooney back among us. His laughter could be heard above that of the entire audience when Judy gave out with her satire."

**FROM LEFT:** At her dressing table, Judy provides a clear view of both her makeup and hairstyle in these reference photographs.

## What They Said

*"All Judy had to do was sing and act like a combination of Gertrude Lawrence,
Greta Garbo, and five other grand ladies of the screen."* —KAY THOMPSON

# Till the Clouds Roll By

METRO-GOLDWYN-MAYER

### CAST:

Robert Walker ............................ *Jerome Kern*

Judy Garland ............................. *Marilyn Miller*

Lucille Bremer ........................... *Sally Hessler*

Van Heflin .............................. *James I. Hessler*

Dinah Shore ............................ *Julia Sanderson*

Van Johnson .............................. *Band Leader*

Paul Langton ................ *Oscar Hammerstein II*

Dorothy Patrick............................... *Eva Leale*

Mary Nash .................................. *Mrs. Muller*

Harry Hayden ........................ *Charles Frohman*

### GUEST STARS:

*June Allyson, Kathryn Grayson, Lena Horne,*
*Tony Martin, Frank Sinatra, Gower Champion,*
*Cyd Charisse, Angela Lansbury, Virginia O'Brien*

### CREDITS:

**Arthur Freed** *(producer)*; **Richard Whorf**
*(director)*; **Myles Connolly and Jean Holloway**
*(screenplay)*; **Guy Bolton** *(story)*; **George Wells**
*(adaptation)*; **Harry Stradling and George J.**
**Folsey** *(photography)*; **Lennie Hayton**
*(musical director)*; **Conrad Salinger** *(orchestra-*
*tions)*; **Robert Alton** *(dance director)*; **Vincente**
**Minnelli** *(Garland sequences)*; **Cedric Gibbons**
**and Daniel B. Cathcart** *(art directors)*; **Edwin B.**
**Willis** *(set decorations)*, **Richard Pefferle**
*(associate)*; **Helen Rose and Valles** *(costumes)*;
**Albert Akst** *(editor)*

### JUDY'S NUMBERS:

*"Look for the Silver Lining," "Sunny,"*
*"Who?" Deleted: "D'Ye Love Me"*

### RELEASE DATE: January 16, 1947
### RUN TIME: 136 minutes

## SYNOPSIS

The melodies of Jerome Kern—and, almost incidentally, the occasional detail about the composer's comparatively sedate private life—lace this all-star biography. By chance, Kern meets Eva Leale, his wife-to-be, when he commandeers her piano for an emergency session of composition. A sluggish taxi causes him to miss the sailing (and ultimate sinking) of the Lusitania. A fictional addition to the story traces Kern's concern for Sally Hessler, the spoiled daughter of Kern's musical associate James Hessler. She storms out of a New York production when her solo in a Kern musical is turned over to the "wistful, lovely, unforgettable" Marilyn Miller (JG) for "the good of the show." Sally ultimately goes her own way, grows up, and to the composer's delight, she finds success singing another Kern number in a Hollywood musical.

**ABOVE:** Judy is seen in "Look for the Silver Lining" (top right) and "Sunny" (center). Robert Walker and Joan Wells (who played Sally Hessler as a child) are pictured bottom right. **OPPOSITE:** Magazine publicity, with Judy in her "Who?" costume

"Citation for 'Best Musical Production of the Month' . . . [The film] will give your brain a two-hour rest. But, oh, how it will delight your ears, your eyes, and your heart. Judy Garland could never dance as Marilyn Miller did, but Marilyn could never have sung as our thrush Judy does—so beautifully."

—COSMOPOLITAN

"Judy Garland plays the late Marilyn Miller as if Miss Miller had foreshadowed Judy Garland herself."

—NEW YORK *MORNING TELEGRAPH*

"After raising quizzical eyebrows several times at the casting of JG as Marilyn Miller, I must now admit that she plays the part astonishingly well. . . . I must say, in all honesty, that it is difficult to think of anyone who could have done so more successfully."

—DANCE FILM NOTES

"Miss Garland's 'Look for the Silver Lining' is socko, and she repeats with 'Sunny' and 'Who?'" —VARIETY

## NOTES

Though technically a guest star in this celebration of Jerome Kern's music, Judy managed to be the film's centerpiece, thanks to cannily selected songs, the expert showcasing provided by new husband Vincente Minnelli, and the opportunity to play Marilyn Miller, a legitimate Broadway legend of earlier decades. The picture itself was another pet project of Arthur Freed, who venerated Kern and whom Kern himself admired and trusted. Unfortunately, the composer died on November 11, 1945, while *Till the Clouds Roll By* was in the early stages of production. The preceding month, he had visited the set to watch and hear Judy at work. Despite a couple of dramatic scenes in the picture, her contribution was primarily musical.

Garland's initial sequence detailed a portion of Miller's opening night in *Sally*, from intermission in a glamorous backstage dressing room to her de-glamorizing costume change, her long walk through a theater corridor and into the wings, and her appearance onstage to sing "Look for the Silver Lining." She also led a circus recreation from Kern's *Sunny*, although the moment in which Marilyn leapt upon a galloping horse and performed acrobatic tricks was done in long-shot

by veteran circus performer Gracie Hanneford. Another of Miller's signature songs, "Who?," was given an elaborate song-and-dance recreation and boasted both vocal arrangement and special material by Kay Thompson. The version as filmed, however, was considerably and unfortunately shortened for the release print of the picture. Conversely, the elimination of the odd "D'Ye Love Me"—performed by Judy with The Arnaut Brothers, a famous clown act—was perhaps a blessing.

With its star-studded cast and glorious musical program, *Till the Clouds Roll By* managed to establish "a new, all-time box-office high for MGM" when it played New York's Radio City Music Hall as the 1946 Christmas show. It was the third biggest money maker of 1947 at London's Empire Theatre and attracted 73,000 customers in three weeks. And although, once again, the studio diplomatically billed the film's stars in alphabetical order, individual cinemas invariably switched the order to best promote the product. Invariably, Judy and Van Johnson were the two greatest selling points.

In first release, *Till the Clouds Roll By* grossed $6.7 million on an investment of $2.8 million.

OPPOSITE: The first chorus of "Who?": Minnelli's riding the camera boom, and Roger Edens is standing center on the staircase, with Robert Alton to his left. **ABOVE**: Aided and abetted by Vincente Minnelli, Dottie Ponedel, and Helen Rose, Judy was effectively glamorized as Broadway star Marilyn Miller (1898-1936).

ABOVE: Marilyn Miller played a circus performer in *Sunny*, thus occasioning this centering-ring recreation of "D'Ye Love Me" with John and Renee Arnaut. OPPOSITE: Judy's directive to "Look for the Silver Lining" is about to be challenged.

## What They Said

*"Till the Clouds Roll By was the first picture that we did when we came back from our honeymoon in New York. Judy was pregnant with Liza, and so I had to shoot three numbers that she did long before [the rest of] the picture was done. They had to fit them in [later], because she was getting bigger every day!"*

—VINCENTE MINNELLI

# The Pirate

METRO-GOLDWYN-MAYER

### CAST:

Judy Garland ..................................... Manuela

Gene Kelly ........................................... Serafin

Walter Slezak...................... Don Pedro Vargas

Gladys Cooper ................................. Aunt Inez

Reginald Owen .......................... The Advocate

George Zucco............................... The Viceroy

Nicholas Brothers ................. Specialty Dance

Lester Allen..............................Uncle Capucho

Lola Deem......................................... Isabella

Ellen Ross......................................Mercedes

### CREDITS:

Arthur Freed (producer); Vincente Minnelli (director); Albert Hackett and Frances Goodrich (screenplay); S. N. Behrman (original play); Harry Stradling (photography); Cole Porter (music and lyrics); Lennie Hayton (musical director); Conrad Salinger (orchestrations); Robert Alton and Gene Kelly (dance directors); Cedric Gibbons and Jack Martin Smith (art directors); Edwin B. Willis (set decorations), Arthur Krans (associate); Tom Keogh and Karinska (costumes); Blanche Sewell (editor)

### JUDY'S NUMBERS:

"Mack the Black," "You Can Do No Wrong,"
"Love of My Life," "Be a Clown."
Deleted: "Love of My Life" (extended
version), "Mack the Black" (original film
opening), "Voodoo"

### RELEASE DATE: June 11, 1948
### RUN TIME: 102 minutes

## SYNOPSIS

Anticipating an arranged marriage on a Caribbean island, beautiful Manuela Alva (JG) is pledged by her Aunt Inez and Uncle Capucho to the pompous, corpulent Don Pedro Vargas, mayor of their tiny village. But Manuela actually dreams of romance with the mysterious pirate of legend, "Mack the Black" Macoco. She also finds herself strangely attracted to Serafin, a strolling player, who hypnotizes her into performing with his troupe.

Despite her engagement to Don Pedro and preoccupation with the fabled pirate, Manuela is pursued by Serafin. He finally pretends to be Macoco, the dreaded, charismatic seaman, after discovering that Don Pedro is actually the retired villain-in-hiding. The wily Pedro conspires to have Serafin hang for Macoco's evil deeds, but the actor and Manuela team and trick the pirate into revealing his identity. This leaves Manuela free to partner Serafin, onstage and off.

**OPPOSITE TOP RIGHT:** Costumes for *The Pirate* accounted for over $140,000 of its budget. **OPPOSITE BOTTOM RIGHT:** Judy sings the first, ultimately deleted, version of "Love of My Life." The song turned up again during the dramatic finale of *The Pirate*—and was thus a reprise of a number the audience hadn't heard before.

## REVIEWS

"A gay, giddy, Technicolor gambol . . . deck[ed] with the best to be had from Metro's talent roster. Escapism pure and simple, but of a highly literate genre, it rates a top box office take. Word of mouth alone should accomplish that. Judy Garland and Gene Kelly sing and dance . . . with a verve that is completely infectious . . . Slam-bang finale is [their] reprise of 'Be a Clown,' that should send payees home in a cloud."
—*DAILY VARIETY*

"WOW! Bright, fast, witty, and wonderfully entertaining. The plot is cute, the musical numbers sensational, and the performances out of this world. It is hit material for any exhibition situation. JG has a role that is admirably patterned to her comedy and vocal talent. Gene Kelly has the part of his career."
—*HOLLYWOOD REPORTER*

"JG is lovely and sings better than ever before. Kelly is the handsomest, most swashbuckling masquerader we've ever seen. The score is magnificent, the picture is skillfully and beautifully directed, and the screenplay is one of the most arresting to come out in many a Hollywood moon."—*MOVIELAND*

"Certainly no effort was spared . . . the cast is star-studded, and the settings and costumes are strikingly handsome. [Yet] *The Pirate* is disappointing, especially with regard to its music. The film has its moments, especially those in which Kelly dominates the screen. JG handles a song as well as ever [and] has several excellent comedy scenes."
—CHICAGO *TRIBUNE*

"*The Pirate* makes probably the most striking use of color on record. But its chief charm is its complete lightheartedness. Sets, songs, characters, and comedy are all devoted to pounding home a single message: it's silly to be serious."—*LIFE*

## NOTES

Most controversial of all Judy's MGM films—both in execution and reception—*The Pirate* was a song and dance adaptation of S. N. Behrman's 1942 Broadway comedy, originally written for Alfred Lunt and Lynn Fontanne. MGM grabbed screen rights to the script and planned to film the story with studio stars Myrna Loy or Hedy Lamarr and William Powell. The property languished until 1946, when Judy and Vincente Minnelli commandeered it for a musical to costar Gene Kelly. By that point, Arthur Freed's seven years of predominantly successful motion pictures had won him carte

blanche at Metro, and his enthusiasm for *The Pirate* equaled that of Minnelli and Kelly. The producer allocated a large budget for the project, and he hired Cole Porter to write its score.

From there, things went repeatedly awry. A full script by Anita Loos and Joseph Than was rejected and had to be completely rewritten by Frances Goodrich and Albert Hackett. Porter contributed several good songs, including (at Kelly's behest) the immediate standard, "Be a Clown." But Judy's principal numbers were vocally arranged by a musically overwrought Kay Thompson. Despite

expert performances from both stars, the film's combination of sophistication and tongue-in-cheek comedy—heightened by Minnelli's directorial flair and gorgeous scenic conceptions—would ultimately mystify average audiences.

As early as preproduction, Judy seemed to sense there were problems in *The Pirate*'s evolving creation and in the appeal it might have for contemporary moviegoers. She gamely forged ahead but came to distrust the artistic hoops through which Minnelli and Thompson were artily expecting her to jump. The film also marked the onset

OPPOSITE: Minnelli's now-famous summation of his leading lady: "When she was ready to go into a scene, [everybody] would be fussing over her, fixing her up. You might tell her twenty things to change in this performance. And God knows she had enough on her mind, and you didn't know whether you were getting through to her or not. But everything would be perfect. She would remember everything." ABOVE FROM LEFT: Garland relaxes on the set. | Preparing for the wedding day sequence. | "Manuela" faces "the ruination of my complete life" with (at least here) a quiet and anticipatory smile playing about her lips.

absences, there was an odd, off-hand approach to the picture's completion. Kelly's "Pirate Ballet" was leisurely done at the end of filming, rather than incorporated into the schedule during one of the lengthy lulls in work. It finally took more than ten months to propel *The Pirate* from preproduction to its sneak previews in autumn 1947. Garland's fears were then borne out by wildly divergent comment cards from test audiences. As a result, the movie underwent major overhauling. "Mack the Black" and "Voodoo" were completely deleted. The latter had already re-filmed in part when Louis B. Mayer and associates found the Kelly-Robert Alton choreography too erotic. Now the number was replaced by an exciting but less hysteric version of "Mack," prepared for Judy by Roger Edens. The double-entendre Garland ballad, "You Can Do No Wrong," was also re-slotted in the plot and re-photographed as a sincere ballad. Her major romantic number, "Love of My Life," was cut, though its reprise remained. It must be noted, however, that hashed about as was its music, *The Pirate* nonetheless later earned an Academy Award nomination for Best Scoring.

Historically, much has been made about Judy's responsibility for the time and cost overruns on the picture, but studio records show that it surpassed its budget by only $100,000—almost precisely the amount incurred by the necessary retakes of Minnelli

of her new five-year contract with MGM and an overwhelming terror of the expected workload to which she'd committed herself.

Such professional pressures were massively compounded by personal difficulties and the rising realization that she had possibly erred in marrying Minnelli. Her growing mistrust of her husband led to irrational jealousy

over the time and joy he shared with Kelly in their mutual hopes for the picture. Whether she was seeking relief from her fears or the resolve to face them, Judy slipped into her most heavy dependence on prescription medication to that time, eventually missing days and weeks of filming.

The production nonetheless dragged on, and beyond Garland's

and Thompson's misfires. Given book-keeping practices, its final $3.7 million tally also included all the earlier, aborted attempts to bring the property to the screen. An initial gross of $2.9 million never even approached a break-even point, and *The Pirate* was the only MGM Garland film to lose money.

Critical reaction ranged from rapturous to dismissive. Even Cole Porter described the final picture as "unspeakably wretched, the worst that money could buy." Still, the film's colorful and romping good spirits, remarkable humor, and energetic achievement have also and always won deserved and vocal adherents.

**CLOCKWISE FROM TOP LEFT:** Costumed for "Voodoo," which was staged (twice), filmed, previewed, and replaced by "Mack the Black"—in the same basic wardrobe. | From all reports, "Voodoo" was a highly sensual and erotic dance duet for Judy and Gene Kelly, but its manic, almost atonal Kay Thompson vocal arrangement defeated the simple Porter melody. | On-set preparation for an early sequence, in which "Manuela" begs to be taken "to see the Caribbean . . . just once before I'm married. It means romance and adventure, and [otherwise] I shall never have any!"

## What They Said

*"For the wedding scene, Judy had three different hair designs that could have been used with her wedding veil; one of them was quite unusual. I said, 'That one, I can do something with. I can really make her look outstandingly quite beautiful.' And Judy wasn't a beauty. But she had an aura about herself and a great gift and a very, very great talent; a wonderful creature, too."*
—MGM HAIR STYLIST SYDNEY GUILAROFF

*"Even in her bad times, when she was functioning, she could—up to her abilities—learn a dance quicker than a dancer. You couldn't give her what you gave Cyd Charisse or Leslie Caron. But within a certain scope, she could learn like that. She could learn a song photographically . . . she could learn a page of dialogue in a glance. She never had any intellectual learning at all . . . and this is why she'd marry [a man] like Minnelli, I'm sure. Because Minnelli was well-read, even though he was not a scholar. And [Vincente and I] thought we were so clever. But when The Pirate opened, we were a hit in one city, and that's New York. [In] the rest of the country, you couldn't give the picture away. The public wouldn't accept Judy in that part. It wouldn't accept me with a moustache on and the curly hair. They wouldn't buy us."*
—GENE KELLY

ABOVE, LEFT, AND TOP OPPOSITE: Visitors to the set: Costar Walter Slezak with his daughter Ingrid, producer Arthur Freed, and year-old Liza May Minnelli.

"My father was not a very patient person, but my recollection is that he was exceedingly patient with Judy and quite patient with [those] kinds of interruptions. He worked very hard to try to keep it together, but personally he would be very upset and very emotional about it. I was not there, and I never saw any confrontations between people. But I think he was probably more vocal about his feelings with Roger Edens or with [a film's] production manager. [Also,] I guess he could figure it out that it wasn't too productive to exacerbate the situation by arguing with the star! But it was difficult."

—BARBARA FREED SALTZMAN,
DAUGHTER OF ARTHUR FREED

The high point of the picture (here with Gene Kelly) and the hit song of the score. Judy later used it as an athletic production number at New York's Palace Theatre in 1956-57 and reprised it on television in 1964.

# Easter Parade

METRO-GOLDWYN-MAYER

### CAST:

Judy Garland ........................... Hannah Brown

Fred Astaire ................................ Don Hewes

Peter Lawford .................. Jonathan Harrow III

Ann Miller.................................. Nadine Hale

Jules Munshin ................................. Francois

Clinton Sundberg .................................. Mike

Jeni LeGon ............................................ Essie

Jimmy Bates ............................ Boy in Toyshop

Richard Beavers ......................... Leading Man

Dick Simmons ............................................ Al

### CREDITS:

**Arthur Freed** (producer); **Charles Walters** (director); **Sidney Sheldon, Frances Goodrich, and Albert Hackett** (screenplay); **Frances Goodrich and Albert Hackett** (story); **Harry Stradling** (photography); **Irving Berlin** (music and lyrics); **Johnny Green** (musical director); **Conrad Salinger, Van Cleave, and Leo Arnaud** (orchestrations); **Robert Alton** (dance director); **Cedric Gibbons and Jack Martin Smith** (art directors); **Edwin B. Willis** (set decorations), **Arthur Krams** (associate); **Irene and Valles** (costumes); **Albert Akst** (editor)

### JUDY'S NUMBERS:

"Everybody's Doin' It Now," "I Want to Go Back to Michigan (Down on the Farm)," "Beautiful Faces Need Beautiful Clothes," "A Fella with An Umbrella," Vaudeville Montage (incorporating "I Love A Piano," "Snooky Ookums," "The Ragtime Violin," "When the Midnight Choo-Choo Leaves for Alabam'"), "It Only Happens When I Dance with You," "A Couple of Swells," "Better Luck Next Time," "Easter Parade." Deleted: "Mr. Monotony"

**RELEASE DATE:** July 8, 1948

**RUN TIME:** 104 minutes

## SYNOPSIS

Don Hewes and dancing partner Nadine Hale are on top of the show business world in 1912. He's also in love with her, but she unceremoniously quits their act to go into a Broadway show and pursue instead a romance with the somewhat under-enthused Johnny Harrow. Drowning his sorrows, Don declaims that he can turn any girl into a professional match for Nadine, and he selects the mystified Hannah Brown (JG) out of a café chorus line for the honor. It turns out that she is hopelessly inept at the ballroom style that marked Don's earlier success, but their act soars when he discovers Hannah's innate talent as a song-and-dance original. The jealous Nadine attempts a brief reunion with her former partner, but her plot is short-lived. She winds up with Harrow, while the newly-engaged "Hannah and Hewes" are the cynosure of Fifth Avenue during the annual Sunday morning Easter Parade.

**LEFT:** A worried "Don Hewes" wonders if "Hannah Brown" is enough of "a peach" to attract male attention wherever she goes. **ABOVE RIGHT FROM TOP:** A Hollywood in-joke: Judy's feathers "molt" in her first performance with Astaire, reflecting real-life trouble he'd had with a Ginger Rogers gown in *Top Hat* (1935). | In the Vaudeville Montage medley, "Don" discovers "Hannah's" real talents: "I Love a Piano."

**OVERLEAF:** Judy does a quick touch-up on the set of the deleted "Mr. Monotony." The costume would turn up again—for keeps—two years later.

"Metro's finest musical of the year, and superlative in every department."

—*MOTION PICTURE HERALD*

"A wonderful show . . . sparkling, tuneful, bright. Judy Garland dances as if she had been Fred Astaire's partner all her life. On her own, she sings and performs with irresistible Garland charm. The exquisite Technicolor shows off her fresh, youthful beauty."    —*HOLLYWOOD REPORTER*

"The perfect screen musical. Judy makes . . . a fine partner with her own lightness of feet, her warm acting style, and her poignant brown-eyed way with a Berlin ballad. She looks as pretty as a china doll in the pre–World War I costumes."

—*COLUMNIST DOROTHY KILGALLEN*

"[It] has but one aim—to entertain—and it hits the mark in all its 103 minutes. Producer Arthur Freed and director Charles Walters give their picture an edge by avoiding the pitfalls common to movie musicals. JG, brilliant versatile in *The Pirate*, shines even brighter [here]. Astaire has never been better."    —*LOOK*

"A musical that excels in every department: story, Technicolor, music, dancing, and all-round good taste. JG gives the finest performance of her career, and Fred Astaire appears better than ever."    —*COUNTRY GENTLEMAN*

"Charles Walters directed, and such entertainment has seldom been seen and certainly not heard before in this splendid guise."

—*MCCALLS*

"This is IT—like the Kentucky Derby or the World Series, you are seeing champions [in Garland and Astaire]. But then, little Judy is in some ways THE Champion. I am chary of the word genius—but I think JG is."

—*MOVIE STARS PARADE*

## NOTES

In late 1946, Irving Berlin began negotiations with Twentieth Century Fox to build a motion picture around his song "Easter Parade." When they refused to meet his monetary requirements—and Arthur Freed offered Berlin the chance to do the film at his desired price *with* Judy Garland—a deal was happily arranged at MGM instead. Berlin contracted to provide eight new numbers for the picture as well as eight standards from his catalog. Among the latter, several titles were suggested that never made the finished product: "Call Me Up Some Rainy Afternoon," "The International Rag," and "The Song is Ended."

Early casting once again paired Judy and Gene Kelly, with Frank Sinatra, Kathryn Grayson, and Red Skelton in support. Vincente Minnelli was to direct the Frances Goodrich-Albert Hackett script. Suddenly, as the storyline evolved, Sinatra, Grayson, and Skelton were out, and Peter Lawford and Cyd Charisse were in. Before the onset of filming, Charisse suffered a work-related injury on another picture, and Ann Miller acquired her role. Just as abruptly, Arthur Freed removed Minnelli from the assignment. Diplomatic historical quotes define this step as action taken on the advice of Judy's psychiatrist. But given the production and creative problems on the still-in-flux *The Pirate*, there also had to be a general sense at MGM that Minnelli's exotic version and vision of Judy was at least in part an incorrect one for contemporary audiences. This is further borne out by the dark, unpleasant *Easter Parade* script drafts that Minnelli approved before his departure.

When Charles Walters came in to replace Minnelli, the new director's first task was to make a legitimate musical comedy of the property. He and screenwriter Sidney Sheldon were on the way to achieving this when a final blow fell. Gene Kelly was known as a highly competitive man, whether in charade-related parlor activities or in backyard athletic contests. On Sunday, October 12, 1947, during one of the regular weekend volleyball matches at the Kelly home, he took verbal umbrage at the lack of concentration of some of the players. One of them was playwright/scenarist Arthur Laurents, who later summarized: "Roaring at the top of his high tenor, [Gene] thrashed his way back to the house, flung open the kitchen door, and swiveled for one final curse. He shrieked and, like Rumpelstiltskin, stamped down so hard on the doorsill that he broke his ankle. And that, dear cineastes, was why Fred Astaire replaced Gene Kelly in *Easter Parade*." (The press was told that the dancer had sustained the injury while rehearsing.)

Once finally underway, however, production went quickly and comparatively smoothly. Sheldon remained on the project, further honing the script, and Roger Edens was credited by Berlin as a major force in the movie's musical sheen. Freed made his contribution by politely rejecting "Let's Take an Old Fashioned Walk" as a duet for the two stars, encouraging Irving to develop a more comic number. This resulted in the film's highlight, "A Couple of Swells." The only musical loss was a sleek and chic Garland performance of "Mr. Monotony," dropped from the picture prior to its premiere.

It took a little more than three months to complete *Easter Parade*, which came in at a cost of $2.5 million—$191,000 under budget. It then grossed $6.8 million, playing extended engagements in every major theater, including seven weeks on Broadway at Loew's State. It was also the biggest draw of 1948 at the Empire in London, pulling in more than 115,000 patrons in three weeks. A year later, *Easter Parade* won the Oscar for Best Score for Roger Edens and Johnny Green, the *Box Office* Blue Ribbon Award, and The Writer's Guild of America Screen Award for Best Written American Musical of 1948.

OPPOSITE, CLOCKWISE FROM TOP LEFT: Hannah—day wear | "Beautiful Faces Need Beautiful Clothes" | Hannah at home | "I Love a Piano"

## What They Said

"Easter Parade is the best picture the little Garland has had so far. She thinks so, too. . . . That child has more talent in that little body of hers than anybody that's been around in a long time. She's a songwriter's dream; I'll go on record as saying that. A songwriter couldn't wish for a better break than to have Judy introduce his new tunes."

—IRVING BERLIN

"The reason I got Easter Parade was not because of my great talent. But Judy and Minnelli had just finished The Pirate, and their psychiatrist said, 'I don't think it's advisable for [them] to do another picture together right away. [That] means all day together and all night together; I just don't think it's a good idea.' And he, I guess, talked them into it. [Meanwhile], Good News had been a success, and Arthur called me in, and he said, 'I think I'm going to give you Easter Parade.' Oh, God. I was almost in tears, you know, with the thrill of it—and double the budget of Good News. But then I read the script, and it was terrible. It was terrible, it was heavy—believe it or not. . . . So I

go to Gene and Judy: 'I have to talk to you seriously. I have no clout, and I'm lucky to get the goddamn thing. But let me tell you something: it stinks. And the audience is going to hate you, Gene, for what you're doing to this poor girl. Because, don't forget, Judy is always sympathetic.' So I'd gotten along very well with Sidney Sheldon [and I told Judy and Gene], 'I think it should be taken away from the Hacketts and see if Sid and I can't work on it and lighten it. It's got to be fun; it's a musi- cal.' So we agreed. Arthur was in New York—they got Arthur on the phone. My name was never mentioned; he wouldn't have liked that. [To him,] I shouldn't have a mind: 'Just shut up and do your job.' I don't mean that cruelly or crudely, but I just thought it was better if it [came] from them. So that's how we got Sid, and Sid—and then I—worked on it. We'd go into the scenes with Judy and Gene, and they loved the lightening of it."

—DIRECTOR CHARLES WALTERS

"The story the Hacketts had written was too serious for a musical. What [their] screenplay needed was humor and a light touch. Irving Berlin had questions and comments as I talked about the possible directions the screenplay could go. I turned in my [work] to Arthur Freed and waited to hear his reaction. Silence. One week [later], his secretary finally called. 'Mr. Freed would like you to be in his office tomorrow morning at ten o'clock to meet Judy Garland and Gene Kelly.' I felt a sudden sense of panic. They would all hate my screenplay.

In the morning, I made a deci- sion. I would go to the meeting. . . . I would listen to their derogatory criti- cisms, and when they were through, I would quit. When Judy walked in, my spirits lifted. It was like seeing an old friend. When I was an usher, I had seen her movies over and over. Her first words were, 'Hello, Sidney. I loved your screenplay.' The door opened, and Gene Kelly came in. 'Author, author,' he said. 'You did a damn fine job.' I was filled with a sudden sense of euphoria. All that worrying for nothing."

—SIDNEY SHELDON

"[MGM executive] L. K. Sidney got me on the phone and asked me if I'd care to come 'home' again. With Irving Berlin's score and the wonderful Judy Garland to play opposite, I was lucky. The part could be made to suit me. I called Gene to find out for sure whether or not he wanted to relinquish his role; he assured me that he could not possibly continue. My retirement was over. Of course, Judy was the star of the picture. And it's a joy to work with somebody like Judy, because she's a super talent, with a great sense of humor. She could do anything. She wasn't primarily a dancer, but she could do what you asked her to do. And she had a great charm, and she was a very big star. She was in good form . . . we had a very good time. [Our numbers together] remain with me as high spots of enjoyment in my career. Her uncanny knowledge of showmanship impressed me more than ever as I worked with her." —FRED ASTAIRE

"I've never seen [Fred] as happy as he was during the making of Easter Parade. It's a wonderful story and a wonderful picture. But to him, the joy came from working with Judy, a girl whose own sense of timing and comedy and perfection is as intense as his. With Judy, the film [for him] was nothing but play."

—ASTAIRE STAND-IN JOE NIEMEYER

OPPOSITE FROM LEFT: Astaire on Garland: "She could do things—anything—without rehearsing and come off perfectly. She could learn faster [and] do everything better than most people." | Astaire and Garland with scenario-saver-supreme Sidney Sheldon. | Relaxing off-camera for the scene in which Hannah Brown and Johnny Harrow "meet cute" for a second time. ABOVE: Judy and Fred—"A Couple of Swells"

"Fred and I agree: With the exception of [his sister] Adele, Judy Garland is the most versatile of all his partners."

—MRS. ANN GELIUS AUSTERLITZ
(MOTHER OF FRED ASTAIRE)

"Fred put me completely at ease. He's a gentleman—and lots of fun to work with." —JUDY GARLAND

"Judy and Fred got along just great—because she's a great pro and a fantastic entertainer, and he was, too. And I think that when you put pros together, it's always a happy union, because they like to work and work hard. And they did."

—ANN MILLER

"I was pleased to be responsible for getting Fred back to work, but every time I see him and Judy singing 'A Couple of Swells,' I do get a twinge of regret."

—GENE KELLY

"Even in the rehearsal hall, long before Judy's teeth were blacked out and her face smudged, the magic of that number was that—while you were laughing—you were so touched by it that you cried. In the rehearsal hall, with Judy in a pair of leotards and Fred in his shirt sleeves and that dreadful piano . . . you were hysterical with the business being devised. And you were crying because it was so touching."

—CONDUCTOR JOHNNY GREEN

# Words and Music

METRO-GOLDWYN-MAYER

**CAST:**

| | |
|---|---|
| Mickey Rooney | *Lorenz "Larry" Hart* |
| Perry Como | *Eddie Lorrison Anders* |
| Ann Sothern | *Joyce Harmon* |
| Tom Drake | *Richard "Dick" Rodgers* |
| Betty Garrett | *Peggy Lorgan McNeil* |
| Janet Leigh | *Dorothy Feiner* |
| Marshall Thompson | *Herbert Fields* |
| Jeanette Nolan | *Mrs. Hart* |
| Richard Quine | *Bob Feiner, Jr.* |
| Clinton Sundberg | *Shoe Clerk* |

**GUEST STARS:**

*June Allyson, Judy Garland, Lena Horne, Gene Kelly, Ann Sothern, Cyd Charisse, Mel Tormé, Vera-Ellen, Richard Quine, and Dee Turnell*

**CREDITS:**

**Arthur Freed** (*producer*); **Norman Taurog** (*director*); **Fred Finklehoffe** (*screenplay*); **Guy Bolton and Jean Holloway** (*story*); **Ben Feiner, Jr.** (*adaptation*); **Charles Rosher and Harry Stradling** (*photography*); **Lennie Hayton** (*musical director*); **Conrad Salinger** (*orchestrations*); **Robert Alton** (*dance director*); **Cedric Gibbons and Jack Martin Smith** (*art directors*); **Edwin B. Willis** (*set decorations*), **Richard A. Pefferle** (*associate*); **Helen Rose and Valles** (*costumes*); **Albert Akst and Ferris Webster** (*editors*)

**JUDY'S NUMBERS:**

*"I Wish I Were in Love Again" (with Mickey Rooney), "Johnny One Note"*

**RELEASE DATE:** December 9, 1948
**RUN TIME:** 122 minutes

**ABOVE:** "Larry Hart" presents . . . Judy Garland. **OPPOSITE:** The camera (left) captures the conclusion of the Garland/Rooney routine. It was the tenth and last time they'd both be billed in the same film.

## SYNOPSIS

The Broadway and Hollywood song-writing partnership of composer Richard Rodgers and lyricist Lorenz "Larry" Hart is traced from their first professional association, circa 1919, to their final production in 1943. After an unsuccessful pursuit of stage star Joyce Harmon, the stable Rodgers marries Dorothy Feiner and enjoys his career, family, and home life.

Jilted by singer Peggy McNeil, the peripatetic Hart turns to alcohol for consolation and ultimately dies of his debauchery. But before Hart's untimely demise, he and Rodgers write some of the best-loved and most fondly-remembered show tunes of their era. Everyone wants to sing them, including Hollywood's Judy Garland, with whom Larry duets at a gala party.

"About the biggest musical film of the year—big, flashy, gorgeous entertainment." —HOLLYWOOD REPORTER

"It's a smash in every sense of the word. It's unfortunate that her two badly-staged routines should have fallen to Miss Garland. Still, they're well worth seeing because of the Garland gal's great artistry." —DAILY VARIETY

"Its chief point is to get as many people through as many routines as quickly as possible. *Words and Music* [is] an unfortunate wedding of the romantic biography and the revue [with] most of the variety stars in the MGM stable, [and] with Rooney and Garland as stand-by box office leads. . . . As ridiculous and confused a musical as has come down the pike in many a year. And it was misuse, not lack, of talent that bogged it down." —HOLIDAY

"JG hardly does herself justice...and is visually startling, appearing thin as a wraith in her first number and coming back immediately for an encore, looking pounds heavier."

—PHILADELPHIA *INQUIRER*

"There's JG doing 'I Wish I Were In Love Again' and being just about the best thing in a movie filled with good things." —MODERN SCREEN

ABOVE RIGHT: Detail from an Italian poster for the film.

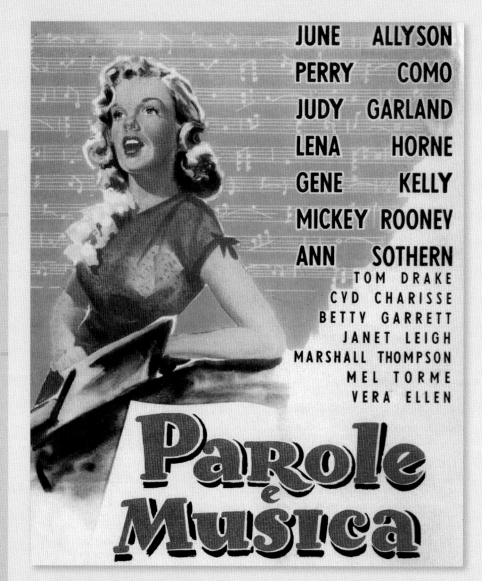

"Welcome to Hollywood!" says Judy Garland. And the honeymooners start on a new life...and new triumphs for the team of Rodgers and Hart!

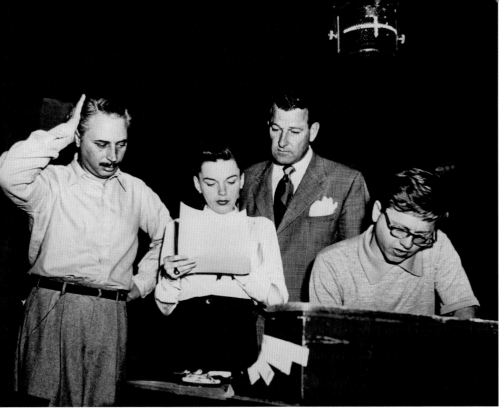

## NOTES

Though involved only in a ten-minute cameo appearance, Judy found her participation in *Words and Music* to be fraught with complication. She was physically frail
and dispirited in spring 1948 but somehow rose to the occasion and, with all the
old elan, prerecorded a duet for the picture with Mickey Rooney on May 28. After
three attempts over three days to get to the set, she was finally able to film both
the song and its preceding scene on June 8. Garland's ongoing malaise left her
unable to complete a second number for the picture and then cost her the lead in
*The Barkleys of Broadway*.

In the throes of a nervous breakdown, she was suspended by MGM for two
months until hastily summoned back to the Culver City lot in mid-September, as
a *Words and Music* sneak preview had resulted in a raft of audience requests for an
additional Garland song. The set pieces and dress extras of nearly four months
earlier were reassembled, and as Judy had been happily eating her way through
a healthy rest cure, the wardrobe department prepared a revision of the Garland
costume to accommodate a less-wraithlike star. Her new dress was suddenly belt-
less; the same could not be said about her bravura rendition of "Johnny One Note."

*Words and Music* enjoyed happy bookings everywhere, including New York's
Radio City Music Hall. At a final cost of $2.8 million, it grossed $4.5 million in its
initial release.

ABOVE FROM LEFT: On May 28, 1948, Judy and Mickey Rooney were reunited to prerecord
their "I Wish I Were in Love Again" duet. From left: conductor Lennie Hayton, Judy, vocal
arranger Roger Edens, and Mickey | Judy and Mickey go for a take. They nailed it on their fifth try.

## What They Said

"It was so ridiculous. In her first
number, she barely casts a shadow.
Then she comes back a minute later,
and she looks like Kate Smith."

—MANAGER CARLTON ALSOP

"As long as she could stand up, [MGM]
would photograph her."

—JOE MANKIEWICZ

"Her weight would vary a great deal,
sometimes during a picture. She presented quite a problem to us for that
reason. She would be a little heavy
and fat, and then she would get very
thin and . . . a little gaunt, and we'd
have to make some compensations
about the way we would light her and
treat her. [But] I think that [her] personality overcame the lack of what you
might consider beauty. She always
seemed rather beautiful to me, because
she was so good."

—CAMERAMAN GEORGE FOLSEY

# In the Good Old Summertime

METRO-GOLDWYN-MAYER

### CAST:

**Judy Garland** ......................... *Veronica Fisher*

**Van Johnson** ................... *Andrew Delby Larkin*

**S. Z. "Cuddles" Sakall** ............. *Otto Oberkugen*

**Spring Byington** ......................... *Nellie Burke*

**Clinton Sundberg** ...................... *Rudy Hansen*

**Buster Keaton** ...................................... *Hickey*

**Marcia Van Dyke** .................... *Louise Parkson*

**Lillian Bronson** ............................ *Aunt Addie*

### CREDITS:

**Joe Pasternak** *(producer)*; **Robert Z. Leonard** *(director)*; **Albert Hackett, Frances Goodrich, and Ivan Tors** *(screenplay)*; **Samson Raphaelson** *(original screenplay)*; **Miklos Laszlo** *(original play)*; **Harry Stradling** *(photography)*; **Georgie Stoll** *(musical director)*; **Conrad Salinger** *(orchestrations)*; **Robert Alton** *(dance director)*; **Cedric Gibbons and Randall Duell** *(art directors)*; **Edwin B. Willis** *(set decorations)*, **Alfred E. Spencer** *(associate)*; **Irene and Valles** *(costumes)*; **Adrienne Fazan** *(editor)*

### JUDY'S NUMBERS:

*"Meet Me Tonight in Dreamland," "Put Your Arms Around Me, Honey," "Play That Barbershop Chord," "I Don't Care," "Merry Christmas." Deleted: "Last Night When We Were Young." Deleted; possibly never filmed: "In the Good Old Summertime" finale*

**RELEASE DATE:** July 1949
**RUN TIME:** 102 minutes

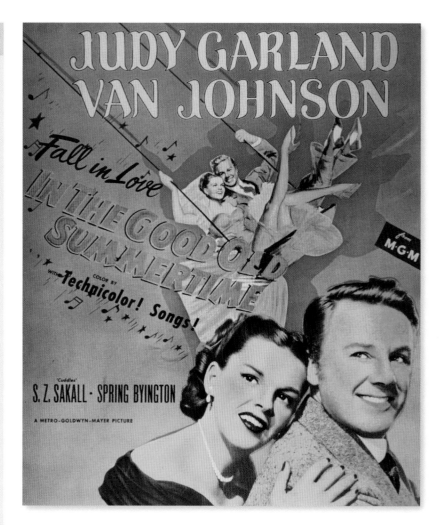

## SYNOPSIS

Andrew Larkin is the head salesman at Oberkugen's, a turn-of-the-century Chicago music emporium. He has hopes for a promotion and even higher hopes for the romantic outcome of the anonymous letter exchange he's conducting with a "Dear Friend." Meanwhile, at the store he remains at odds with pert Veronica Fisher (JG), who has virtually added herself to the staff, blithely demonstrating songs and instruments to delighted customers.

Away from work and unbeknownst to Andy, Veronica is also sustained by an ongoing correspondence with "Dear Friend." The Fisher-Larkin workplace feud serves as a backdrop for the romance of Otto Oberkugen and store cashier Nellie Burke, as well as for two ultimately unrequited crushes: Oberkugen's nephew Hickey dreams of Veronica, while classical violinist Louise Parkson longs for Andy. Everything is resolved by Christmas Eve, when Andrew passionately reveals to Veronica his own recent discovery: they are each other's "Dear Friend."

CLOCKWISE FROM TOP LEFT: Aunt Addie (Lillian Bronson) was at first cast with Spring Byington, but the latter moved up to the role of Nellie Burke when it was decided not to use Mary Astor in that part. | The silent-comedy genius and staging suggestions of Buster Keaton artfully embellished several *Summertime* sequences. | Judy and Van "meet cute" in a head-on collision outside the Chicago post office. (Their slapstick bits came courtesy Buster Keaton.) | Metro borrowed S. Z. Sakall from Warner Bros. to play "Otto Oberkugen."

# REVIEWS

"Another good old Metro musical. . . . Thanks to efficient research, *Summertime* has a deceptively substantial appearance. Its authentic period sets and costumes are persuasively gay, and the whole film is redolent of early German-American *Gemutlichkeit*." —TIME

"It is not minimizing the contributions of the other fine artists in the film to define [Judy Garland's] appearance in this musical remake as a Garland triumph. The Garland style is uniquely her own but still reminiscent of the great showmanship of such immortals as [Nora] Bayes, [Sophie] Tucker, [Eva] Tanguay, and [Blossom] Seeley. Producer Joe Pasternak and director Robert Z. Leonard show their sensitivity to the Garland artistry with a film that is airy, charming, and delightful entertainment."

—HOLLYWOOD REPORTER

"It is a leisurely paced show. It is so leisurely that at times it slows down to a crawl. The need for a bit of smartening up here and there is evident. When Miss Garland offers the half-dozen or so vocals, the proceedings adopt a discernible sparkle and a pointed-up entertainment quality." —FILM DAILY

"JG, looking more like her pretty, perky self than she has for a long time, carries the major weight of this musical on her sturdy shoulders. She gives a likable performance, but the story is pretty thin, and the plot lacks action. The film's brightest spots are the musical numbers." —CHICAGO *TRIBUNE*

## NOTES

Originally planned for June Allyson and Frank Sinatra (or Robert Walker or Gene Kelly), *The Girl from Chicago* was Joe Pasternak's "Americanization" of *The Shop Around the Corner*, a 1940 MGM vehicle for Margaret Sullavan and James Stewart. Pasternak took their romance-in-a-Budapest-perfumery, reconfigured it for a turn-of-the-century Chicago music store, and retitled it after an evergreen song of 1902. At the last minute, Allyson's commitment to *The Stratton Story* left Pasternak without a star. MGM awarded him Judy as her replacement, and additional songs were instantly, gleefully added to the script.

The supporting cast provided further entertainment value. Box office champ Van Johnson had been befriended (and dated) by Judy soon after his arrival in Hollywood nearly a decade earlier, and he had almost played opposite her in *Meet Me in St. Louis*. In contrast to Garland and Johnson as *Summertime*'s young romantics, Spring Byington and S. Z. Sakall were well-matched for charm as an in-love couple of senior citizens. Legendary comic actor Buster Keaton won his role on sheer talent. He was asked to develop a slapstick fall for the actor who would play a

ABOVE SEQUENCE: "Play That Barber Shop Chord": Ken Darby's vocal group, The King's Men, did the prerecording, but their quartet sound was lip-synched in the film by Charles Smith (*Babes in Arms*), Joe Niemeyer (Fred Astaire's stand-in), George Boyce, and Eddie Jackson (one-third of the great team of Clayton, Jackson, and [Jimmy] Durante).

junior shop clerk. When the Keaton routine proved invaluable, director Robert Z. Leonard instigated a script rewrite so that the comic could create the part himself. Virtuoso violinist Marcia Van Dyke—cousin to the late Woody Van Dyke, ace Metro director—provided excellent classical music balance for the movie score.

Principal photography for *Summertime* was completed in less than ten weeks, and Judy's sole regret was the deletion of a favorite number. By her own admission, "I was always fighting to get 'Last Night When We Were Young' into a picture." But its almost art-song melody and lyric (and Garland's emotional rendition) meant that "Last Night" was somewhat out of place in the light-hearted Pasternak piece, and the film moved forward more quickly without it.

Audiences made *Summertime* one of the top-grossing pictures of 1949, and it provided MGM with a $3.4 million return on a $1.5 budget. In later years, the basic *Summertime* plot was adapted yet again for an original Broadway production, *She Loves Me* (1963), and subsequently, the Tom Hanks-Meg Ryan update, *You've Got Mail* (1998).

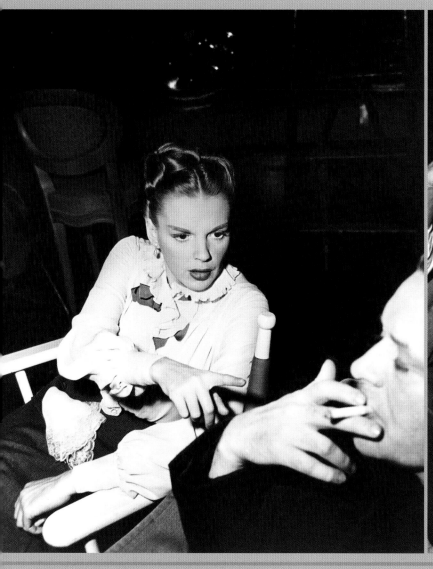

## What They Said

*"When we did* In the Good Old Summertime *with her, there was evidence that she'd been making too many pictures, and she was being forced to do too many things. And in some of the instances, she had to receive assistance to get onto the stage—in the way of a nurse with a needle or a doctor with a pill of some sort, in order for her to get up to the performance point. Because she literally wore herself to pieces."*

—VOCAL ARRANGER KEN DARBY

*"Mr. Mayer called me into the office—I always trembled when I got called out to Mr. Mayer on the red carpet! And he said, 'What did you do to Judy?' I thought, My God, what did I do?! 'What do you mean, Mr. Mayer?' [He said,] 'It's the first time we've finished on one of her pictures early.' I said, 'Well, I kept her happy, I kept her laughing. I had a gag every morning on her mirror when she came into the dressing room. . . . She just needed love. You just tell her she's beautiful, and keep her giggling.' They don't make people like Judy Garland anymore. She was a natural. Spontaneous talent. She wasn't crazy about rehearsing. She'd rehearse it once, and then shoot it. And she'd throw ad lib remarks in the scene. And I'd ask, 'Why did you . . . ?' She said, 'Keep it loose. Just keep it loose. You go by the book too much!' Lesson Number One from Miss Garland. And she was right."*

—VAN JOHNSON

*"I have said that Judy was an accomplished artist from the first. What she had gained in the years [since* Presenting Lily Mars*] was heart, depth. . . . But her heart was troubled. I don't know why. I can only report that [there were times during* In the Good Old Summertime*] she did not show up for work. This is quite a serious matter. Shooting schedules are carefully prepared. All sorts of things, running to vast expense, complicated arrangements—this is what a shooting schedule involves. . . .*

*In my view, a great artist is entitled to a lot more latitude than, let us say, a producer. That quality that makes her great makes her feel more deeply. I knew that my star's failure to appear stemmed from no lack of seriousness about her work. I determined to bear with her and trust she would feel my complete belief in her as actress, a singer, and a woman. Van Johnson, Jani Sakall, all of us felt— and you don't often feel this way in Hollywood—that we would accommodate ourselves gladly to work with Judy. There was never a word uttered in recrimination when she was late, didn't show up, or couldn't go on. Those of us who worked with her knew her magical genius and respected it."*

—PRODUCER JOE PASTERNAK

**OPPOSITE, CLOCKWISE FROM TOP LEFT:** In conversation with frequent musical stager/ choreographer and great friend Robert Alton | Both stars were known for their humor— and their life-long ability to laugh out loud | Preparing for her "meet cute" scene with Van Johnson | Nurse Duffy and Momma Judy oversee the activity as thirty-three-month-old Liza Minnelli prepares for her show business debut. Judy addressed the nanny as "a wonderful nurse and such a lovely friend," adding "Mr. Minnelli and I are so grateful to you for taking such beautiful care of our child."

# Summer Stock

METRO-GOLDWYN-MAYER

## CAST:

Judy Garland ............................. *Jane Falbury*

Gene Kelly ...................................*Joe D. Ross*

Eddie Bracken......................... *Orville Wingait*

Gloria DeHaven........................*Abigail Falbury*

Marjorie Main ..................................... *Esmé*

Phil Silvers .................................. *Herb Blake*

Ray Collins.......................... *Jasper G. Wingait*

Nita Bieber.............................. *Sarah Higgins*

Carleton Carpenter................................. *Artie*

Hans Conried .......................*Harrison I. Keath*

## CREDITS:

**Joe Pasternak** *(producer)*; **Charles Walters** *(director)*; **George Wells** and **Sy Gomberg** *(screenplay)*; **Sy Gomberg** *(story)*; **Robert Planck** *(photography)*; **Harry Warren** and **Mack Gordon** *(music and lyrics)*; **Saul Chaplin** *(music and lyrics to "All for You," "Heavenly Music")*; **Harry Warren, Saul Chaplin,** and **Jack Brooks** *(music and lyric to "You Wonderful You")*; **Harold Arlen** and **Ted Koehler** *(music and lyric to "Get Happy")*; **Johnny Green** and **Saul Chaplin** *(musical directors)*; **Nick Castle** *(dance director)*; **Conrad Salinger** and **Skip Martin** *(orchestrations)*; **Cedric Gibbons** and **Jack Martin Smith** *(art directors)*; **Edwin B. Willis** *(set decorations)*, **Alfred E. Spencer** *(associate)*; **Walter Plunkett** and **Helen Rose** *(costumes)*; **Albert Akst** *(editor)*

## JUDY'S NUMBERS:

"If You Feel Like Singing, Sing," "(Howdy Neighbor) Happy Harvest," "Portland Fancy," "You Wonderful You" (and reprise), "Friendly Star," "All for You", "Get Happy," "(Howdy Neighbor) Happy Harvest" finale

**RELEASE DATE:** August 1950

**RUN TIME:** 110 minutes

## SYNOPSIS

Jane Falbury's (JG) Connecticut farm is in trouble. In debt, bereft of farmhands, and with only the stalwart Esmé on site, Jane commandeers a tractor on additional credit from the store run by her mousy fiancé Orville Wingait and his father, Jasper. But her principal hope lies in the imminent arrival of her kid sister, Abigail, who is expected to help with the coming harvest. Instead, Abby turns up with Joe Ross, Herb Blake, and the full cast of *Fall In Love*. The stage-struck girl has recklessly committed the Falbury barn for use as a summer theater.

Jane is nonplussed but allows the troupe to stay in exchange for their (initially questionable) aid on the farm. The staid townsfolk are askance at the interlopers; Joe realizes that he's falling out of love with Abby and in love with Jane; and the clueless Abby turns prima donna and deserts the show with hambone actor Harrison I. Keath. With two days remaining until the opening performance, Joe is forced to play the male lead himself, and he turns to Jane to replace Abigail. They triumph as a couple, professionally and personally.

LEFT, FROM TOP: The film got off to a buoyant beginning with Judy's free-spirited "If You Feel Like Singing, Sing" and—moments later—a rambunctious "(Howdy Neighbor) Happy Harvest." The latter was prerecorded as a mini-production number; instead, Judy finished it solo, poking fun at herself with a fortissimo final note. | Whether under long-term contract or the studio's acquisition-for-the-picture, singular talent was rife in virtually every MGM feature. (In this case: Eddie Bracken, Marjorie Main, Gloria DeHaven, Carleton Carpenter, and Phil Silvers). Here, Marjorie Main and Judy cast, respectively, disapproving and envious glances at Gloria De Haven and Gene Kelly.

"Delightful summer entertainment—fresh, attractive-looking—with some of the best, intimate singing-and-dancing numbers ever put on the screen. Judy's great voice and great way with a song sock across her numbers. In 'Get Happy,' looking stunning and thin, [she] is nothing short of magnificent. Her appearance drew a hand from the preview audience (all newspapermen), just as it will in general release."

—HOLLYWOOD REPORTER

"While there is a nifty line-up of new tunes, it is 'Get Happy' that walks away with song honors. It's the old, wonderful Garland who sells the tune. . . . Kelly and Miss Garland also indulge in a jivey barn dance routine that has value."

—DAILY VARIETY

"In the course [of the film], Miss Garland changes weight twice and loses ten years before the final reel is ended. All of which does not in the least detract from . . . the young lady's ability to sell a song and make the contract stick. . . . The effective choreography is in 'Get Happy,' which [JG] accomplishes with the assistance of eight agile males, pink-shirted, and lighted like something out of *The Cabinet of Dr. Caligari*."

—DALLAS *DAILY TIMES HERALD*

"It is Kelly's show from beginning to end. Miss Garland is less casually assured [but] she sings fetchingly."

—NEW YORK *HERALD TRIBUNE*

"The spirited and joyful air of *Summer Stock* principally is provided by JG, who endows the songs and romance with all her abundant and showman-like talent. She gives every sequence and note a full measure of devotion."

—KANSAS CITY *STAR*

**ABOVE FROM TOP:** Not your average Connecticut barn: Judy, Gene Kelly, and company open their show with "All for You." | Metro's trade paper proclamation about preview reactions to the picture

**ABOVE SEQUENCE:** The twenty-year-old "Get Happy" got permanently revived, thanks to Judy's idea, Saul Chaplin's vocal arrangement, Skip Martin's orchestration, Chuck Walters' staging, and Vincente Minnelli's costuming concept. Theater audiences regularly broke into applause at the song's conclusion, and no less an admirer than playwright Edward Albee was part of one such crowd. He later said, "Nothing has instructed and gratified me more than the time she convinced a bunch of afternoon movie watchers that a strip of celluloid was the real thing."

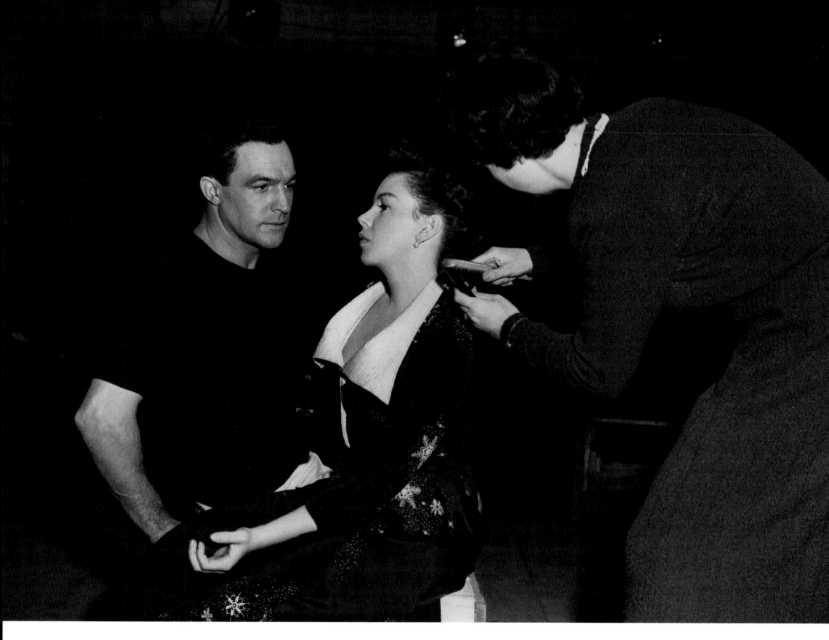

ABOVE: Preparing for the scene in which "Joe Ross" teaches "Jane Falbury" about grease paint, hokum, and the magic of boy-meets-girl-in-song-and-dance. A late addition to the film score, "You Wonderful You" became a happily accepted standard, as well as a later, identical, television duet for "Rob and Laura Petrie" (Dick Van Dyke and Mary Tyler Moore).

## NOTES

Joe Pasternak hoped to reteam Garland and Mickey Rooney for *Summer Stock*, thus bolstering her Hollywood return after the aborted *Annie Get Your Gun*. But by 1949, Gene Kelly was infinitely better box-office insurance than Mickey, and Kelly agreed to do the old-fashioned, "let's put on a show in the barn" picture as a favor to Judy. Director Chuck Walters approached the project on the same level.

Much has been written about the problems of completing *Summer Stock*,
and there's no question that Garland's frequent absences from the set were a major contributing factor. But it's important to add a couple of other facts as well. The production itself was oddly disorganized. It was originally scripted to reprise "If You Feel Like Singing, Sing" and "Dig-Dig-Dig For Your Dinner" for the show-within-a-show finale, and it wasn't until the picture was well underway that the creative staff realized that additional new songs would better serve the project. There
were delays while these were written, arranged, and rehearsed.

Then, as with *The Pirate*, Gene Kelly's tour de force routine was finished last. The number made inspired use of old newspapers and a creaky floor board as dancing adjuncts, but its completion helped push *Summer Stock* to a six-month total production schedule. While this was no more lengthy than that of the especially lavish Freed-unit product of preceding years, *Summer Stock* ran up against

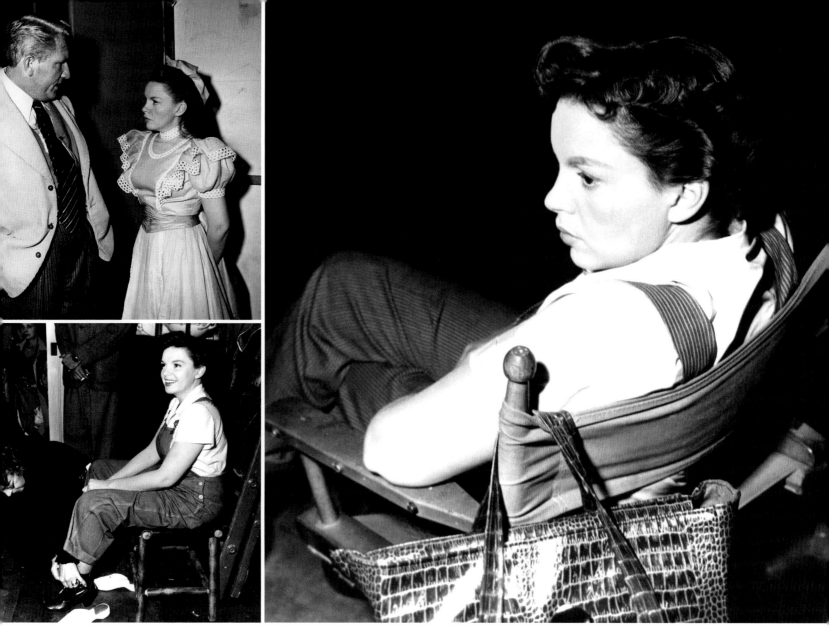

TOP LEFT: Spencer Tracy on a break from *Father of the Bride*; Judy on a break from the reprise of "You Wonderful You." ABOVE RIGHT: Off-camera and on, "Jane Falbury" was alternately musing or merry, and the picture won Judy critical plaudits. *Time* hailed her "unerring way with a song" and "one of Hollywood's few triple-threat girls."

new MGM honcho Dore Schary, who was less than sympathetic to musicals and (what he viewed as) indulgent film making. Regardless, and whatever the hold-ups, the final cost of *Summer Stock* was $2 million—only $43,000 over its original budget. Walters would humorously later recall his disbelief at the ebullience inherent in the film's rushes: "How dare this look like a happy picture?!"

*Summer Stock* remains one of the most entertaining of all Garland movies, whether enjoyed for song, dance, or script. Judy is partnered by Kelly in the super-charged "Portland Fancy"—arguably the best terpsichorean duet of her career. She wisely opted out of a hillbillies-and-howling-dogs routine, "Heavenly Music," electing instead to deliver "Get Happy," which remains one of the half-dozen archetypal Garland performances. The costarring and featured players make consistently energetic and compelling comedy contributions as well, from Phil Silvers to Eddie Bracken, Marjorie Main, Gloria DeHaven, Hans Conried, and Ray Collins.

When the box office was tallied for the month of September 1950, the only MGM picture in the top five was *Summer Stock*. It surpassed the million-dollar mark in receipts in just its first one hundred engagements, a 10 percent increase over the business for *In the Good Old Summertime*.

## What They Said

"It took us six months. . . . Six months is a terribly long time. [But] never once did I hear a cross word, a tart comment, a bitter crack, on the part of any member of the crew or the cast. They all understood. Gene Kelly rates a special word. He said, 'I'll do anything for this girl, Joe. If I have to come here and sit and wait for a year, I'd do it for her. That's the way I feel about her.'"

—PRODUCER JOE PASTERNAK

"We loved her, and we understood what she was going through. And I had every reason to be grateful for all the help she had given me."

—GENE KELLY

"I played her sister. Prior to that, we were just very good friends, but I'd never worked with her. So to film with her was . . . like a treasure for me, because she was the most incredible person. The funniest woman I'd ever been around. I mean, forget any stand-up comic or comedienne you want to talk about; she was hysterical. Great sense of humor. [And she] could make you cry faster than anybody in the world; I mean she was an actress—superb. And just a terrific lady with a terribly mixed-up life. Everything seemed going in wrong directions."

—GLORIA DEHAVEN

"She was the best actress I ever worked with. We used to 'overlap' each other—talk while the other actor is talking and have them answer you and make it seem as though it's the most natural thing in the world. From an acting standpoint, you use that for comedy, and Judy could do that so beautifully. Forget about singing; she was the best actress."

—EDDIE BRACKEN

"As far as I was concerned, she was a joy to work with. To begin with, there was no such thing as 'teaching' her a new song. You'd just play it for her, and she'd sing it back to you. I mean, the first time it happens to you, it's like magic. And she always got more out of a song than you expected. The choreographer was a man named Nick Castle; he had the same reaction. He would teach her a step, and she'd know it immediately. And—I remember so vividly!—Nick staring at her: 'I don't believe it!' And she said, 'Oh, come on; I'll forget it tomorrow, you know!' But that's what she was like to work with."

—COMPOSER/VOCAL ARRANGER
SAUL CHAPLIN

"Summer Stock was my first ulcer. And [there] was no help around the studio . . . gossip spreads, regardless of the size of MGM. And the bets were all over the lot that we'd never finish it; that's how bad it was. We were going through absolute torture. And Gene was right in there, helping; he was marvelous.

We [finally] finished the picture and realized that we didn't have a big payoff number for Judy. She'd gone up to Carmel with a hypnotist to try to help her mental problems and with her weight. And she was only there, I think, a week and half. But we needed the number. And she said, 'I want 'Get Happy.' I want Chuck to [stage] it; I'll give you a week. And I want to wear the outfit that was cut out of Easter Parade.' So that was a nice little challenge. People always thought that 'Get Happy' was taken out of another picture, because in that short of time, she was back to her trim figure. But it was all bloat—just water retention from nerves and pills. Once the pressure was off, she looked absolutely great. And it was only about two weeks later."

—CHARLES WALTERS

**OPPOSITE:** Perhaps Judy's final portrait sitting at MGM; she's decked out in the "All for You" wardrobe.

# THE ONES THAT GOT AWAY

Although only the loss of the first three assignments is to be regretted, Judy Garland began work on five feature films in which she was ultimately replaced. The "back stories" of the problems besetting each production often involve conflicting reports from the principal participants. Representative examples of differing memories are presented below.

## THE BARKLEYS OF BROADWAY (1949)

A METRO-GOLDWYN MAYER PICTURE.

**Produced by Arthur Freed, directed by Charles Walters.**

Conceived as a sort of spiritual sequel to *Easter Parade*, *The Barkleys of Broadway* centered on fictional Josh and Dinah Barkley—a triumphant, modern-day husband-and-wife team of musical theater stars. In the story, their personal and professional success is short-circuited by British playwright Trevor Huntington, who persuades Dinah to forsake song-and-dance for drama. The film's principal roles were created for Judy, Fred Astaire, and Peter Lawford; in rewrites, the playwright became a Frenchman and was recast with Jacques Francois. Harry Warren and Ira Gershwin were signed to do an original score, while Betty Comden and Adolph Green crafted the plot and script. (Across early drafts, their ultimately unused titles for the picture ranged from a generic *Judy Garland Story* to *The Stars Are Shining* to *You Made Me Love You*.)

Astaire started rehearsals for his solo numbers on May 17, 1948. Over four days in early June, Judy's stand-in Betty O'Kelly partnered with him, while Judy worked on *Words and Music*. But thereafter, Garland was less and less in shape to take on a new assignment. The preceding eighteen months had subjected her to the ongoing deterioration of her marriage to Vincente Minnelli; periodic but increased periods of prescription medication dependence and abuse; the extensive problems of filming (and then redoing portions of) *The Pirate*; the strain of completing *Easter Parade* on schedule and under budget; at least two stays in sanitariums for nervous collapse and withdrawal; and the stressful knowledge that several major productions were awaiting her at the studio. By contract, Judy owed them two such films each year.

Frail, fragile, and medication-propelled, she managed ten days of *Barkley* rehearsals and wardrobe fittings from June 14 through July 1, missing three days due to illness. But she was unable to work for the next two weeks; by July 17, and after consulting with Judy's doctor in hopes that she might still rally, producer Arthur Freed was forced to drop her from the picture. She was replaced by Ginger Rogers, with whom Astaire had done nine already-legendary films at RKO studios between 1933 and 1939.

An emotionally disheartened, physically depleted, and professionally suspended Judy collapsed. But over the next two months, she was able to rally, withdraw from pills, and regain a healthy amount of weight. In late September 1948, she returned to Metro to record and film an additional song for *Words and Music*. At that time, she also made at least two visits to the set of *Barkleys*, one of which so intimidated Rogers that director Chuck Walters had to ask a hurt and angry Judy to leave the soundstage. Seeing Garland go, Astaire could only sympathize, "What are they doing to that poor kid?"

## What They Said

*"I was elated when Arthur Freed told me he had started work on another one for Judy and me. We liked the story by Betty Comden and Adolph Green. When they read their original script to us in Arthur's office, we flipped with delight and said we'd have a hard time following them in the parts. They are noted for their brilliant readings of their own material. When it came time to start, I was disappointed to find that Judy could not make it because of illness. Although we decided to wait as long as possible in hopes that she might recover, we were bitterly disappointed, as she advised the studio to go ahead and replace her. The whole show having been written with Judy in mind, this situation presented a major problem."*

—FRED ASTAIRE

*"By now, I was just a mechanical hoop they were rolling around. I was sure I wasn't going to make it, but it didn't matter. The rehearsals began, and my migraine headaches got worse. I took any kind of pill to stop them, but they didn't stop. I went for days without sleep . . . but I kept on. I started to be late . . . and started to miss days. Finally, I was fired . . . they sent a telegram."*

—JUDY GARLAND

*"On the first day of work, I went down to the rehearsal hall to see Fred. He was sweet and friendly, but I could see he was slightly disappointed. [He and Judy had] just worked together on* Easter Parade, *and I knew Fred had a slight crush on her. Though I had nothing to do with her being ousted, I could tell she blamed me for her dismissal. [Later,] she came on the set and looked daggers at me. Judy, Fred, and I had a few photos taken together. [But] . . . she was fooling around with the crew and holding up the shoot. In the end, she had to be physically removed from the set."*—GINGER ROGERS

**RIGHT:** Judy made at least two visits to *The Barkleys of Broadway* soundstages. But whatever on-set tensions supposedly accompanied her are nowhere apparent as she relaxes with old friend Oscar Levant and jokes with Fred Astaire and Ginger Rogers.

"ANNIE GET YOUR GUN"

JUDY GARLAND is first of an All-Star cast to be announced. It will be produced in Technicolor by Arthur Freed, producer of "Easter Parade," "Words and Music" and many more Big Ones.

Approaching its 3rd year on Broadway and still packing them in. The nation will watch eagerly for this great Irving Berlin show when M-G-M brings it to the screen!

**ABOVE**: Advance trade paper ad for the film, heralding its Garland association.

"Doin' What Comes Natur'lly": The costume in which Annie finally gets her Frank.

## ANNIE GET YOUR GUN (1950)

A METRO-GOLDWYN-MAYER PICTURE.

**Produced by Arthur Freed, directed (ultimately) by George Sidney.**

*Annie Get Your Gun* was a great 1946 Broadway triumph for both star Ethel Merman and songwriter Irving Berlin. After a year of negotiations, Berlin saw to it that motion picture rights for the show were sold to MGM. In addition to their top dollar offer, Arthur Freed had specifically assured Berlin that the picture would be made with Judy Garland.

A fictionalization of the life of sharpshooter Annie Oakley, the film encountered script and (apart from Judy) casting difficulties early on. While he'd scheduled rehearsals for October 1, 1948—and the onset of principal photography for November 1—Freed ultimately had to postpone everything until spring 1949. In the interim, Judy was assigned to *In the Good Old Summertime*. But *Annie*'s preproduction problems persisted. Early scenarios included most of the show's score, including both "Moonshine Lullaby" and "I Got Lost in His Arms" for Judy. They were inexplicably, unfortunately dropped, and the latter was replaced by an ill-conceived reprise of "The Girl That I Marry." A lesser outtake from the Broadway score, "Let's Go West Again," was shoehorned into the script as well.

With everyone from Bing Crosby to Roy Rogers, John Raitt, Cary Grant, Dan Dailey, and Perry Como rumored in the running, the role of Frank Butler finally went to Howard Keel, American-born star of the London production of *Oklahoma!* But further problems grew out of Judy's marital and medication issues. To combat the latter, she was subjected to a series of electroshock therapy treatments. Meanwhile, she and Minnelli officially separated on March 30, 1949. In the midst of it all, Freed named the irrational Busby Berkeley as director of *Annie*, which almost effectively sealed Judy's fate.

**LEFT AND OPPOSITE**: A series of costume tests for *Annie Get Your Gun*. Hair and makeup seemingly were not a consideration here, but Judy modeled her complete wardrobe across several days; it's apparent that she felt better on some occasions than others. Each costume is identified by caption as to the plot point (or song) it would accompany.

nie goes on the road and discovers there's no business like show business.

"They Say it's Wonderful"

A star is born, thanks to Colonel Buffalo Bill.

Annie makes her solo debut.

Chief Sitting Bull adopts Annie in a formal (musical) ceremony.

Annie and the Wild West Show set out for their triumphs abroad.

Annie comes home to America.

Dressed to recapture the love of Frank Butler at New York's Brevoort Hotel.

The original show dialogue would have trouble getting past the movie censors: "I'll wear my low-cut-in-the-front-dress; I'll show him a thing or two!"

Ever more a martinet (and given to shouting, declamation, and endless, repetitive rehearsal), Berkeley was possibly the single worst choice to helm a major Garland musical in 1949. His manic demands led to a serious accident for Keel just as filming began; a month later, Berkeley's ineptitude was finally acknowledged by the studio, and he was replaced, almost overnight, by Judy's champion, Charles Walters. But it was too late. Her own exhaustion and medication dependence had occasioned delays and lost days. In a black comedy of miscommunication—and mistimed letters of alternate threat and dismissal from the front office to Garland—the production was abruptly shut down on May 10.

Within hours (and playing the company game), Judy took public responsibility for the situation: "I don't blame the studio for suspending me. I've been a bad girl for not getting to work on time. Studios are run to make money. They can't take chances with careless people like me." Later, when told Betty Hutton would be imported from Paramount to play Annie Oakley, Garland added, "I'm glad that if anyone had to replace me, it was Betty. I'd rather the part went to her than to anyone else. I'm sure she'll have the same love for the role that I have. She's a good trouper." Although at least one legend would have it otherwise, Betty later recalled that Judy was generous and kind to her during her subsequent weeks of work at MGM on *Annie*. When the film opened as one of the box office hits of 1950, Hutton enjoyed an enormous personal triumph in the role.

## What They Said

*"Judy put me at my ease at once and showed me what I should have known all the time: the people with real talent want you to have a break. Judy was my first friend in Hollywood, [and] I was thrilled to death to work with her. [But] she was very tired, and I don't think she was too happy with Busby Berkeley. On the second day of shooting, I had to come from behind a backdrop at a full gallop on horseback. I did it about six times; it was fine—the camera[man] was happy, everybody was happy. Not Buzz. He said 'One more.' And the horse lost his footing at a full gallop on the sharp turn, fell on me, and I broke my ankle. So they had to shoot around me for about six weeks. And Judy had no time off—and she needed time off. She just fell apart. It was terribly sad. She just ran out of energy."* —HOWARD KEEL

*"There was enormous fanfare, because they paid more money for [Annie] than they'd ever paid for any other property. So I started rehearsals, and I was still a very tired and a very distressed woman. I remember I started to lose my hair; my hairline started to recede badly. But I went through all the rehearsals and all the costume fittings. We made all the prerecordings. And, unfortunately, they put Buzz Berkeley on the picture. Now, I think he's a wonderful director; I think he did*

*a fine job with the earlier pictures. But psychologically, Buzz represented all the years of Benzedrine to work as hard as we worked [to] just exhaustion; you know how Buzz was. And to tell you the truth, he was in a very bad mental state himself doing* Annie. *And I said [to the executives], 'I don't think we're a very good combination right now.' But they said, 'Oh, we know what we're doing; you just do as you're told.'*

*So . . . we did a couple of scenes, and I knew I wasn't good. I was just in a daze. My head wouldn't stop aching. They had to keep putting black in my hairline because of my hair falling out so badly. And I had these heavy costumes on, trying to play a terribly funny role. But I just kept plugging away, and finally I was doing a number called, 'I'm An Indian, Too'—where they make [Annie] an Indian and where the boys threw me around; Bob Alton was [choreographing] it. And I just didn't know what I was doing. I had this migraine headache constantly. And I started being late again . . . So they sent me another notice, dismissing me, at noon time. Well, I really blew my top. And again I rushed to the phone and tried to get everybody, and nobody was in their offices. They would send these notices and then leave for their homes. Or if they didn't leave for their homes, they'd leave word with their secretaries not to put me through—which was a very, very cruel thing to do. Because it doesn't give you any chance to say . . . maybe we can get this straightened out. No—just complete dismissal. And I knew I was in for a public beating, and I got a hell of one."—*JUDY GARLAND (1960)

# ROYAL WEDDING (1951)

A METRO-GOLDWYN-MAYER PICTURE.

**Produced by Arthur Freed, directed by Stanley Donen.**

It was first noted in an MGM memo of January 11, 1949, that Broadway scenarist/lyricist Alan Jay Lerner was scripting *Niagara Falls*, an original musical comedy screenplay for production by Arthur Freed. The very next day, a follow-up memo tersely continued, "Niagara Falls atmosphere being eliminated . . . the story will concern American entertainers going to London to entertain at the time of a royal wedding." Lerner went on to fashion the American entertainers as present-day prototypes of Fred Astaire and his sister Adele, who'd performed together from the time they were preteens, beginning in 1906. Their career encompassed vaudeville, Broadway, and London's West End until Adele's marriage into the peerage in 1932 and Fred's emergence as a solo performer.

It took Lerner just over a year to solidify the scenario for what had been retitled *Royal Wedding*. He also wrote the film's lyrics to music by Burton Lane, and both

CLOCKWISE FROM LEFT: Judy was venerated by producer Arthur Freed, although—a week after this picture was taken—it was his abrasive comment during her costume tests ("What are *you* made up for?") that decimated the star. | Judy's twenty-eighth birthday was celebrated during *Royal Wedding* preproduction in one of the MGM rehearsal halls. She was joined by husband Vincente Minnelli, Gene Kelly (here *sans* toupee), and the film's director, Stanley Donen. | The dancers in Garland's films adored her. Many Metro coworkers would forsake all other assignments to tour with Judy "live" during the 1950s.

the revised plot and songs happily harked back to the 1947 marriage of Princess Elizabeth of England to the Duke of Edinburgh. Meanwhile, Arthur Freed's initial plan (at least as of April 14, 1950) was to team Astaire with Vera Ellen as his fictional sister. Shortly thereafter, however, June Allyson was assigned the role; Fred began his own rehearsals on May 1, and June joined him ten days later. But by May 19, she had to confess, "Suddenly, I didn't know what was happening. I felt weak. I felt nauseated. I felt faint. I was in awe of Astaire—but not that much! I went directly to my doctor. And from his office, I called Fred excitedly and said, 'Fred, I want you to be the first to know: I'm pregnant!' There was a stunned silence. Then a horrified voice said, 'Who *is* this?!'"

Hastily, a vacationing Judy was summoned back to MGM on May 22 to discuss the picture; she started work the next day. But director Charles Walters then requested that the studio replace him. As much as he personally and professionally venerated Garland, he'd just undergone several months of pressure during the filming of *Summer Stock*, and he freely admitted he couldn't face another immediate association with her. So, Stanley Donen, in his first major solo assignment, began work as director of *Royal Wedding* on May 24.

Despite Donen's later erroneous claims ("We could not get her to come in"), Judy reported for rehearsals and fittings on all eighteen of her scheduled work days between May 23 and June 16. She was late in arriving for more than half of them but, once on site, performed "brilliantly," according to Saul Chaplin; Johnny Green of the Metro music department also found her a model of cooperation. However, the ambitious, rehearsal-prone Donen was scarcely the correct match for the quick-to-tire, quicker-to-learn-a-routine Garland. On Friday, June 16, she appeared for wardrobe tests and was cheered to the rafters by the crew for her glamorous get-up. A harried Freed sauntered by, unthinkingly deprecated her appearance, and the enormously insecure star was shattered. When Donen requested she appear the next day for a mere hour's rehearsal, she opted out, and the Metro hierarchy—under the unsympathetic regime of new production head Dore Schary—went into action. By late afternoon on June 17, Judy was again suspended; by June 21, Jane Powell was rehearsing her role in the film.

## What They Said

*"June Allyson and I started a few numbers with choreographer Nick Castle and were going along well when things began to happen. First of all, little June arrived one morning, after about ten days, and told us she could not go on with the picture because she was expecting a baby. Now we had a problem. Who could we get? Originally, Chuck Walters had agreed to direct, but he retired to take over some other assignment. The studio submitted the script to Judy [and she] readily*

*accepted, much to the jubilation of us all. We now could resume after a week's quandary. I was delighted that Judy and I could get together again after the false start of* Barkleys. *We went back to rehearsals. Although still without a director, we could go ahead with the dances. After about two weeks, Judy was taken sick and could not rehearse for several days. We waited and soon realized that it would not be possible for her to make it. There were five weeks gone, and we had no leading lady and no director. I began to wonder if we would ever get this picture made."*

—FRED ASTAIRE

*"Judy had no choice but to say 'yes', even though she was only in the second week of what was supposed to be a six months' rest period. If she refused the offer, the studio could suspend her and wouldn't have to pay her salary."* —JUNE ALLYSON

*"Last Friday, when Judy went on the set to have her clothes tested, she was gay and happy. Everybody said how well she looked and how pretty her dresses were. Then came a producer who said she didn't, and the smile on her face went out."*

—COLUMNIST HEDDA HOPPER

*"[After* Summer Stock*], I took off for Carmel by myself and took a house for six months. I was there exactly two and a half weeks when I got a call from the studio about* Royal Wedding. *That's when I made the biggest of the many big mistakes in my life. I reasoned that I had been so humiliated by the studio and the press that, if I returned, I could look all right again. So I returned to Culver City. I plunged into my work. I learned seven dance routines, a lot of songs, got fitted for costumes—and it happened again. The weight had to come off, so they put me back on Benzedrine and the crash diet. Even my system couldn't stand it anymore; I just couldn't make it. So, MGM did the same thing again. Fired. Another telegram. Another beating in the press. That's the last time I ever worked at MGM. Farewell, Alma Mater."* —JUDY GARLAND (1960)

ABOVE: On their arrival in California to begin *Harlow* rehearsals, Judy and fiancé Mark Herron (left) were greeted by her children, Lorna and Joe, as well as cast member Barry Sullivan. Lorna holds an enlargement of the trade paper ad for the production.

# HARLOW (1965)

AN ELECTRONOVISION PRODUCTION.

**Directed by Alex Segal.**

Irving Shulman's graphic and controversial 1964 biography of Jean Harlow created new interest in the 1930s film actress. As a result, producer Joseph E. Levine immediately began work on a lavish biopic starring Carroll Baker and based on Shulman's work. At the same time, an exploitative Bill Sargent rushed into production with an alternate retelling of the Harlow saga, built around Carol Lynley. Sargent's hastier approach made use of the Electronovision process, in which performances were captured on high resolution videotape and later transferred to film via kinescope for theatrical release. Judy was announced for the role of Harlow's "Mama Jean" in Sargent's picture on March 11, 1965.

She withdrew from the cast on March 22, and at least one later press report offered that "Sargent canned her" when she failed to turn up that day for rehearsal. Garland's management, however, cited scheduling conflicts, referencing the preparation required for Judy's April 5 singing appearance at the Academy Awards. Fresh from her stint as "The Baroness" in *The Sound of Music*, Eleanor Parker agreed to replace Judy, but within twenty-four hours, she bowed out as well, to be supplanted by Ginger Rogers. Sargent's *Harlow* was completed in eight days of videotaping, the results of which were then edited for release on May 14. The film was neither a critical nor a box office success.

## What They Said

*"Honey, I'm not drunk, I'm not on drugs, and I'm telling you this is a piece of a junk, and I'm getting out!"*

—JUDY GARLAND TO COSTAR CAROL LYNLEY ON THE SET OF *HARLOW*

# VALLEY OF THE DOLLS (1967)

A TWENTIETH CENTURY FOX RELEASE.

**Produced by David Weisbart, directed by Mark Robson.**

Jacqueline Susann's novel *Valley of the Dolls* was published in February 1966 and quickly rose to long-term, best-seller status. Graphic descriptions of sex, drugs, alcohol abuse, and the more tawdry aspects of show business won the book scurrilous notoriety, much of it derived from the author's barely-disguised fictionalizations of the lives of Garland, Ethel Merman, Carole Landis, Marilyn Monroe, and lesser denizens of the entertainment world. (When Susann died in 1974, it was estimated that *Valley* had sold 17 million copies. At the time of Judy's passing, five years earlier, *New York Times* critic Vincent Canby trenchantly observed, "Judy lived [her life] and died still worrying about money, and Jacqueline Susann wrote it, as if it were a comic strip, and made a million dollars.")

Hollywood understandably rushed to capitalize on the book's infamy, and Twentieth Century Fox attracted world-wide media coverage when they signed Judy to play "Helen Lawson" in the picture. An aging Broadway diva, Lawson was the story's Merman prototype and—as Garland later, mischievously proclaimed— "the only one in the book that doesn't take pills." To announce Judy's participation, Fox held a massively-attended New York press conference on March 2, 1967, and she fielded the sometimes pointed journalistic queries with characteristic humor. (Reporter: "Miss Garland, the book deals with pills to some extent. Have you found that prevalent around show business people?" Judy: "Well, I find it prevalent around newspaper people.")

In mid-April, Garland reported to Fox in Hollywood and tested her wardrobe, makeup, and hair styles in fine fettle. She was further cheered by the affection and veneration shown her by the crew and by costars Barbara Parkins and Patty Duke— the latter playing Susann's obvious rip-off of Judy herself. But Judy only shakily managed to prerecord her one song for the soundtrack, and for all the intended good will, her customary insecurities were further magnified by the indifferent handling she received on set from director Mark Robson. Once again medicated— whether in terror or rebellion—she was unable to perform as requested. Garland's lack of cooperation can also be traced to her own evolving emotions about the picture. At first overjoyed at being asked to return to the screen, she had gradually come to feel dismay and dissatisfaction at the caliber of the script, the nature of the story, and the inherent exploitation of her position.

After some sporadic attempts at filming Judy's first scene—all of which footage was deemed unusable—Fox was forced to fire her on April 27 and managed to garner even more press over her dismissal. (She was eventually replaced by Susan Hayward.) Garland was distraught and publicly railed against the studio; by mid-summer, however, she had embarked on a triumphant fifteen-city, eighty-performance, "comeback" concert tour, including her third record-breaking engagement at New York's Palace Theatre. When *Valley of the Dolls* was released in December 1967, its box office was also record breaking, but the picture itself won nearly universal critical scorn. And virtually everyone was glad that Judy Garland had not been a part of it.

## What They Said

*"She never should have been hired in the first place, in my opinion. She obviously needed the money . . . but I thought it was cheap and tawdry to ask her to play the part. And it made me sad that she had reached the point of having to take this stupid role, playing opposite someone who was reputedly playing her. . . . It's undignified to have to do such a thing, and even though she did a lot of undignified things, she was basically a dignified person. At this particular time, Judy was not in very good shape, to say the least. But she was so sweet [and] cute . . . you just wanted to hug her all the time. . . . I mean, the very first day [she was on the set], it was like going to Mecca. And she was charming—and funny, oh! very funny! I worshipped her. She made me laugh every time she looked at me. But the director, who was the meanest son-of-a-bitch I've ever known in my life, he kept this icon—this little sparrow, very thin at the time—waiting and waiting. Had her come in at 6:30 in the morning, and he wouldn't even plan to get to her until four in the afternoon.*

*She was very down-to-earth; she didn't mind waiting. What I minded was there were gentlemen around her who supplied her with wine and other things, so that when she finally did get called to the set, she couldn't function very well. At any rate, instead of trying to talk to Judy, the director decided that some [assistant] should talk to her, and she crumbled. She just crumbled. And she was fired. And that was devastating. [That] was really the end of the movie for all of us. It was so ugly, so unkind, that even if people had cared before, nobody gave a damn now. The producers may have been justified in terms of her being unable to work, but remember, I didn't think they were justified in hiring her in the first place. Also, they were a little too ready with a replacement. They had gotten their PR mileage out of the situation; the 'Judy comeback' stories had created extraordinary publicity for the film. And now she was expendable. And that was the last I saw of her, until [later that] year when she was appearing at the Palace, in tiptop shape and doing a great show . . . wearing her costume from* Valley of the Dolls!*"*

—PATTY DUKE

*"Wasn't that a terrible picture?!"*—JUDY GARLAND (1968)

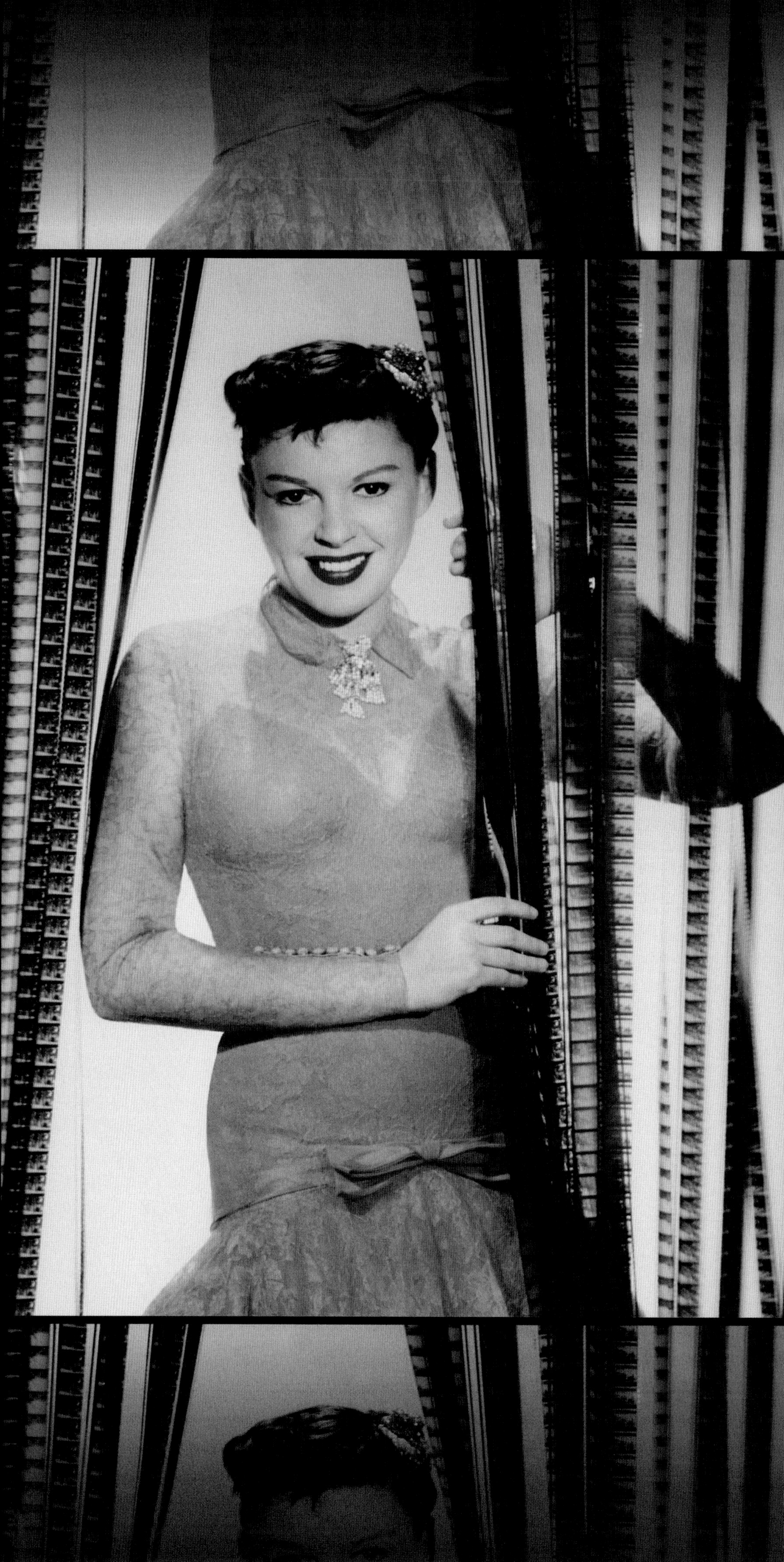

# crowning a career

1954–1963

The last nineteen years of Judy Garland's life were much more about live performances, television appearances, and recordings than they were about motion pictures. Indeed, discounting the two movies for which she loaned just her voice—the all-star *Pepe* and the cartoon *Gay Purr-ee*—she made only four feature films between 1954 and 1962. But two of those pictures remain classics of their respective genres, and she received Academy Award nominations for both of them. To a lesser degree, the other two have their own significance. One dealt with intellectually disabled children, long before that topic became mainstream. The other provided Garland with a much-venerated, bravura showcase and, as it turned out, a suitable finale to her screen career. All four offered a greater thematic diversity than any of her MGM vehicles, reflecting both the changing times and Garland's growing maturity as an actress and woman.

The greatest of these—both in terms of contemporary reaction and that of succeeding generations—was *A Star is Born* (1954), which Judy had wanted to do as a musical at MGM more than a decade earlier. Corporate executives thought the drama too heavy for a twenty-year-old Garland, even with the leavening addition of songs. (The concept of *Star* as a film musical was similarly dismissed by the studio hierarchy when Gene Kelly wanted Metro to buy the rights as a vehicle for him in the late 1940s.) But Judy's international stage "comeback" in 1951 and 1952 resonated so strongly within the film industry that husband Sid Luft—representing himself as producer—was able to negotiate a nine-film option deal with Warner Bros. Three of those pictures would star Judy, and *A Star is Born* was to be the first.

Preproduction, filming, and the editing and scoring of *Star* covered two years, and the final 181-minute result was proudly heralded and received as "the *Gone With the Wind* of musicals." Whether in front of or behind the cameras, all involved were at the top of their form and determined to provide Garland with an extraordinary, unprecedented return to motion pictures. Director George Cukor was Judy's equal in striving for perfection, and the finished product stands as one of the finest musical dramas in Hollywood history: clear-eyed, humorous, celebratory, disturbing, and a strong indictment of the pros and cons of the industry at that time. As they completed their work, Cukor spoke of Judy: "She is perfect in the picture. She's cooperative, tireless, energetic, and—I say this objectively—absolutely magnificent."

Unfortunately, any box-office success or potential Academy recognition for *Star* was squelched by Warner Bros.' post-premiere tampering—and augmented by a minor media undertow that (however inaccurate in part) held Garland accountable for any and all delays in the *Star*-making process. As a result, the studio didn't pick up its option for future Garland/Luft productions. A little over a year later though, they definitely wanted Judy back to play the title role in *The Helen Morgan Story*. Around the same time, Nunnally Johnson implied that his meetings with Garland regarding her appearance in *The Three Faces of Eve*

health and increasing weight through the rest of the decade made screen work less likely as well.

In December 1960, Luft relinquished control of Garland's career to Freddie Fields and David Begelman, then at the onset of their managerial/agency partnership. The two men would wreak their own havoc on Judy's health and professional affairs, but their initial focus and savvy led to her greatest comeback, covering all media. The Fields/Begelman plan to re-launch Garland as a motion picture actress was made easier when, within a few weeks of their takeover, Stanley Kramer approached them about casting her in the all-star *Judgment at Nuremberg* (1961). Her role across three scenes was brief, but it was built to provide the turning point of the courtroom drama, and Judy was more than up to the task. Kramer first introduced her character in the final scene before the film's intermission; she was seen in profile in silhouette, which gave audiences the opportunity to both recognize her and to adjust to the concept of a thirty-eight year old, heavier Judy Garland. In her final scene, her character approaches hysteria when a defense attorney browbeats her for refusing to lie about a fabricated intimacy with an elderly Jewish man who had befriended her as a girl. Years later, Liza Minnelli told Garland biographer Gerold Frank that her mother had acknowledged summing up memories of father Frank Gumm

for Twentieth Century Fox eventually fell apart because he could no longer "get to her." A firm RKO offer to star Judy in a musicalization of *Alice Adams* went virtually unacknowledged. In every case, there was reluctance on the part of the studios to take on Sid Luft as a major part of the production package. Meanwhile, Luft preferred to keep Judy onstage in Las Vegas, New York, or on tour, as the cash flow from such enterprises was greater. Her own as her acting subtext for the scene. (The author reported Minnelli's comment but seemingly missed its possible connection to the factually different, yet tormenting stories heard by a confused Baby Gumm three decades earlier.)

The most lightweight of Judy's latter-day film ventures came when she was signed to speak and sing the leading role in the artful feature-length cartoon *Gay Purr-ee*. The orchestration and underscoring were written and conducted by Garland's new musical director, Mort Lindsey, and his charts for "Paris Is a Lonely Town" and "Little Drops of Rain" provided her with two excellent concert pieces as well. For a brief period in 1962—and to promote *Gay Purr-ee*—Judy was singing the latter song in her act in lieu of "Over the Rainbow." (She confessed to a Chicago reporter, "I think I've wrung that one pretty dry.")

Of the two films Garland made in 1962, *A Child is Waiting* was the most ambitious in theme and statement. The Stanley Kramer production about a school for challenged children was prestigiously launched at a gala Washington, D.C. dinner/preview, benefiting the Joseph P. Kennedy, Jr. Foundation. Members of the First Family, led by President and Mrs. John F. Kennedy, honored Garland and costar Burt Lancaster on that occasion, with the President warmly acknowledging Judy—with him on the dais—as "our old friend."

Finally, *I Could Go on Singing* was based on an earlier CBS-TV drama which had starred Judy's "screen mother" of years past, Mary Astor. The story was musicalized for Garland and, though not much more than a Technicolor soap-opera-with-songs, it managed to win almost universal raves for its star. Even critics who justifiably qualified their enthusiasm for other aspects of the production came out in her favor, and the customarily acerbic *Time* magazine admired, "If the Judy who once stole Andy Hardy's heart has gone somewhere over a rainbow of hard knocks and sleeping pills, Garland the actress seems here to stay." *I Could Go on Singing* debuted in London, "to an audience divided between titled admirers and professional people of stage, films, and press." The latter had been flown in from the United States on a publicity junket for the picture, and as the correspondent for the Boston *Globe* continued to marvel, "[It was] one of the most extraordinary premieres I've ever seen. The cheers that rang out for this . . . small, lithe, and lovely young woman were deafening. People stood up as if she were the queen herself."

Yet for all the accolades, *I Could Go on Singing* did comparatively little business. Brian Baxter of London's National Film Theatre later opined that Judy's original movie audience didn't necessarily want to see their heroine grown, "possibly resenting their lost youth through hers." And

though there would be further film offers, Fields and Begelman had, by that time, sold Garland into weekly television, as there was much more money in such contracts. (The fact that the duo didn't fight to place Judy into more commercial screen vehicles in the early 1960s—including *Gypsy*, which was mentioned for her—remains a further comment on their managerial savoir-faire.)

But there's really no reason to regret "what wasn't"—at least not when "what is" remains so present, palatable, and persuasive. From her first feature film to her last, Judy Garland's through-line remains the immediacy and impact of her talent, personality, and reality, from "I can sing; ya wanna hear me?!" to "Love does funny things when it hits you this way: I could go on singing. . . . "

Let the professionals tell it. A 1936 Kansas City review for *Pigskin Parade* enumerated the reasons for the film's appeal, and the most succinct of his estimations was the simple phrase "Judy Garland! Judy Garland!! Judy Garland!!!" Twenty-seven years later, when critiquing *I Could Go on Singing* for the London *Sunday Times*, Dilys Powell was a bit more analytical but no less enthusiastic: "It is for something beyond acting that one cherishes this elated little creature. It is for the true star's quality. The quality of being."

# A Star is Born

## CAST:

Judy Garland .......................... *Esther Blodgett,
renamed Vicki Lester*

James Mason .......................... *Norman Maine*

Jack Carson .................................. *Matt Libby*

Charles Bickford .......................... *Oliver Niles*

Tom Noonan .......................... *Danny McGuire*

Lucy Marlow ............................... *Lola Lavery*

Amanda Blake .......................... *Miss Ettinger*

Irving Bacon ........................................ *Graves*

Hazel Shermet ..................... *Libby's Secretary*

Glenn Williams .......................... *James Brown*

Lotus Robb ............................. *Miss Markham*

## CREDITS:

**Sidney Luft** *(producer)*; **Vern Alves** *(associate producer)*; **George Cukor** *(director)*; **Moss Hart** *(screenplay)*; **Dorothy Parker, Alan Campbell, and Robert Carson** *(original screenplay)*; **William A. Wellman and Robert Carson** *(story)*; **Sam Leavitt** *(photography)*; **Harold Arlen and Ira Gershwin** *(music and lyrics)*; **Leonard Gershe and Roger Edens** *(music and lyrics to "Born in a Trunk")*; **Ray Heindorf** *(musical director)*; **Skip Martin** *(orchestrations)*; **Richard Barstow** *(dance director)*; **Gene Allen** *(production designer)*; **Malcolm Bert** *(art director)*; **George James Hopkins** *(set decorations)*; **Jean Louis, Mary Ann Nyberg, and Irene Sharaff** *(costumes)*; **Folmar Blangsted** *(editor)*

## JUDY'S NUMBERS:

*"Gotta Have Me Go with You," "The Man That Got Away," "Trinidad Cocoanut Oil Shampoo Commercial," "Born in a Trunk" (incorporating "I'll Get By," "You Took Advantage of Me," "Black Bottom," "The Peanut Vendor," "My Melancholy Baby," and "Swanee"), "Here's What I'm Here For," "It's a New World" and reprise, "Someone at Last," "Lose That Long Face." Deleted: "It's a New World" finale reprise, "When My Sugar Walks Down the Street" dropped from "Born in a Trunk").*
*Never recorded: "Green Light Ahead," "I'm Off the Downbeat," "Dancing Partner"*

**RELEASE DATE: September 29, 1954
(Los Angeles world premiere)
RUN TIME: 181 minutes**

OPPOSITE: Don McKay and Jack Harmon partner with Garland for "Gotta Have Me Go with You." At Judy's request during prerecording, vocal arranger Hugh Martin pulled a "fish face" to break her up at the moment she needed to laugh for the soundtrack. LEFT: In costume for "Born in a Trunk"/"Swanee"

## SYNOPSIS

Screen legend Norman Maine is the preeminent attraction at Hollywood's "Night of the Stars" benefit. Per custom, he's also drunk and only saved from making an onstage disgrace of himself by the quick thinking of band vocalist Esther Blodgett (JG). Once sober, Maine goes looking for the girl. Hearing her sing in an after-hours club, he discovers she possesses extraordinary talent. He convinces her to precipitously quit the band and opt for a screen career, but her decision is thwarted by his alcoholic disappearance on location to make a film.

When they are finally reunited, Maine secures Esther a contract at the Oliver Niles Studio, and publicist Matt Libby sets the wheels of her ascent to stardom in motion by having the girl rechristened Vicki Lester. In her first film, she is an overnight sensation. Esther and Norman marry soon after.

The subsequent, increasing demand for Esther's pictures are contrasted by the studio's abandonment of the no longer cost-effective Maine. After several episodes of drunken public embarrassment, the actor overhears Esther's plan to abandon her success and go away with him. He sacrifices his life to save hers, and she in turn becomes a recluse. Only her long-time musical arranger Danny McGuire is able to convince her that her withdrawal from the spotlight is just what her husband most feared. She returns to the benefit stage where they'd first met and proudly introduces herself as "Mrs. Norman Maine."

LEFT: The film's production number, "Born in a Trunk," traces the career arc of a singing hopeful. Working toward success means delivering "The Peanut Vendor" in a series of dives.

## After-hours at the Downbeat Club

"The Man That Got Away" was filmed three times until all parties were satisfied with the camera work, lighting, composition, and approach. The first two attempts featured Judy in Mary Ann Nyberg costuming; the ultimate rendition had her in a dress by Jean Louis.

**ABOVE FROM TOP:** The first version | As seen in the film—and a moment described in the *New Yorker* in 2010 as "one of the most astonishing, emotionally draining musical productions in Hollywood history, both for Garland's electric, spontaneous performance and for Cukor's realization of it."

**RIGHT:** Danny McGuire (Tom Noonan) was right to be leery of Esther's initial sympathy for alcoholic film actor Norman Maine; she tells McGuire she's quitting her job with him to pursue a Hollywood screen test.

BELOW FROM LEFT: Unbeknownst to Esther, Maine has been shanghaied to a film location—and she waits for his call that never comes. | Norman Maine (James Mason) finally returns and is beset by Esther's neighbors when he finally tracks her down at a seedy boarding house. Cut from the film after its premiere, the sequence featured Garland and Mason with Geraldine Wall, Mary Young, Barbara Pepper, Lauren Chapin, and Nancy Kulp.

## REVIEWS

"*A Star is Born* could well be among the top money-makers of all time, for entertainment such as this will not soon be forgotten. It could be with us for a long, long time. One of the finest measures of its quality is that it does not seem overlong. *Star* far surpasses the [1937] original in entertainment content, in every visual and technical property, and obviously in business possibilities."

—*MOTION PICTURE DAILY*

"Miss Garland's rich and spirited singing of a nice selection of Harold Arlen songs is matched by her versatile performance of an undisguised sentimental role. You can believe she has merited stardom from the demonstrations of talent she gives. This is something that few pictures about sensational artists can call upon them to do. Mr. Mason's performance is a sharply nettled and flexible one, revealing a tormented ego if not a clearly understandable man."

—NEW YORK *TIMES*

"Exploiting the razzle-dazzle of Hollywood as it has never before been explored or exploited in a picture, *Star* last night put a brilliantly shining crown upon the dark-tressed head of Judy Garland. A resplendent movie throng, completely in the mood for adulation, took part in the figurative coronation ceremony at probably the most remarkable premiere ever held in the film city."

—LOS ANGELES *TIMES*

"[*Star*] gives Judy THE chance of her career to really showcase the talent that turned her into an entertainment great at a relatively early age. She handles comedy with ease, drawing laughs without straining. Her vocal efforts are incomparable. . . . As for her dramatic quality, Miss Garland reaches her peak. Jack Carson does an outstanding job . . . and Charles Bickford's interpretation is excellent."

—LOS ANGELES *DAILY NEWS*

"Warner Bros. laid $6,000,000 on the line last night and rolled a seven. The biggest movie gamble in years sure paid off for the studio and JG. For all I know, they're still cheering down at Hollywood and Vine. . . . The picture is first rate. It has class and distinction, [and it] cinches an Oscar for JG come next Academy Award time. She turns in a beautiful acting job, as well as singing her heart out."—LOS ANGELES *MIRROR*

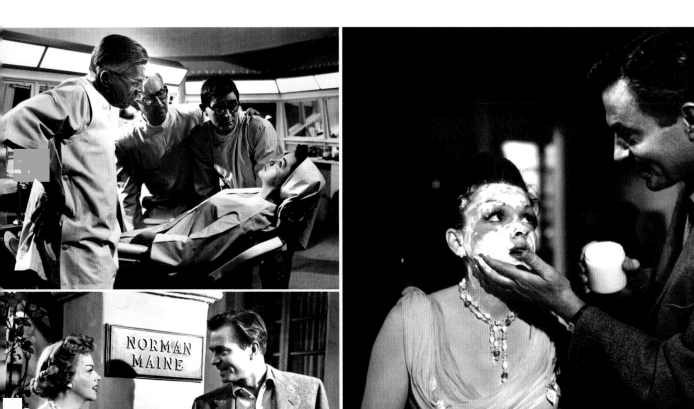

**TOP LEFT**: Makeup whiz Ettinger (Rudolph Anders, left) despairs over Esther's problematic face prior to her screen test. Associates Joe Dougherty and Alan DeWitt are equally discouraged. **ABOVE AND RIGHT**: Horrified by what the "experts" have done to Esther, Norman attempts to correct their errors.

## NOTES

David O. Selznick's *A Star is Born* was an instant cinematic classic when it premiered in 1937. Fourteen years later, Judy and Sid Luft launched their plan to musicalize the story as the first Garland screen vehicle since the dissolution of her MGM contract. The William Morris Agency at that time represented Judy. Reflecting the affection held for her within the industry, Morris agency president Abe Lastfogel expressed to coworkers his "every wish that Judy's picture be given every help within our power." Thus, across many months of preparation, Garland and Luft were able to achieve a co-production deal with Warner Bros., as well as a stellar cast, staff, and crew.

The list of actors considered for the male lead in *A Star is Born* eventually included everyone from established luminaries to relative newcomers. Among them: Cary Grant, Henry Fonda, James Stewart, Humphrey Bogart, Tyrone Power, Laurence Olivier, Gregory Peck, Frank Sinatra, Robert Taylor, Ray Milland, Burt Lancaster, Robert Young, Richard Burton, Montgomery Clift, Stewart Granger, and Glenn Ford. In April 1953, Jack L. Warner advised scenarist Moss Hart, "We are still optimistic about getting [twenty-nine-year-old] Marlon Brando. . . .

We deleted a couple of references in the script sent him as to the twenty years he had been drinking, etc." The role finally went to James Mason.

Hart carefully expanded, adapted, and updated the 1937 script to reflect the Hollywood film industry of the early 1950s, simultaneously creating an outstanding showcase for Judy. When she read his final draft, she responded, "If I can only say it the way you've written it, *I'll be home*! God bless you." Harold Arlen and Ira Gershwin worked closely with Hart to determine the best places in his scenario to slot at least six new songs, and George Cukor—delighted at the opportunity to finally work with Garland—signed to direct the picture. A decade had passed since he'd almost helmed *Meet Me in St. Louis*, and even before that, he'd provided her with brief but substantial counsel during a transitional moment in the filming of *The Wizard of Oz*.

The history of *A Star is Born* is a tumultuous one. Through a complicated mix of issues, it was an enormously long shoot, from mid-October 1953 through July 1954. A switch-over to the new CinemaScope process a couple weeks into filming meant starting the picture from scratch. The seamless amalgamation of story

**ABOVE:** Once more herself, Esther still needs Maine's encouragement. "Of course you're scared! We all are! What made you think you wouldn't be?" he declaims.

and song resulted in a rough cut that ran well over three hours; in *Star*, Warner Bros. basically made two full-length feature films. Garland's emotional, physical, domestic, and prescription medication problems contributed their own havoc, especially as principal photography moved into its fourth and fifth months.

There was conflict over a production number to end the first half of the planned "road-show" picture, and Luft finally went outside the *Star* talent pool to MGM for help from Roger Edens. Edens and Leonard Gershe then crafted a fifteen-minute medley of standards and new material under the title, "Born in a Trunk." But, as James Mason noted years later, "We never had a producer. Sid Luft was an amateur." So the problems were often compounded or ignored rather than addressed as *Star* ground on.

Yet enthusiasm for the picture's prospects never wavered. Professionals who saw *Star* in preview were unanimous in their exultation. Unfortunately, at the last minute, Warner Bros. decided to eliminate the film's intermission and show it in its 181-minute entirety, without the special handling that had always been the intent of its creators. Nonetheless, the picture drew huzzahs when it premiered, and its impact was best summarized by the trade publication *Box Office Digest*. They reported that *Star* "opened up at better than three times the average business and appears to be building from day to day . . . [this is] the top business of 1954 and is also the biggest box-office hit Warner Bros. has had in many years. Furthermore, it will prove to be a good repeat picture, as so many of the early theatergoers have expressed their desire to see it again."

Despite all this, and in an effort to placate some exhibitors (who declared that a shorter movie would mean an additional lucrative screening per day), Warner Bros. unceremoniously cut thirty minutes from the film just two weeks after its opening. There was an immediate public and critical outcry, as most cities never got to see the full picture. Business fell off; "A Star is Shorn" declaimed Bosley Crowther in the New York *Times*. Although bringing in nearly $6 million in initial release, *Star* lost money, thanks to its nearly $6 million budget, including prints and advertising.

At the end of the year, the picture was often omitted from the "ten best" lists for 1954 because (as the *Saturday Review* bluntly stated) "its distributors hacked away at it since the original release." There was still some recognition. The National Board of Review cited it for excellence, as did many individual critics. In its showings abroad (still in truncated form), *Star* broke records at the Warner Theatre in London, and in its European premiere, receipts topped those for *A Streetcar Named Desire*. Judy won the Golden Globe as Best Actress in a Musical or Comedy, plus the *Look*, *Picturegoer*, and *Film Daily* awards; the latter polled the nation's reviewers and specifically noted Garland's victory over the competition "by [an] overwhelming

ABOVE FROM TOP: Patricia Rosamond and Bobby Sailes partner Judy in "Lose That Long Face"; the little boy in the hat is Tom Nolan. | The original "Love Theme from *A Star is Born*": Years before "Evergreen," Judy sings "It's a New World" to James Mason as their characters honeymoon in a small motel.

OPPOSITE FROM TOP: Judy & Company perform "Swanee" | To the delight of the soundstage musicians, Esther happily accepts Norman's proposal.

margin." But she lost the Best Actress Oscar to Grace Kelly in *The Country Girl*, and *Star* missed out in each of its other Academy Award categories as well: Best Actor, Best Color Art Direction, Best Scoring of a Motion Picture, Best Color Costume Design, and Best Song. The song which earned the nomination, "The Man That Got Away," charted for both Garland and Frank Sinatra, topped out at number twenty-two and twenty-one, respectively; the annual *Downbeat* awards cited Judy as their Best Vocal Performer and Female Musical Personality of the Year.

*A Star Is Born* somehow withstood all its excesses, pro and con, to acquire and maintain instant stature as Judy Garland's preeminent motion picture performance. Any further proof of that claim was vociferously provided in 1983—amidst enormous whoopla and excitement—when the entire film was virtually restored. Working with other Warner Bros. veterans, savvy archivist Ronald Haver unearthed the complete 181-minute *Star* soundtrack, along with footage for three deleted musical numbers. He then used raw stock footage and stills to cover most of the missing dialogue sequences, and the finished product became an international fundraising, film festival, revival house, and home video success. Though still five minutes short of the original release, Haver's exemplary assemblage provided at least an approximation of what Cukor, Garland, and their coworkers intended and—however briefly—achieved in 1954.

LEFT: "Vicki Lester" wins her Oscar for *A World for Two*.

**CLOCKWISE FROM TOP LEFT:** Hairdresser Helen Young and Judy's stand-in, Betty O'Kelly, with Garland on location for the drive-in/nutburger scene (cut after the film's premiere) | Fifteen years earlier, it was director Cukor who had eliminated Judy's blonde wig and heavy makeup while revising the look of Dorothy Gale for *The Wizard of Oz* | The mutual admiration society in full sway: Judy, scenarist Moss Hart, and director George Cukor | Judy and *Star* dance director Richard Barstow enjoy a visit from Warner Bros.'s own Doris Day, then filming *Lucky Me*.

## What They Said

*"It's the biggest picture and the toughest I've ever been in; I never worked so hard in my life. James Mason had to give me a good sock in the face at [the] Academy Awards rally. Well, it had to be right and realistic, you know. So James gave me seventeen vigorous blows in the cheek [before we got the scene]. He was terribly sorry and apologetic, but my face took a real beating. My husband couldn't stand to be on the set. . . . [But] I'm sadistic about this picture! I love to make people cry—and they do. Clark Gable sat right behind me at a screening and bawled like a baby. Afterwards, Deborah Kerr came up to me and said, 'Hello,' and burst into tears and cried for a half hour."*—JUDY GARLAND

ABOVE: Between takes of the elopement
sequence

*"Judy is completely enchanting. She is one of the wittiest and most intelligent
creatures I have ever known and certainly one of the few actresses who is a person
in her own right, apart from her talent. There's something very appealing about
her. . . . One wants to protect her—[to] take her in your arms, and make sure that
no harm befell her."*—SCENARIST MOSS HART

*"Judy is the hardest worker I've ever seen. And Ina Claire said the same thing. She
saw Judy doing some scenes, and she said that after Judy put in three hours on a
set, she should go home in an ambulance. I'm an old athlete myself—football and
track and so on. And I tell you that, in a four-minute song, Judy uses up as much
energy as if she ran a mile at top speed."*—PRODUCER SID LUFT

"Judy's a great, great talent. I loved working with her. After so much TV, where a whole show is done in a day, it was a pleasure to spend a day on a one-minute scene. Director George Cukor wanted perfection; so did Judy. I didn't see any displays of temperament, but when Judy wasn't ready for a scene, she wouldn't do it. That's good sense—not temperament—if you can afford the luxury of being sensible in this racket. It was like the old days of picture-making, with lots of time, lots of money, and lots of talent."

—JACK CARSON

"When Ira Gershwin and I wrote [the songs for] A Star is Born, we knew exactly—or we thought we knew exactly—the things that Judy could do well. And we were fortunate enough to get 'The Man That Got Away,' which is one of her identifying songs. When you hear it, you immediately think of Judy."

—COMPOSER HAROLD ARLEN

"'The Man That Got Away' was all done in one long take, the whole musical number. I do [that] whenever I can, for you get a very complete sort of result. I did it with Judy because she could sustain it. It isn't easy for an actor or actress to carry a long take—you have to be strong. The 'Someone at Last' number was carefully rehearsed—very carefully rehearsed. She gave it the effect of improvisation, but it was created to give that impression.

[In A Star Is Born,] James Mason's performance was terribly good, very moving, but I don't think it was the equal of Garland's. I thought she was absolutely staggering. She did this extraordinary scene where she [screamed and] cried. And she'd never before done such an emotional scene on the screen. We did it once. And then I said, 'Let's do it again; it's great,' without any [further] comment. And we did it again. And then I said [to her], 'It's just thrilling.' And she said, 'Well, if you come around to my house, I do it every afternoon at five o'clock. . . .'

[Elsewhere] in the construction of the picture, she did the most moving and heart-rending scene in her dressing room. And then she went right from that into a comedy number. I thought she was remarkable. I said to her, 'Well that's rather like Laurette Taylor.' And Marguerite Taylor, who later wrote a book about her mother, saw the same resemblance. I was a great admirer of Laurette Taylor, with whom I had done two stage plays, and unconsciously, I suppose that I must have passed something of her on to Judy. And that very often is the way one stimulates an actor's imagination.

It's awfully nice if [a picture] looks beautiful—[and] gives the impression of verisimilitude. But if you've got some good stuff, that's [where] the vitality is. That is the heart's blood of the whole thing. You can do a picture about movies, like A Star Is Born—well, that's a very special experience. Her problems are special to movie actresses. But if you get beyond that, to the [general human] truth of it, then you move the audience. And Judy did, with this extraordinary performance."

—DIRECTOR GEORGE CUKOR

OPPOSITE CLOCKWISE FROM TOP: February 24, 1955: Well into her eighth month of pregnancy, Judy accepts the Golden Globe Award from Rock Hudson | Dancing with close friend Frank Sinatra at the Grove. Earlier in 1954, he'd enjoyed his own comeback in *From Here to Eternity*. | The Los Angeles *A Star is Born* premiere was the first to be nationally televised. Jack Carson and emcee George Jessel welcome Judy and Sid Luft to the proceedings.

# Pepe

COLUMBIA PICTURES

## CAST:

Cantinflas ............................................. *Pepe*
Dan Dailey ......................................... *Ted Holt*
Shirley Jones ........................... *Suzie Murphy*
Carlos Montalban ........................... *Rodriguez*
Vicki Trickett ...................................... *Lupita*
Matt Mattox ....................................... *Dancer*
Hank Henry ...................................... *Manager*
Sue Lloyd ......................................... *Carmen*
Carlos Rivas ........................................ *Carlos*

## GUEST STARS:

*Billie Burke, Maurice Chevalier, Charles Coburn, Bing Crosby, Michael Callan, Richard Conte, Tony Curtis, Bobby Darin, Sammy Davis, Jr., William Demarest, Jimmy Durante, Jack Entratter, Zsa Zsa Gabor, "The Voice of Judy Garland," Greer Garson, Hedda Hopper, Joey Bishop, Ernie Kovacs, Peter Lawford, Janet Leigh, Jack Lemmon, Dean Martin, Jay North, Kim Novak, André Previn, Donna Reed, Debbie Reynolds, Edward G. Robinson, Cesar Romero, and Frank Sinatra*

## CREDITS:

**George Sidney** (director/producer); **Jacques Gelman** (associate producer); **Dorothy Kingsley and Claude Binyon** (screenplay); **Leonard Spigelgass and Sonya Levien** (story); **L. Bush-Fekete** (original play); **Joe Mac Donald** (photography); **Johnny Green** (musical director); **André Previn and Dory Langdon** (music and lyrics to "Faraway Part of Town," "That's How it Went, Alright"); **Hans Wittstatt, Johnny Green, and Dory Langdon** (music and lyrics to "Pepe"); **André Previn** (music and lyrics to "The Rumble"); **Augustin Lara, Maria Teresa Lara, and Dory Langdon** (music and lyrics to "Lovely Day"); **Eugene Loring and Alex Romero** (dance directors); **Ted Haworth** (art director), **Gunthere Gerszo** (associate); **William Kiernan** (set decorations); **Edith Head** (gowns); **Viola Lawrence and Al Clark** (editors)

## JUDY'S NUMBER:

*"The Far Away Part of Town" (vocal only; heard on the soundtrack as Dan Dailey and Shirley Jones dance)*

**RELEASE DATE: December 21, 1960**
**RUN TIME: 195 minutes**

## REVIEWS

"Even after having been sliced by twenty-five minutes for showing in this country, *Pepe* at two hours, fifty minutes, is still disastrously long on wind and short on charm and appeal. Guest stars (the film's publicity claims thirty-five, I only made it twenty-four, and that includes, if you please, the 'voice' of Judy Garland) appear at odd intervals throughout without rhyme or reason."

—*FILMS & FILMING*

Review of the soundtrack album: "A Colpix long-playing record made up of all sorts of stuff from . . . *Pepe* is distinguished only in one band. Here, JG delivers a bluesy piece called 'The Far Away Part of Town' in a manner that makes the remainder of this enterprise seem exceedingly shoddy as it puts Bing Crosby, Maurice Chevalier, and some others through labored paces."

—NEW YORK *DAILY NEWS*

## SYNOPSIS:

Alcoholic film director Ted Holt has fallen on hard times in Hollywood. All he has to his name is a horse he bought in Mexico and Pepe, the faithful groom who follows the horse everywhere. Holt is eventually redeemed by the love of aspiring actress Suzie Murphy, but before that happens, the three principals encounter more than two dozen celebrities during their career-related adventures in and around Los Angeles, Las Vegas, and south of the border. Early in their association, Holt and Suzie share a romantic dream dance as Judy Garland is heard singing "The Far Away Part of Town" over a nearby radio.

**OPPOSITE FROM LEFT:** Cover art for the "original soundtrack album" | As *Pepe* preproduction continued in early 1960, a series of trade paper announcements heralded the latest "name" additions to the cast.

## What They Said

*"You'll tune up all the hi-fis and tune in even your tin ears to 'The Far Away Part of Town,' as tracked for Pepe by Judy Garland and Andre Previn. Judy's 'Far Away' is WAY far out, her best in years."*—COLUMNIST MIKE CONNOLLY

*"On the far side of the continent, I'd watched Judy Garland on the screen of the local movie house and wanted to be her. Now, I'd written [a song] for her. It was like one of the plots of her movies. A decision came down from the top. She shouldn't appear. Someone thought she was too overweight. I didn't think so. I'd have taken her under any conditions. At our first meeting, she was in radiant spirits. She had us in stitches with stories of the great days at MGM. She wickedly mimicked prissy leading ladies and rough, tough heroes. As for the not-so-great days, she struck back with the same humor. The most awful story had the most hilarious punch line. She dealt with adversity by laughing her head off. Andre and I played several songs for her. She liked them all. I was deeply grateful for her generosity. Many singers resent the fact they don't write the words they're interpreting. Judy had admiration and respect for the writer. To me, she seemed to be so secure in her own talent, she would never need to waste time resenting that of others. In Pepe, her sound soared gloriously over the trivial action on the screen. In my opinion, she was never in better voice. Thanks to her, I had my first Academy Award nomination, together with Andre. We were on our way."*—DORY LANGDON PREVIN

## NOTES

*Pepe* was conceived as a showcase for Mexico's beloved Cantinflas, an internationally popular comic actor who'd won American stardom in *Around the World in Eighty Days* (1956). Perhaps the most elephantine of all "all-star" musicals, *Pepe* garnered (at best) mixed reviews but achieved a $4.6 million gross in the United States alone. It also tallied seven Academy Award nominations: Best Color Cinematography, Best Color Art Direction, Best Sound, Best Scoring of a Musical Picture, Best Film Editing, Best Color Costume Design, and Best Song. "The Far Away Part of Town," which earned the last nomination, was Judy's contribution to the soundtrack.

# Judgment at Nuremberg

UNITED ARTISTS/ROXLOM FILMS

### CAST:

**Spencer Tracy** .................. *Judge Dan Haywood*

**Burt Lancaster** ........................... *Ernst Janning*

**Richard Widmark** .............. *Colonel Ted Lawson*

**Marlene Dietrich** .................. *Madame Bertholt*

**Maximilian Schell** ........................ *Hans Rolfe*

**Judy Garland** ............... *Irene Hoffman Wallner*

**Montgomery Clift** ................. *Rudolph Peterson*

**William Shatner** ............ *Captain Harrison Byers*

**Werner Klemperer** .......................... *Emil Hahn*

**Kenneth MacKenna** ........ *Judge Kenneth Norris*

### CREDITS:

**Stanley Kramer** *(producer/director)*; **Philip Langner** *(associate producer)*; **Abby Mann** *(screenplay and story)*; **Ernest Laszlo** *(photography)*; **Ernest Gold** *(music)*; **Clem Beauchamp** *(production manager)*; **Rudolph Sternad** *(production designer)*; **George Milo** *(set decorations)*; **Joe King** *(costumes)*; **Frederick Knudston** *(editor)*; **R. Richtsfeld, Laci Ronay, L. Ostermeier, Hubert Karl, Lyn Hannes, Egon Haedler, Pia Arnold, Frank Winterstein, Albrecht Hennings, R. Eglseder, and Hannelore Winterfeld** *(German crew)*

**RELEASE DATE:** December 19, 1961
**RUN TIME:** 187 minutes

## SYNOPSIS

American judge Dan Haywood is assigned to preside over the 1948 Nuremberg trials, held to determine the accountability of four German judges who had supported and participated in the Nazi regime. He listens to the angry prosecution put forth by U.S. Colonel Ted Lawson and the impassioned defense of Germany's Hans Rolfe. He is subject to the tormented testimony of sterilization victim Rudolph Peterson and to horrifying film footage taken at the concentration camps. Away from the courtroom, Haywood is confronted by an informal spokesman for the German people in Madame Bertholt, widow of a German general who had been executed after the war.

The trial reaches its emotional peak when Irene Hoffman (JG) is summoned to recount the horrors of her own earlier prosecution at the hands of two of the present defendants, Ernst Janning and Emil Hahn. After refusing to participate in a Nazi plot against an older Jewish man who had been kind to her and her family, Hoffman had been sentenced to two years in prison for perjury, and the Jewish man had been executed. In the end, Haywood reads out a verdict of guilty against the four judges, citing the opinion that international law and morality must always override national law.

**OPPOSITE BOTTOM FROM LEFT:** Judy prepares to face a movie camera for the first time in nearly seven years. | Kramer and Garland on the set. When they first discussed the role, he broached the topic of salary. Her reply: "How much do you want me to pay you to play it?" | Minnesota meets Milwaukee: The girl from Grand Rapids and the gentleman from Wisconsin had already known each other for twenty-five years.

ABOVE FROM LEFT: Arriving in Berlin for the premiere of the film and interviews with the international press: (from left) Werner Klemperer, Stanley Kramer, Judy, and Maximilian Schell | At the conclusion of the premiere, West Berlin mayor Willy Brandt (third from left) honored the stars and the producer/director: Montgomery Clift, Kramer, Judy, Richard Widmark, and Schell.

## REVIEWS

"The astute Stanley Kramer once again attacks a vital problem of our time . . . and with production staging of incisive quality, and cast selections and performances which rank among the best of any year, he has a film of outstanding importance and significance. [This] is a motion picture of uncompromising reality strong and vital, splendidly done, and certain to add new stature to the reputations of its producer and the members of its distinguished cast. Judy Garland is excellent as the woman who was a victim of one of the judges on trial, accounting for a highlight of the film as she recounts her experience."

—*MOTION PICTURE HERALD*

"The best thing about *Judgment at Nuremberg* is that it makes you think. . . . Mr. Kramer was resolved to make a picture that would absorb and entertain, [and] he plainly intended this drama to excite contemporary thought and give us a little elevation for reflecting on the problems of our times. . . . Two pathetic witnesses who have suffered grave injustices are played with expert deftness by JG and Montgomery Clift."

—NEW YORK *TIMES*

"[It] is the most important American picture of the year. Mr. Kramer throws a cold, revealing light upon international morality—the morals of nations. [He] has mounted a picture that is obviously expensive, loaded with message, and consistently absorbing. . . . JG pours into her moments the same instinctive, sure intensity that characterizes her ballads."

—*SATURDAY REVIEW OF LITERATURE*

"We take exception to only two members of the star-studded cast: Montgomery Clift and JG. Each has a small, important part. Each gives a brilliant performance. It is a performance, however, many lesser known but equally as competent actors could duplicate. The problem seems to be that the appearance of these 'stars' distracts the audience, and Mr. Kramer's great feeling of reality is lost while they are on the screen."

—*NEWSDAY*

## NOTES

Judy returned to the screen for the first time in seven years to play a small but pivotal role in this Stanley Kramer drama. The producer/director had originally considered Julie Harris for the part, and the January 1961 announcement that he'd cast Garland resulted in a year-long surge of media and public interest which culminated when the picture premiered in Berlin the following December. *Judgment at Nuremberg* enjoyed critical and financial success, thanks to the combination of Abby Mann's script, Kramer's sure touch, the work of the other stars and actors, and Garland's three intense sequences. Domestically, the film's gross was estimated at nearly $10 million.

To prepare for the vocal challenge inherent in playing a German hausfrau, Judy worked daily with a Greenwich Village dialect coach recommended to her by actress Uta Hagen. While the film unit did some actual location work in Nuremberg, all of Garland's scenes were filmed in Los Angeles in March 1961.

The film was cited by the New York Film Critics as one of the Ten Best Pictures of the Year, and it won two Academy Awards: Best Actor (Maximilian Schell) and Best Screenplay Based on Material from Another Medium (Abby Mann). *Nuremberg* was nominated for nine additional Oscars: Best Picture,

Best Actor (Spencer Tracy), Best Supporting Actor (Montgomery Clift), Best Supporting Actress (Judy), Best Direction (Kramer), Best Black and White Cinematography, Best Black and White Art Decoration, Best Film Editing, and Best Black and White Costume Design.

That year, Garland lost both the Oscar and the Golden Globe Best Supporting Actress awards to Rita Moreno of *West Side Story*. Some compensation came when the Hollywood Foreign Press Association recognized her instead with the Golden Globe Cecil B. DeMille Award for her "outstanding contributions to the entertainment industry throughout the world."

## What They Said

*"For* Nuremberg, *I chose [a] singer, Judy Garland, to portray a frumpy, highly emotional German hausfrau who doesn't have a musical note in her throat. I must admit I agonized quite awhile over this one. Judy's personal problems were well-known in the industry, but the very disorders that made it difficult to work with her fitted perfectly with the role. Though she may have been difficult for directors to handle, she had lost none of her skills as an actress, and they were all wonderfully evident in this role. One need say no more than to note that, despite her fame, she was able to make herself eminently believable as an anonymous German hausfrau."*

—STANLEY KRAMER

*"I adore Stanley. He called my manager, Freddie Fields [and] said he had no doubts about me.* Judgment at Nuremberg *is an important picture, but he never questioned me about my so-called unreliability. He didn't question my weight. He treated me like an actress . . . and what that did for me! If Stanley ever wants me to play a leper on Molokai, I'll do it."* —JUDY GARLAND

*"Judy asked me, 'Can you hit me more, off-camera?—be tougher on me?— because then I can feel more, I can give more.' She had to break down and get tears, and so I did it for her, much more than what [was] written in the script. I invented a lot of things until she finally*

*broke down. Then afterwards, she sent me flowers and a little note, 'Thank you for being so mean to me.' And then we went for dinner—I invited her—and we drove along the beach. By chance, they were playing her songs on the radio; it was an open, rented car, so she sang for me while we were driving. [Later] I changed over to the classical station, and there was Mozart's 'Jupiter Symphony.' And she said, 'You know, I've never listened to Mozart.' And we came back to The Beverly Hills Hotel, and we sat in the car for an hour, listening to Mozart. And at the end, she cried. Then I took her hand; I will never forget that moment."* —MAXIMILIAN SCHELL

# Gay Purr-ee

UPA/WARNER BROTHERS

## CAST:

Judy Garland ........................ *voice of Mewsette*

Robert Goulet .................... *voice of Jaune Tom*

Red Buttons.................... *voice of Robespierre*

Paul Frees........................... *voice of Meowrice*

Hermione Gingold ............................. *voice of Mme. Rubens-Chatte*

Mel Blanc ............................. *voice of bulldog*

Morey Amsterdam .............................. *narrator*

Joan Gardner .......................... *multiple voices*

Julie Bennett .......................... *multiple voices*

## CREDITS:

**Henry G. Saperstein** (executive producer); **Lee Orgel** (associate producer); **Abe Levitow** (director); **Steve Clark** (sequence director); **Dorothy and Chuck Jones** (screenplay); **Ralph Wright** (additional dialogue); **Ben Washam, Phil Duncan, Hal Ambro, Ray Patterson, Grant Simmons, Irv Spence, Don Lusk, Hank Smith, Harvey Toombs, Volus Jones, Ken Harris, Art Davis,** and **Fred Madison** (animation); **Harold Arlen** and **E. Y. Harburg** (music and lyrics); **Mort Lindsey** (musical arrangements); **Earl Jonas** (production manager); **Robert Singer, Richard Ung, "Corny" Cole, Ray Aragon, Edward Levitt,** and **Ernest Nordli** (production designers); **Victor Haboush** (art director); **Don Peters, Gloria Wood, Robert Inman, Phil Norman, Richard Kelsey** (color styling); **Ted Baker, Sam Horta,** and **Earl Bennett** (editors)

## JUDY'S NUMBERS:

Gay Purr-ee *overture,* "Take My Hand, Paree," "Roses Red, Violets Blue," "Little Drops of Rain," "Paris is a Lonely Town," "Mewsette"

**RELEASE DATE:** November 9, 1962
**RUN TIME:** 85 minutes

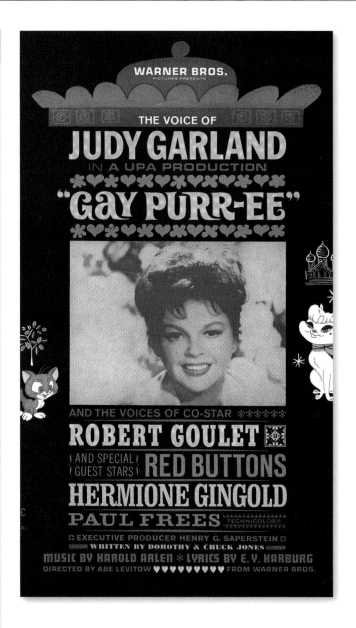

## SYNOPSIS

French country kitty Mewsette (JG) longs for life off the farm. Forsaking devoted admirer Jaune Tom and his sidekick Robespierre, she departs for the sophistication of Paris, where she is quickly taken over by the sleek Meowrice. He dazzles her with visions of romance and acclaim, placing her in the glamorizing paws of Mme. Rubens-Chatte at her Salon de Beaute Pour Felines.

What Mewsette doesn't realize is that Meowrice has sold her in marriage to a fat cat in Pittsburgh, and that she will be shipped to the United States as soon as she's completed her makeover. Jaune Tom and Robespierre race to save her, encountering adventures everywhere from the sewers of Paris to the gold fields of Alaska. They finally manage to rescue Mewsette—and Meowrice is bundled off to America instead.

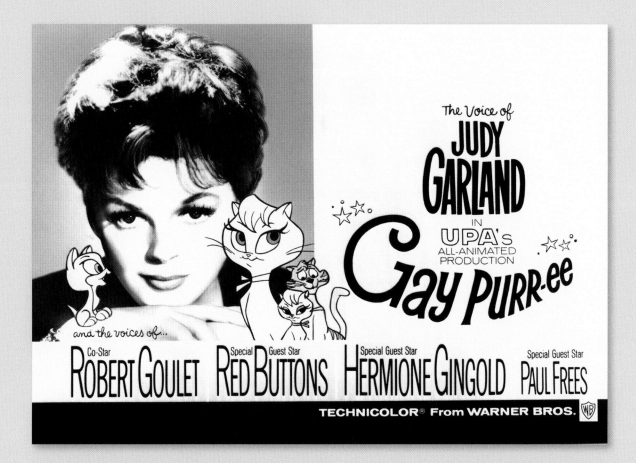

The Voice of
JUDY GARLAND
IN UPA's ALL-ANIMATED PRODUCTION
Gay Purr-ee

*and the voices of...*
Co-Star ROBERT GOULET    Special Guest Star RED BUTTONS    Special Guest Star HERMIONE GINGOLD    Special Guest Star PAUL FREES

TECHNICOLOR® From WARNER BROS.

## REVIEWS

"A happy item of entertainment, perhaps with its greatest appeal to the youngsters, but with unquestioned fun and entertainment inherent for all ages."

—*MOTION PICTURE HERALD*

"This cartoon feature has two major assets: JG's warm voice, singing some pleasant songs by Harold Arlen . . . and some artistic backgrounds. Another interesting and skillfully executed feature consists of portraits of Mewsette done in the style of noted artists— Renoir, Modigliani, Picasso, etc. While I thought the animals did not exude the whimsical sort of charm we have come to expect of cartoon characters, it's moderately entertaining fare which youngsters will probably enjoy."

—CHICAGO *TRIBUNE*

"Judy Garland, as the voice of Mewsette, yowls enchantingly." —*TIME*

"Goulet's voice doesn't eclipse his cat the way Judy does hers. Always ready to belt out a song, or squeeze the last heart-throb out of a lyric, Judy gives the full treatment to [her numbers]. One expects her to sweep aside the feline characters, step downstage front, and talk it over with the audience. . . . A frail little lady, Mewsette sounds strong enough to rough up Meowrice and his slinky black assistants with one paw tied behind her back. It's just too much Judy for this sort of cartoon feature."

—CHICAGO *DAILY NEWS*

ABOVE: Judy poses with Robespierre, Mewsette, and a smaller icon of Mewsette with Jaune Tom.

**ABOVE**: At the prerecording sessions for the songs from *Gay Purr-ee*, Judy worked with Robert Goulet, conductor/orchestrator Mort Lindsey, and long-time friend and musical advisor Kay Thompson.

## NOTES

In 1961, United Productions of America was happily known for its innovative cartoon shorts, celebrating the nearsighted "Mr. Magoo" or the indefatigable "Gerald McBoing-Boing." *Gay Purr-ee* was the company's second feature-length cartoon, and Judy's involvement was at least in part predicated on the fact that Harold Arlen and E. Y. Harburg (composer and lyricist of *The Wizard of Oz*) would be writing songs for the picture. Maurice Chevalier's rumored role as narrator was ultimately taken by Morey Amsterdam. Meanwhile, UPA originally hoped to sign Gene Kelly as Garland's vocal costar; in the end, she was partnered for the first time by Robert Goulet, with whom she would later do two television shows.

Judy recorded her musical numbers and dialogue for *Gay Purr-ee* in three weeks of sessions in Los Angeles in November 1961. The cartoon debuted a year later, at a total production cost of $1 million. UPA and Warner Bros. then spent an additional $900,000 on advertising. To help launch the feature, Garland promoted it on national television and made in-person appearances at the Chicago "world premiere" and at more than a dozen New York movie theaters. The film's elaborate tie-in with Friskies cat food also helped spread the word, and the cartoon eventually won the *Parents* Magazine Family Medal. But *Gay Purr-ee* was perhaps too special and specialized in its approach to artwork, song, and storytelling to achieve mass appeal. It failed to return a profit, although it later became a happily embraced television and home video favorite.

## What They Said

*"It's our goal to present on a CinemaScope screen the most beautiful graphics ever drawn, taking the 1880–1910 Impressionists as our models—that was, you know, the richest period in the world of art. There never was a time when so many greats were in the same place at the same time. I decided to be different and write it as a musical. Cartoon features have been made with music, but only* Snow White *was a true musical. [And] if it were to be about art, it had to be set in France."*

—UPA PRESIDENT HENRY SAPERSTEIN

*"It's all about French pussycats. I play Mewsette, a farm pussycat who decides to go to Paris, where I'm immediately picked up by Hermoine Gingold—a fat, horrible, pink cat who runs a . . . a . . . cat house! Hermoine transforms Mewsette—that's me—into a very glamorous cat. Oh, I really look beautiful; I never looked this good in my heyday. From now on, I think they'll have to draw me in. . . . Anyway, I find out that they're fattening me up for an old cat in Pittsburgh. Now, I didn't want to go Pittsburgh; I wanted to go to Paris. So I ran away. But they get this gang after me—the 'Meow-fia.' The Meow-fia is after me, and I run through the streets. I lose all my glamour; my mascara is running, and I become all matted. So I decide to jump into the river—the Seine. But before I jump, I stop to sing, which I guess is the usual thing to do before you jump, you know, do a quick thirty-two bars."*

—JUDY GARLAND, INTRODUCING A SONG FROM
*GAY PURR-EE* TO A CONCERT AUDIENCE (1962)

Garland and Goulet made the promotional rounds of New York theaters to herald *Gay Purr-ee* in early December 1962. Feeling that just talking up the audiences wasn't sufficient entertainment, Judy pressed her costar and their force of security guards into an a cappella rendition of "There's No Business Like Show Business." Per the New York *World-Telegram*, Judy "worked out a razz-ma-tazz ending for the song where she joined in with a few of her famous high notes . . . She got the 14 'cops' onstage and went into her conducting routine like a demented Bernstein. The act was a smash."

# A Child is Waiting

UNITED ARTISTS

**CAST:**

Burt Lancaster......................*Dr. Matthew Clark*

Judy Garland ............................*Jean Hansen*

Gena Rowlands.... *Sophie Widdicombe Benham*

Steven Hill.............................*Ted Widdicombe*

Paul Stewart ...................................*Goodman*

Gloria McGehee.................................. *Mattie*

Lawrence Tierney.................. *Douglas Benham*

Bruce Ritchey.................. *Reuben Widdicombe*

John Marley ...................................... *Holland*

Billy Mumy........................................ *Student*

**CREDITS:**

**Stanley Kramer** *(producer)*; **Philip Langner** *(associate producer)*; **John Cassavetes** *(director)*; **Abby Mann** *(screenplay and story)*; **Joseph LaShelle** *(photography)*; **Ernest Gold** *(music)*; **Marjorie D. Kurtz** *(music and lyric to "Snowflakes")*; **Nate Edwards** *(production manager)*; **Rudolph Sternad** *(production designer)*; **Joseph Kish** *(set decorations)*; **Howard Shoup and Joe King** *(costumes)*; **Gene Fowler, Jr. and Robert C. Jones** *(editors)*

**JUDY'S NUMBERS:**

*were integral to the story line and not musical performances, per se: "Snowflakes" and reprise, "The Beer Barrel Polka"*

**RELEASE DATE: January 14, 1963**

**RUN TIME: 105 minutes**

STANLEY KRAMER presents
**BURT LANCASTER
JUDY GARLAND**

A
CHILD
IS
WAITING

co-starring
GENA ROWLANDS   STEVEN HILL

Written by ABBY MANN
Directed by JOHN CASSAVETES
Associate Producer · PHILIP LANGNER

A MOTION PICTURE THAT GIVES SO MUCH... GOES SO FAR... LOOKS SO DEEP INTO THE FEELINGS OF MAN AND WOMAN!

## SYNOPSIS

Despite her teaching inexperience, Jean Hansen (JG) has a background in music, which leads Dr. Matthew Clark to take her on as an instructor at the Crowthorn Training School—a facility for mentally challenged youngsters. Jean's own vulnerability enables her to bond with student Reuben Widdicombe, whose parents have forsaken him. Against Clark's wishes, Jean manipulates the divorced and remarried Sophie Widdicombe Benham into a visit, but the woman is emotionally unable to reunite with her son. From afar, Reuben witnesses his mother's abrupt departure and is further traumatized at being abandoned yet again.

The guilt-ridden Jean offers to resign, but thanks to Clark's stern tutelage, she gradually comes to realize that unconditional love and overt sympathy aren't healthy for these children. She returns to her music class, disciplining Reuben and preparing the students for a Thanksgiving pageant. Reuben makes a monumental effort to recite the finale poem of the program and is quietly rewarded by the unexpected presence of his father, Ted Widdicombe. When Clark selects Jean to welcome a recalcitrant new boy to the school, she knows that she has earned the doctor's trust.

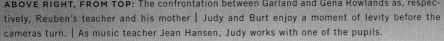

ABOVE RIGHT, FROM TOP: The confrontation between Garland and Gena Rowlands as, respectively, Reuben's teacher and his mother | Judy and Burt enjoy a moment of levity before the cameras turn. | As music teacher Jean Hansen, Judy works with one of the pupils.

COTTAGE
A

# REVIEWS

"Although the picture at times rambles and occasionally gets lost in discursive byways of no help to the main theme, when it catches fire, it lights a matching flame in the spectator and at its best is deeply moving. [The] sequences of the children bursting through their handicaps to speak and behave with normality are poignantly done. The scenes . . . of the parents are less penetratingly sketched and are sometimes prolonged beyond their value. JG, as something of a lost child herself, projects a tremulous and bittersweet characterization. The final scene, in which some unexpected improvisation apparently occurred, is Miss Garland's, and a good one."—*HOLLYWOOD REPORTER*

"A simple, intelligent, and moving film. Cassavetes . . . has gotten a series of utterly convincing, low-key performances from his cast (despite a few moments of heart-tugging professionalism in Miss Garland's acting)." —*SHOW*

"A disturbing, unnerving, and yet encouraging drama, *A Child is Waiting* tears the heart out as it looks deeply and honestly into the subject of mental retardation. [But] this is not a sudsy tear-jerker. [The Lancaster and Garland] performances, in two most difficult roles, are well-nigh faultless. Extremely able support is given by Gena Rowlands, Stephen Hill, and Paul Stewart, among the adults."

—PITTSBURGH *POST-GAZETTE*

"I don't think *A Child is Waiting* will need any crusaders, but I feel like one in writing about it. It affected me more strongly than any movie I can recall. I think that everyone should see it. It is difficult to think of the actors as actors. They seem to have become the people they are playing. The lift at the finish is breathtaking." —MINNEAPOLIS *TRIBUNE*

"Lancaster gives a strong and reserved performance. JG gives a very quiet but deep and effective sympathy to [her] role. The [central] boy is played by Bruce Ritchey with a naturalness that is a credit to director Cassavetes, but it is the really retarded children whose faces will dwell in the memory."

—*KINEMATOGRAPH WEEKLY*

OPPOSITE: A deleted moment: Judy leads the children on "Visitors' Day." ABOVE: Judy and Bruce Ritchey's characters bond with the aid of "Mr. Machine," a classic early 1960s toy.

## NOTES

A number of *Judgment at Nuremberg* participants were reunited in *A Child is Waiting*, and its company was both bolstered and emotionally inspired by the presence of special-needs children from Pacific State Hospital who were, in effect, playing themselves. Those youngsters were augmented on screen by actual child performers (including Billy Mumy, Butch Patrick, and Brian Corcoran); the principal boy of the story was portrayed by professional actor Bruce Ritchey.

Stanley Kramer had earlier considered Ingrid Bergman, Elizabeth Taylor, or Katharine Hepburn for Garland's role. His own commitments kept him from directing *Child*, and after a scheduling conflict sidelined director Jack Clayton, that task was assigned to comparative newcomer John Cassavetes. Cassavetes's style—alternately improvisational or confrontational—was anathema to Judy and Burt Lancaster, who somewhat bonded in their confusion over his approach and intent. Finally beginning to succumb to the strain of more than twelve preceding months of overwork, Garland responded by missing days of the *Child* schedule. Still, the picture was completed in less than three months, and Kramer ultimately oversaw its final edit himself.

*A Child is Waiting* was given a gala Washington, D.C. send-off at a benefit screening for the Joseph P. Kennedy Foundation in December 1962. Despite that honor—and considerable critical praise and comprehension—the film was (perhaps not unexpectedly) a financial failure. Its topic and "cause" were then still too far afield for public assimilation or mass audience involvement.

## What They Said

*"Controversy about this movie? In a world where you almost have to choose sides on everything, can there be more than one side of the subject of helping retarded children? [At first,] I just wanted to hug them and protect them. But I realized they didn't want protection—they wanted to be accepted. These children want affection, yes, but most of all they need to be accepted as human beings. They need to feel useful."*

—JUDY GARLAND

*"All children must be accepted and loved for what they are. Our everyday contact with these children made everyone care for them. It had been agreed that the greatest actors in the world could not portray them as accurately as the children themselves. They had delightful humor; they deported themselves so well and were very responsive to direction. Working with them cleared up our own misconceptions. We hope with all our hearts that our movie will clear up a lot of public misconceptions."*

—BURT LANCASTER

*"Whatever artistic fulfillments the picture reaches, the utilitarian value could be enormous. If people saw this picture and understood something of the problems of mentally retarded children—and [would] not laugh at them—this would be an enormous achievement. What better way to do this than to have people watch the children themselves and let their simplicity and honesty speak for themselves? No words that I could ever write could ever do it that eloquently."*

—SCENARIST ABBY MANN

*"It would really be silly for me to comment about Miss Garland, because I [didn't] really know her. As an audience, I'm a member of her vast admiration society, and I thought she had the potential to be a really great actress."*

—DIRECTOR JOHN CASSEVETES (1972)

OPPOSITE TOP: Judy listens as the men speak: Burt Lancaster and director John Cassavetes. OPPOSITE BOTTOM: Judy stops for reference photos of her Howard Shoup wardrobe for the film.

*"Judy Garland was a gem. As a person. Every way you can think of—a gem. Top drawer. Wonderful. Beautiful. Touched everybody. She really did have it all—lucky girl. And a hard-working one. MGM only touched . . . what she could do. She was a magnificent 'classic' actress—emotionally and spiritually. She gave it a frame; she could make it a rectangle or a big square; anyway you wanted it. But, boy, she really had it to develop it. She felt it inside; came from there. Deep. I was lucky to recognize it."*

—STANLEY KRAMER

A CHILD IS WAITING. PROD. 16903
COSTUME DEPT.
CH.No. JUDY GARLAND AS JEAN
INT. WARD—SC.
JOE KING WGCD

A CHILD IS WAITING. PROD. 16903
COSTUME DEPT.
CH.No. SCS. 168 THRU 190
JOE KING WGCD

# I Could Go on Singing

BARBICAN FILMS / UNITED ARTISTS

### CAST:

Judy Garland ............................Jenny Bowman

Dirk Bogarde ..............................David Donne

Jack Klugman............................George Kogan

Aline MacMahon .......................................Ida

Gregory Phillips.....................................Matt

Russell Waters ...........................Mr. Reynolds

Pauline Jameson.......................Miss Plimpton

Jeremy Burnham ...................Hospital Surgeon

Gerald Sim.......... Palladium Assistant Manager

David Lee............................................Pianist

### CREDITS:

**Stuart Millar and Lawrence Turman** (producers); **Ronald Neame** (director); **Mayo Simon** (screenplay); **Robert Dozier** (story); **Arthur Ibbetson** (photography); **Saul Chaplin** (musical supervisor); **Mort Lindsey** (musical score); **Harold Arlen and E. Y. Harburg** (music and lyrics to "I Could Go On Singing"); **Wilfred Shingleton** (production designer); **John Hoesli** (set decorations); **Edith Head, Beatrice Dawson, and Evelyn Gibbs** (costumes); **John Shirley** (editor)

### JUDY'S NUMBERS:

"I Am the Monarch of the Sea,"
"Hello, Bluebird," "It Never Was You,"
"By Myself," "I Could Go On Singing"
(under opening credits and as the film finale)

**RELEASE DATE: March 6, 1963**
**(London world premiere)**
**RUN TIME: 99 minutes**

## SYNOPSIS

International singing star Jenny Bowman (JG) is in London for a concert engagement at the Palladium. Prior to her opening, she seeks medical attention from David Donne, a renowned throat specialist. Not at all coincidentally, she'd had a love affair with the surgeon a dozen years earlier but didn't want to relinquish her career for married life. He subsequently wed another, only to discover that Jenny was about to have his baby. Keeping secret the child's identity and parentage, he and his wife adopted the boy. Now, near forty and personally adrift, Jenny asks to see her son.

Against his better judgment, Donne—a widower—escorts the star to Matthew's school. She is an instant sensation with the lad and his friends, and she invites him and his father to her premiere at London's famed Palladium. When the surgeon is called to Italy, Matt undertakes the trip to London on his own. Against the recommendations of her manager, George Kogan, and dresser, Ida Mulligan, Jenny revels in Matt's company for several days, until Donne returns to angrily confront her. Their argument is overheard by Matt, who realizes they are his real mother and father. He then has to decide with which parent he will live.

Jenny quickly comprehends the boy's dilemma and relinquishes him, but the heartbroken star then goes out drinking, spraining her ankle in the process. Donne comes to her aid, admits his long-standing love, but helps her to realize that her place is onstage. An hour late and limping, Jenny returns to the Palladium and overwhelms the sold-out crowd, doing what she does better than anyone else.

**ABOVE:** Judy selected "It Never Was You" for her *I Could Go on Singing* repertoire as it was Dirk Bogarde's favorite song. Her accompanist was revered British jazz pianist David Lee, who'd played for several of her 1960 concerts abroad. **OPPOSITE:** On location at the London Palladium: the intended but ultimately unused opening sequence of the film.

# REVIEWS

OPPOSITE, CLOCKWISE FROM TOP LEFT:
Phillips, Judy, and Laurie Heath after the
boys' school production of *H.M.S. Pinafore*.
| Kogan to Bowman (or Klugman to Garland):
"This is your job . . . you do it better than
anybody else in the world." | "Here I am
for my Luise Rainer bit" was Judy's quip
when she arrived on set to film her dramatic
telephone sequence—referencing the MGM
actress and her 1936 monologue in *The
Great Ziegfeld*, which resulted in an Oscar
for Rainer. | Though later rumored to have
been ad-libbed, the extraordinary hospital
sequence was actually rehearsed for hours
before its one-take capture for posterity.
From left, Neame, Bogarde, Garland. | The
no-nonsense persona manifested by Aline
MacMahon was ideal support for Garland,
here with Gregory Phillips.

"*I Could Go On Singing*, without Garland, is unthinkable. With her, for all its faults and they are many, it has moments of infinite richness and variety. . . . She can work effortlessly from comedy to drama, as she does here in her long final scene with Dirk Bogarde; she can bring a glimmer of tragedy to her role, as she does here in one last telephone conversation with her son; she can sustain the longest and most searching of close-ups without faltering."

—*FILMS & FILMING*

"The Magna Carta was signed in 1215. Shortly thereafter, JG sang 'Over the Rainbow,' and ever since, she has had her special place in the hearts of millions. There she sits, up in the left auricle, her lower lip quivering and a tear in her eye, and everybody just loves her. She sings a number of songs in *I Could Go on Singing*, but singing isn't really what she does anymore. Acting is not exactly what she does, either. And glamour surely isn't what she's selling: Edith Head's costumes, especially one unflattering red number, make her look downright potty. But she's, well, Judy Garland. And we love her. We have to love her. It's part of our way of life, like cookie jars, and baseball, and oral hygiene, and the call of the open spaces. And for people who like this kind of thing, this is the kind of thing they'll like." —*NEWSWEEK*

"There are not many actresses around who are as exciting and shattering to encounter as Judy Garland. . . . Her art is captured in scenes you will remember long after you have forgotten the story. Unforgettable is the incident on the first night at The Palladium, when she stands in the wings and awaits her entrance. That glimpse tells everything about the fantastic demands with which the great entertainer is faced, both artistically and humanly. In the concert numbers, she radiates a complete magic. It is fascinating how, by virtue of her strong personality, she gives the (in themselves not important) songs a dramatic function. What an artist. Judy Garland stands alone. Experience her."

—*POLITIKEN* (DENMARK)

"Judy proves she is still one of the movie greats. No matter . . . an improbable plot. No matter, too, that Judy is now middle-aged and plump. As she belts out song after song, or reveals what show business has given her— and what it has taken away—you know you're in the presence of a topflight performer." —*GOOD HOUSEKEEPING*

"Judy hits a new high . . . a peak and then some. Her portrayal will be remembered at Oscar-nominating time. Oh, such potent entertainment!"

—*MIAMI HERALD*

## NOTES

Almost in spite of itself, Judy's final film remains a worthy valedictory to her motion picture career. A somewhat autobiographical role and performance were later defined and then congratulated by historian Foster Hirsch as "tabloid-level exploitation that Garland, astonishingly, manages to redeem by her truthful, low-key, improvisatory acting style."

Originally titled *The Lonely Stage* and filmed entirely in England, *I Could Go on Singing* gave Judy the opportunity to act with close friend Dirk Bogarde; to combine song and drama for the first time since *A Star is Born*; and to sing four numbers at one of her "home" venues, the London Palladium. Two of the musical interludes— "By Myself" and "It Never Was You"—were actually photographed on a recreation of the Palladium stage at Shepperton Studios. The second of these was additionally noteworthy in that Garland sang the entire song "live" on camera, rather than lip-sync it to a prerecorded track, as was the custom in movie musicals. The exciting vocal arrangements were the work of Saul Chaplin, her compatriot from MGM's *Summer Stock* a decade earlier. Mort Lindsey, Judy's concert conductor of the preceding fourteen months, provided rousing orchestrations for the numbers and composed and recorded the film underscoring as well.

Overworked and exhausted at the time, Garland missed or was late over a number of days during the shooting schedule. And, as with several of her other films, the scope of such delays has since been inordinately exaggerated in the retelling across the ensuing decades. But *I Could Go on Singing* was completed in just twelve weeks (between early May and late July 1962) and came in as budgeted at $1.4 million. The film took its new title—changed by United Artists just a month prior to the premiere—from the picture's one original song, written for Judy by Harold Arlen and E. Y. Harburg.

Though far from a box-office bonanza, the movie captured both on-and-off-stage glimpses of the mature, in-concert Garland and includes several sequences that were recognized, even on first exhibition, as virtual documentary. Years later, such parallels have been (whether or not correctly) even more embraced. It's perhaps enough to note that, as "an end-of-career testimonial," Judy's work in *I Could Go on Singing* was linked with that of Charlie Chaplin in *Limelight*, as Foster Hirsch appreciatively realized that the two "always acted with an emotional ripeness that chafed against generic limits."

**ABOVE:** Poster for foreign release: *L'Ombre du Passe* (Belgium) **OPPOSITE:** Judy's real-life hairdresser Al Paul and actor Jack Klugman watch as "Jenny" is poised to make her supercharged first entrance.

Judy at the Palladium: "Hello, Bluebird" was the first footage shot for the film.

The audience rises to her in acclamation. Mort Lindsey is the beaming conductor.

FROM TOP: Phillips, Neame, Garland, and co-producer Stuart Millar reunite in London on March 5, 1963, at a press conference touting the film's release. | Judy's fortieth birthday was celebrated by the crew, costars, and Judy's children with a "Palladium stage" proscenium cake. From left: Joey and Lorna Luft, Judy, Gregory Phillips, Liza Minnelli, and Dirk Bogarde. OPPOSITE: At the Stoke Poges location: director Ronald Neame, Gregory Phillips, and Judy

## What They Said

*"We have wanted to do this movie with Judy for nearly three years. That was long before the Judy Garland comeback, when no company would risk making a movie with her. Robert Dozier, a close friend, originally wrote* The Lonely Stage *as a TV script. He had the idea that the script could be adapted for Judy, with the locale to be England. We always had our own faith in her talent, and our own hunch that she'd come back."* —PRODUCERS STUART MILLAR AND LAWRENCE TURMAN

*"The thing I remember most about Judy was that she was a great storyteller. I loved her; I adored her. When we finished the picture, we had become kind of friends. [At one point,] the director of the movie wanted to reshoot a scene. Judy asked why. He told her, 'Well, let's just say there's a little man inside that tells me to.' Judy said, 'Well, I'll just have to crawl inside you and kill that f------ little man!'"* —JACK KLUGMAN

*"When Mr. Neame took me into Miss Garland's dressing room . . . [she] gave me a big hug and said, 'Hello, darling!' It was marvelous, and so quick I forgot to be frightened. 'Come and sit down by me,' she said, and the next thing I knew, we were discussing the part, and I felt as if I'd known her all my life. All through the film, [she and Dirk Bogarde] were both wonderful to me. They are so completely natural, with no 'side' at all. It was the most friendly job I ever had. We used to rehearse all our scenes together and discuss every detail. [And] she would always come down to the studio to read my lines off for me. When you have to do a scene in which you're alone—but talking to someone off-camera—most stars let someone else read the lines off. But Judy used to say, 'How can he be expected to act as if he's trying to talk to his mother, and she isn't there?' This often meant her coming to the studio when she might have had a day off, but she never minded. I thought she was tops [before], but now that I've worked with her, I know she's the greatest star of them all."* —GREGORY PHILLIPS

*"I knew Judy very, very well and closely for about ten years. I did her last movie with her, but [Hollywood and the system] killed Judy. They've killed anybody of any sensitivity. People said how brave I was to be in a film with Judy Garland. I wasn't brave, I wasn't self-sacrificing. I wrote [a lot] of her material for that movie, and one of the greatest privileges of my acting life was to work with that actress. And she was a monster, she was monstrous, but she was magic."* —DIRK BOGARDE

"In many ways, it was a horrendous experience, but in many ways, it was also a wonderful experience, because the whole unit—everybody—we all loved this lady, no matter how many problems she gave us. And she gave us problems: not being there and even half-hearted suicide attempts. Every few days, there would be a drama. But through it all, we loved her, and I'm very, very glad I made that film. It's not a great film, but it's become sort of cultural. [And] when she was on the set, she was highly professional and extremely good; the trouble was getting her there. She was scared stiff; it was a fear that she had. There were several shots in that picture when Judy was really good, [and] I just kept going and never cut. She does one scene on the telephone; it was always planned to cut to the little boy she was talking to. [But] I couldn't believe Judy. I had to stay with her, and we never cut away from her. It was all done in a close shot. Dirk knew Judy very well; he never took a screen credit, but he wrote a lot of the dialogue in that picture. When we came to the hospital scene, I planned to do a two-shot, fairly far back . . . and then I was going to go to close shots to finish the sequence. We rehearsed five or six times, we started to shoot, and then suddenly, the most extraordinary thing happened. It wasn't a scene anymore; it was Judy, as she had been many times in her own life. She more or less remained with the dialogue, but it wasn't exactly as written. Dick, being a consummate actor, adjusted to it and responded to it. And I thought, 'My God, I am never going to get this again; I'll never be able to match it when we go into close shot.' So I [gestured] to the man tracking the camera, [and] the focus man adjusted the focus. . . . And the scene went on. And there was a little bit of magic."

—DIRECTOR RONALD NEAME

"It was so brilliant that there is no way I can explain it to you. We all stood around in hushed silence, and when she was finished . . . such a cheer went up, because suddenly in this scene, she was complaining about her life, in a way—about 'I've given all this to show business, and what has show business given to me?' That's what the speech was all about; it was wonderful. It's a good movie, by the way; it's well worth seeing, and she's wonderful in it. It's partly the story of her life. [Also,] we did one thing which was never done: we recorded the songs in a studio with an audience, and we recorded their applause, because she was going to do the songs in the picture at the Palladium, where there was an audience. But she always sang better with an audience."

—ASSOCIATE PRODUCER/MUSICAL SUPERVISOR SAUL CHAPLIN

**OPPOSITE AND ABOVE:** The title song/finale of *I Could Go on Singing* was filmed in front of a live audience at the Palladium, with pick-up shots made on the theater stage mock-up at Shepperton Studios the next day. After going on a martini spree and spraining her ankle, "Jenny Bowman" arrives an hour late for a concert. Tossing aside her furs ("I just shot 'em"), she gets down to business; the initially disgruntled audience is swiftly charmed and repeatedly interrupts her rendition with thunderous applause. Bereft of both lover and son, Jenny is back where she belongs—on the (however) lonely stage.

# INDEX

## A

Abbott, Bud, 122
Adams, Lee, 217
Adler, Stella, 176
"After You've Gone," 179
Agee, James, 13
Ager, Cecilia, 94
Ager, Milton, 94
*Aimee Semple McPherson Story, The*, 218
Akst, Al, 200
Albee, Edward, 14, 279
Alberni, Luis, 164
Alexander, Shana, 94, 127
*Alice Adams*, 217, 300
*All About Eve*, 217
"All For You," 278, 282–83
"All I Do is Dream of You," 130–33
Allen, Lester, 250
Allen, Steve, 49
Allyson, June, 49, 194, 199, 208, 211, 214, 216, 272, 291–92
"Alone," 131
*Alone* (album), 36
Alsop, Carlton, 269
Alton, Robert, 11, 53, 127, 246–47, 254, 274–75, 289
"America," 160
"America the Beautiful," 123
*American in Paris, An*, 13
*American Symphony*, 210
Ames, Leon, 202, 204
Amsterdam, Morey, 326
*Anchors Aweigh*, 212, 214
Anders, Rudolph, 308
Anderson, John Murray, 241
Andrews, Julie, 218
Andrews Sisters, 122
*Andy Hardy Comes Home*, 87
*Andy Hardy Meets Debutante*, 126–33
*Andy Hardy* series, 9, 13, 77, 236
  see also individual movies
Ankrum, Morris, 236–37
*Anna & the King of Siam*, 215
*Annie Get Your Gun*, 32, 223, 280, 286–89
*Applause* (Broadway musical), 217
Arlen, Harold, 309, 317, 326, 339
Armed Forces Radio, 27, 44–45
"Army-Navy Screen Magazine No. 20," 123
*Arnaut Brothers, The*, 247
Arnaz, Desi, 211
Arnold, Edward, 211, 238
*Around the World in Eighty Days*, 319
*Arthur Murray Party, The*, 37
Astaire, Adele, 211, 265, 289

Astaire, Fred
  *The Barkleys of Broadway* and, 284–85
  *The Belle of New York* and, 212
  *Broadway Melody of 1939* and, 210
  *Cabbages & Kings* and, 214
  *The Duchess of Idaho* and, 215
  *Easter Parade* and, 11, 222–23, 258, 262, 264–65
  *Finian's Rainbow* and, 214
  *Funny Face* and, 211
  *Royal Wedding* and, 289, 291–92
  *That's Entertainment!* and, 10
  World War II and, 28
  *Yolanda and the Thief* and, 213
  *Ziegfeld Follies* and, 238, 241
Astor, Mary, 90, 93–95, 190, 202, 204–5, 271, 301
Aubrey, James, 40, 218–19
Austen, Jane, 214
Austerlitz, Ann Gelius, 265
Avedon, Richard, 47

## B

"Babbitt and the Bromide, The," 241
*Babes in Arms*, 26, 63, 108–15, 119, 126, 139, 185, 199, 211, 273
*Babes in Hollywood*, 209, 212
*Babes on Broadway*, 115, 123, 126, 162, 164–71, 199
Bacall, Lauren, 214, 217
Bacon, Irving, 229, 302
Bainter, Fay, 164, 168, 180, 185
Baker, Carroll, 293
Baker, Kenny, 232, 234, 236–37
Ball, Lucille, 28, 219, 234, 238
"Ballad for Americans," 168
"Ballin' the Jack," 178–79
Bancroft, Anne, 218
*Band Wagon, The*, 13
Bannett, Marcella, 21
Barker, Patricia, 180–81, 188
*Barkleys of Broadway, The*, 223, 269, 284–85
Barnes, Binnie, 68
Barrymore, John, 207
Barstow, Richard, 53, 314
Bartholomew, Freddie, 29, 63, 75, 80, 90, 93–95, 119, 210
Bates, Jimmy, 258
Baum, Frank, 100
Baxter, Anne, 213–14
Baxter, Brian, 301
Baxter, Warner, 118
"Be a Clown," 253
Beavers, Richard, 258
Beckett, Scotty, 90–91, 94–95
Beery, Wallace, 24
Begelman, David, 38–41, 300–301

Behrman, S. N., 253
Bell, Marion, 238
*Belle of New York, The*, 212
Benchley, Robert, 68
*Ben-Hur*, 205
Bennett, Tony, 49
Benny, Jack, 44
Benson, Sally, 204, 212, 216
Berg, Harold, 117
Bergen, Polly, 217
Bergman, Ingrid, 213, 331
Berkeley, Busby
  *Annie Get Your Gun* and, 286, 288–89
  *Babes in Arms* and, 108, 113–15
  *Babes on Broadway* and, 123, 164, 168
  *Girl Crazy* and, 199–200
  *For Me and My Gal* and, 172, 177, 179
  *Strike Up the Band* and, 134, 136, 138–39, 141
  working relationship with, 127
Berle, Milton, 122
Berlin, Ellin, 218
Berlin, Irving, 11, 214, 218, 222, 262, 264–65, 286
Bernhardt, Sarah, 166, 168
Bernie, Ben, 62
*Best Foot Forward*, 49, 200
Bickford, Charles, 302
"Bidin' My Time," 199
Bieber, Nita, 276
"Big Revue, The," 116–17
*Big Store, The*, 185
*Big Time, The*, 211
"Bill," 25, 212
Blake, Amanda, 302
Blake, Gladys, 130
Blandick, Clara, 96
Blane, Ralph, 11, 126, 192, 204, 241
*Bloodhounds of Broadway*, 215–16
Bloom, Ken, 15
Blue, Ben, 172, 176, 190, 211
Blyth, Ann, 216
Bogarde, Dirk, 217, 334, 336–37, 339, 342, 345
Bogart, Humphrey, 308
Boles, John, 190
Bolger, Ray, 36, 49, 96, 98, 103–4, 106–7, 232, 234
*Bonanza*, 40
Booth, Shirley, 217
"Born in a Trunk," 303, 311
*Born in Wedlock*, 217
*Born to Dance*, 209
*Born to Sing*, 168–69
Bowron, Fletcher, 162

"Boy Next Door, The," 222
Boyce, George, 272–73
Boyd, Stephen, 212
Boyd, William, 215
"Boys and Girls Like You and Me," 207
*Boys Town*, 113
Bracken, Eddie, 276–77, 281–82
Brady, Fred, 204
Brady, Judy, 215
Brady, Ruth, 224, 229, 232, 236–37
Brady, Scott, 215
Brando, Marlon, 308–9
Brandt, Willy, 322
Brazzi, Rossano, 217
Breakston, George, 84, 128
Brecher, Irving, 212
Bremer, Lucille, 202, 204, 213–14, 238, 244
Bressart, Felix, 229
Brice, Fanny, 11, 78–80, 82, 238, 241
*Brigadoon*, 216
Brissac, Virginia, 134, 138–39
*Broadway Melody of 1937*, 24, 62, 71
*Broadway Melody of 1938*, 65, 68–73, 75, 80, 156, 211
*Broadway Melody of 1939*, 210
*Broadway Melody of 1940*, 210
"Broadway Rhythm," 24, 181, 185
*Broadway Rhythm*, 211
*Broadway: The Golden Age*, 14
Bronson, Lillian, 270–71
Brooks, Rand, 109
Brothers, Nicholas, 250
Brown, Charles D., 74
Brown, Joe E., 213
Brown, Nacio Herb, 75, 131, 157, 185
Bruce, Virginia, 156
Brynner, Yul, 215
"Bubbles," 118
Bubbles, John, 54
Buck, Pearl S., 212
"Buds Won't Bud," 131
*Bundles for Britain*, 45
Burke, Billie, 78, 96–97
Burke, James, 144
Burnham, Jeremy, 334
Burton, Jim, 52
Burton, Richard, 308
"But Not for Me," 199–200
Butch and Buddy, 122
Butler, David, 64
*Butterfield 8*, 217
Buttons, Red, 324
"By Myself," 14, 339